Breaking the Rules

11/14/07

Breaking the Rules

KURT WRIGHT

**REMOVING THE
OBSTACLES TO EFFORTLESS
HIGH PERFORMANCE**

CPM Publishing
Boise, Idaho

ISBN 0-9614383-3-9

Library of Congress Catalog Card # 98-92446

Jacket design by Dunn+Associates

CPM Publishing books are available at special quantity discounts to use as premiums and sales promotions, or for use in corporate training programs. For more information, please write to the Director of Special Sales, CPM Publishing, 3452 Riva Ridge Way, Boise, ID 83709-3809. Or contact your local bookstore.

This book is dedicated
in loving memory
to my Grandmother, Averil Wright,
in whose eyes her eldest grandson
could do no wrong . . .
and to my wife, Patricia,
who fanned that faint spark
until it became the ceaseless flame
of feeling truly believed in.

Table of Contents

Foreword

My first experience of Kurt Wright's extraordinary understanding of questions occurred in 1989 when he invited me to participate in a 12 hour long "Dialogue For Visionary Leaders." He engaged six of us in a most insightful dialogue around the question, "When was the last time you can remember giving all you've got to achieve some goal or complete some task?"

I came away with a greatly heightened appreciation of the power of intuition and the role of properly framed questions in the intuitive process. I've always had a good appreciation of intuition, but found it most encouraging to realize there is a systematic way for us to increase our use of the intuitive mind. I think it is easy to overlook its tremendous power to sort and organize, and to find patterns and where things fit. I found it particularly important to appreciate the intuition's ability to convey to our rational mind a solution or a way forward to fulfill our vision. As a practical matter, these are things we do not get by relying on the rational mind alone.

My second experience with Kurt came when he conducted a team dialogue with my division operating committee at 3M Pharmaceuticals. That was probably a major turning point—for me as well as for the whole group of people who worked very closely together—because we came to appreciate what was needed to take advantage of the intuitive power of our team. It built the trust considerably and helped us create an environment where people did not have to be defensive. This greatly strengthened relationships among everyone on our management team.

We all learned to embrace the whole notion of working to find the value in everyone's contribution. We also learned the importance of attributing no negative value to the things we didn't necessarily agree with or didn't feel made a strong contribution. It was okay to attribute a kind of zero value to something, but the whole interaction becomes more productive when we are all looking for the positive value that can be created. The resulting trust level fueled a creative synergy within our group that allowed us to achieve much more than we could have ever done using a more conventional approach.

Using the material Kurt presents so effectively in *Breaking the Rules*, we were able to build an environment in which team members weren't penalized for what they put out. People came to feel as if they could just give their best with no prospect of a negative situation or a penalty being associated with that. We each came to trust that others would be looking for the value of our contribution. It was getting that set of behaviors and expectations into a group of people who already had a great deal of mutual respect for each other that really enhanced the overall productivity and effectiveness of that group. It moved us to a higher level of effectiveness.

Our resulting ability to create a common vision was something that really provided the focus for our management team. It was one of the greatest benefits we extracted as a team from our work with these principles. The elements of high trust, building on strengths and then having a common vision that the whole group could really subscribe to made a large contribution to our success within the division.

Without the trust, we may have been able to create a vision, but we wouldn't have had the environment in which we could put everything into realizing it. It's the ability to achieve WHOLEHEARTED commitment, and a sense that no one had a territory to protect that made the difference. It became a very shared undertaking with a real feeling that we were operating in a cultural relationship where we could all just open up and contribute fully without constraint and pull things together from the group to provide the maximum forward energy.

This is the picture of potential benefits I would paint for readers of *Breaking the Rules*. There is a power here that will help you to be more effective, to be a higher performer, and hopefully have less pain associated with that. There is also a power here that can help you become an effective member or leader of high performance groups.

I believe that if your desire is to establish a high performance group, or to put yourself on a roll personally, reading Breaking the Rules can show you how. You will come away knowing that to do so, you must learn to ask the questions and establish the kind of high-trust mentor-coaching relationships that Kurt describes. Even greater value could be achieved with entire teams working through this 'rule-breaking' material together.

W. George Meredith
Executive Vice President
3M Company
St. Paul, Minnesota

Chapter One

Being On a Roll

This book is about being on a roll. Notice I did not say learning to be on a roll. This is because I believe our natural state is to be on a roll, and getting back to that state involves a lot more unlearning than learning. Being on a roll is the product of a state of mind that leads to WHOLEHEARTED commitment, and this state of mind is only reached when we follow the guidance of our hearts, rather than allow ourselves to be ruled by our heads. To be on a roll, we must break free of rules that keep us out of touch with our hearts—so we can get back to the effortless ease of WHOLEHEARTED commitment.

In this book you will discover why our conscious, rational minds are attempting to play an unintended role of master over our intuitive minds, and why they are failing so miserably at it. You will learn how our rational minds are perfectly designed instead to be servants to our inner, intuitive minds. You will also learn the steps taken by effortless high performers to develop this more productive relationship. Hence, this book invites us to unlearn many intellectually based rules about how things should work and replace them with a practical, proven, intuition-based system of self-management. This system is based on asking RIGHT QUESTIONS. As we learn to practice it together, we will each move back toward a state of WHOLEHEARTED commitment and effortless high performance. When applied at an organizational level, mastery of this self-management system as a leadership style can lead to effortless high performance there as well.

I invite you to join me now as we explore a fundamental question which has led to all of the insights presented in this book: "What are you and I like at our very best?" Over the past 27 years, my relentless pursuit of answers to this question has transformed my life. It is now my intent to make the life-transforming benefits of this question available to everyone who chooses to read this book.

What Are We Like At Our Best?

So, what *are* you like at your best? When does it happen? What is your level of awareness about this for yourself as we begin this journey? For example, when things are going especially well for you—i.e., when you are truly on a roll—have you taken time to really explore how and why you got there? Or, are you like most people who wait until they fall off their roll and then wonder what's wrong? Could it be possible we have been asking the wrong questions . . . and at the wrong time? If we wait until we're down and then try to figure out what's wrong, we are failing to learn the key steps required to get ourselves back to our natural state of being on a roll. This is why it is so important for us to discover how and why people get on a roll. We have much to gain by recalling and exploring our own experiences of being in this wonderful state, whether we are someone who enjoys being on a roll much of the time, or if we just aspire to get there in the future.

This book explains why we must make a fundamental shift in our approach to asking questions—from one of inquiring about what is not working, to one of learning to identify and build upon what *is* working. But it doesn't stop there. It shows exactly how to bring this shift about, and how this will allow us to reach higher levels of personal achievement—and do so with less effort than we may have ever thought possible. In other words, we are about to explore a set of insights that can bring us back to a natural style of inquiry found to be always at work in people who are WHOLEHEARTEDLY committed and on a roll. By adopting this style of inquiry, each of us can return to and remember how to sustain ourselves in the euphoric state of effortless high performance—which I again propose is our naturally intended state.

A quick example will show what kind of results can be achieved by making this simple shift. The president of a printing company in California once asked if my approach could help him solve a costly problem of rework. As he went on to describe his concern, I learned that in a typical month seven percent of his printing orders had to be redone because of errors. I also learned this had been going on for years, in spite of many different attempts to solve the problem, and that it was eating up much of the company's profits. During dialogue with the company's management team, I encouraged them to shift their focus of inquiry onto what produced perfect orders rather than why others contained errors. Their agreement to make a shift didn't come instantly, but soon included most team members. After several years of failed attempts to "solve" their seven-percent rework problem, it took that team only 30 days to move the plant's output from 93% to 97% perfect. Output went on to exceed 98% perfect during four of the following 12 months.

The ideas being set forth here actually grew out of a life-changing experience which occurred for me in October of 1970. By way of background, I can tell you I grew up with a failure pattern. I grew up with a wonderful father who just happened to judge it "not okay" for me to need attention. As a result, he made it a point to withhold any attention from me for doing things well. In response, I learned to fail in order to get his attention. It worked every time. Among other things, this is a personal story of how I came to recognize my failure pattern, and how I managed to remove it as an obstacle in my life. It is also about how, in the process, I was able to develop a model to help me and others achieve our goals in life with effortless ease.

Psychological Theory?

Some readers may be tempted to view the insights offered here as psychological theory. That would be puzzling, however, since the field of psychology is so focused on the study of sick people to find out what's wrong. My approach has been exactly the opposite: it has been to study the super-well to find out WHAT'S RIGHT. Besides the many fresh insights produced by this approach, it also exposes the painfully high cost we incur as a society for our all-pervasive "find-what's-wrong-and-fix-it" mind-set. It also reveals why efforts to manage change that rely on "yet another theory" to fix WHAT'S WRONG are destined to fail. Thus, it is surely not my intent to continue this practice here. I seriously question the need for yet another theory when, deep inside us at an intuitive level, each of us already knows all we need to know to be at our best. Yes, that is a core finding from my study. Here is another.

No Advice, Please

Those who operate most of the time in the state of effortless high performance didn't get that way by following advice given by others. This is why I've delayed writing this book for several years. I simply do not wish to reward anyone for looking to me for answers. In this book I have no intention of giving advice. Instead, I shall raise wonderful questions which are used to find your own answers deep within. Thus, if you are accustomed to looking outside yourself for answers, and hope to find those in this book, you may encounter some initial discomfort with the approach used here. My findings convince me that being at our best is a natural state which *cannot* be accessed via the overlay of "yet another theory." Asking ourselves and being asked RIGHT QUESTIONS (in order to regain conscious access to what we already know intuitively) is a path far more certain to put our lives on a permanent roll.

The key to getting on a roll and staying there is learning to frame questions in such a way that they cannot be processed analytically. When we do this correctly, our questions are automatically processed by our intuition. When applied personally, the intuition-based system of inquiry being introduced here has proven far more productive, and at the same time less stressful and more fulfilling, than any other I have ever seen. This intuition-based approach to inquiry can also be applied directly to organizations—and to teams of people who work together. Using this approach, team members have often enjoyed far higher levels of cooperation, commitment and motivation than they had ever seen before, or perhaps had even thought possible. Visionary leaders give us a wonderful glimpse of this system of inquiry in practice.

Visionary Leaders

My experiences from studying visionary leaders for many years have made a significant contribution to my understanding in the area of effortless high performance. One experience in particular will be instructive. *Business Week* ran a cover story in its 1/25/85 issue entitled, "The New Corporate Elite." This story featured 50 visionary leaders from American businesses, and was the first time I can recall visionary leadership being given such high visibility. For me, the article's high profile was a welcome validation of my commitment, since by that time I had already dedicated nearly 15 years of my life to the study of visionary leaders.

After reading the article, I was prompted to write a letter to several of the leaders identified. I wished to extend my congratulations for the example they were setting, and to include a complimentary copy of an article I had written about how visionaries think. Eventually I sent letters to 43 of the 50 leaders. This correspondence created an opportunity for me to personally interview five featured leaders, only four of whom turned out to be true visionaries. My experience with the fifth leader, the non-visionary, was a watershed. It gave me a first glimpse into the vast difference between those who are vision-driven and those who are theory-driven.

A Surplus and Abundance World View

The first four leaders I interviewed—those I later came to realize were true visionaries—demonstrated a consistent and remarkable openness to new ideas. It was as if they simply couldn't wait to get another idea to help lift their vision to another level. In contrast, it was as if the leader who was theory-driven had to hold every new idea at arm's length until he could confirm it would not risk upsetting his theories of how things should work. It felt energizing to be in dialogue with the four who were vision-driven. After leaving my meeting with the leader who was theory-driven, I felt emotionally drained. It felt like we were adversaries, and for no apparent reason. This felt very different from all of my dialogues with true visionaries, where an awesome sense of partnership always seems to occur. By seeking to understand these differences, I learned how the thought process practiced by visionaries works to generate a surplus of creative energy. This excess energy allows them to sustain a "surplus and abundance world view," which leaves them completely open to new ideas. This is a very different picture than the illusory world view of depletion and shortage, which is initially created by and then reinforced by the theory-driven thought process.

You may as well know right now that it will be impossible for any of us to experience WHOLEHEARTED commitment and become effortless high performers as long as we remain theory-driven. No amount of good advice will get us there either. The natural and self-sustaining source of creative energy needed to enjoy this level of commitment is simply not available to us as long as we continue to look *outside* ourselves for answers. Hopefully this book will not reward anyone for looking to me for answers. Instead, it will equip us all to look more skillfully *inside* ourselves—not to our egos or intellects, but to our hearts and our intuition—where the only true answers for guiding our lives await our discovery.

Organizations Can Be Put On A Roll, Too

Since the very beginning of my study I have noticed striking similarities in the way organizations and individuals function. It soon became apparent to me that any insights I might gain into what each of us is like at our best as an individual must be equally valid when applied to an organizational entity as a whole. In this context, perhaps it would be helpful to present a case study. The following experience provided many insights into how my findings could be applied to the task of putting an entire organization on a roll.

The situation presented itself as follows. I received a call from a client who for the preceding year had been doing an excellent job of implementing our intuition-based system of management within his area of responsibility. This client found himself suddenly placed in charge of a huge software development project which was deeply in trouble. The project consisted of a $100 million effort involving some 400 software engineers who were 38 months into a 60-month government contract requiring them to deliver a distributed bus system for running a piece of military equipment. The technical requirements of the contract were so complex that the team slipped its schedule in each of the first 38 months of work on the contract. By the time my client asked me to look at the situation and make recommendations, work had fallen an estimated 18 months behind schedule. Everyone was particularly concerned about a contract stipulation of $30 million in penalties if the team remained 18 months behind schedule at the 48-month milestone— a mere ten months away.

Fortunately, my client was a true visionary. He had also experienced the power of our intuition-based system of management during the previous year. As a result, he looked upon his new situation as a perfect opportunity to demonstrate to the entire company the power of asking RIGHT QUESTIONS. We both knew if we could simply change the question the team was running on from "What's going wrong?" to "What's going right?" we'd have the problem licked. My client also knew that the crisis would allow him to justify a budget large enough to assure full implementation of our system within the troubled project. Once he secured a budget commitment for $150,000, he issued me an employee badge and put me to work. He added, "There's more money where that came from if you need it, so don't come out of there until you've got it right." (Talk about a consultant's dream!)

My vision for how to turn this situation around was to get everyone on the team running on the same question—in precisely the same manner as visionary leaders run on a single galvanizing question. I knew my success depended on choosing a question powerful enough to capture everyone's imagination and lead to WHOLEHEARTED commitment. I also knew the only way I could ever hope to identify the perfect question would be to fully immerse myself in the energy of the project for a few days.

I began by taking teams of 18 to 20 engineers off-site for a two-day team dialogue designed to bring about a fundamental shift in thinking from WHAT'S WRONG to WHAT'S RIGHT. (This book is intended to produce a similar outcome.) I also found the intense interactions which always took place in the team dialogues to be a perfect place for me to get fully engaged in my search for the perfect question. From the work I had done with visionaries, I knew what kind of a question it would take to truly capture their attention. The moment of insight occurred in the second week, when it dawned on me that our question had to be: "What will it take to finish this project a week early?" This question met every one of the criteria I had identified.

It was fascinating to watch people's initial reactions. On the surface, of course, the question was preposterous. It was considered by most to be totally impossible, but this was one of the criteria it had to meet in order to work. It was so preposterous, in fact, that on more than one occasion I found myself being summoned into a supervisor's office and sternly advised to stop asking this question. First one, and then another, would say to me with great conviction, "These people are engineers, Kurt. They know this can't be done. You'll just destroy your credibility if you keep asking this question." In response, of course, I had to thank them profusely for saving my skin. I then went right back out into the hallways and continued asking my preposterous question.

Later in the book, after we have developed a better framework within which to understand their implications, we will explore several aspects of this case in much more detail. For now I will just let you know I completed my commitment to the project in six weeks. I used only $90,000 of the $150,000 budget, and left after describing to my client all of the reasons I now felt the project would succeed. Some eight months later, this critical phase of the project was completed right on schedule—exactly on the 48 month milestone date, and $15 million under budget. Add the $15 million savings to the vanished $30 million penalty risk, and we have a $45 million payoff. All of this from a mere six-week effort to shift the mode of thinking from WHAT'S GOING WRONG to WHAT'S GOING RIGHT among 400 software engineers. Some folks would say that's a pretty good return on investment for breaking a few rules. From my perspective, it's not an uncommon experience at all when WHOLEHEARTED commitment is engaged.

Chapter Two

Setting Expectations

A Vision Is Born

My story began in the fall of 1970, with my participation in a "goal in life contest" as part of the Dale Carnegie Sales Course®. By then I had already attended the regular Dale Carnegie Course® three times, beginning in 1959 as a senior in high school, where I was the youngest person in the class and badly in need of a boost in self-confidence. (I could very well be one of their classic success stories.) Yet even though my desire to better myself ran pretty deep—I had been through the regular course three times by 1970—I had somehow missed the concept of setting goals. In addition, I had still not completely conquered my fear of speaking in front of a group of people.

As I began thinking about what goals to set and how to compete in this contest, I recalled the powerful advice of Ralph Waldo Emerson, who once said, "Do the thing you fear to do and the death of fear is certain." Those words struck a chord with all of my insecurities and unresolved fears of speaking in public. Somehow they also managed to move my thinking out beyond those fears to a place where I was able to set a goal of becoming a nationally famous motivational speaker by the

11

age of 40. Now if you had known me at the time—at least through the 29-year-old self-doubting eyes with which I saw myself—you would have surely seen the impossibility of my reaching any such goal.

After setting this seemingly unreachable goal, I began to wonder how in the world I could ever achieve such an impossible dream. Something then prompted me to go back and examine my success patterns. Perhaps it was just a standard part of the course, but I had never done anything like that before, and it was quite an eye-opener.

The greatest success I could remember up until then took place at my first job out of college as a commodities trader for the Pillsbury Company in Minneapolis. As I reviewed those successes, an obvious pattern emerged. Every big success had taken place when I was going against the crowd. My trading style was clearly "contrarian," and it taught me a key lesson: The crowd is *always* wrong. If the past 30 years is any indication, this lesson will continue to serve me well throughout the rest of my life.

I learned the importance of being able to read and understand a crowd's direction, and then take this as a clue to begin my search for the truth in exactly the opposite direction. I knew better than to think the opposite would *always* be true, but it has always been the most promising place for me to begin my search for the truth. This has proven to be an important philosophy for guiding my decisions ever since.

While reviewing these principles, and the gratifying success they had brought my way, a wave of embarrassment welled up in me. I suddenly realized I was right in the middle of the biggest crowd I had ever known, competing with everyone in sight at figuring out WHAT'S WRONG. I was a flaw-finder's flaw finder, a critic's critic. It instantly became obvious to me. I would never be able to distinguish myself or reach my goals by continuing to compete with the fault-finding crowd.

Just as this thought struck me, a vision began to unfold. I saw myself as a lone player on an empty stage, with no competition, no distractions of any kind to prevent me from distinguishing myself as the best on the planet at figuring out WHAT'S RIGHT. I was nearly overwhelmed by the simplicity of it—by the very elegance of it. I suddenly knew I could count on everyone to remain caught up in the race of finding WHAT'S WRONG and trying to fix it. I knew it would never occur to anyone to compete with me until I was so far ahead of the crowd it would be no use for anyone to even try to catch up with me. What an exhilarating feeling!

This experience inspired me to begin a quest to discover what each of us are like when we are at our very best. I began by setting out to identify and focus on people in business who consistently have more energy left over at the end of a day than at the beginning—after having outperformed their peers and competitors all day long. All of my observations are based on key findings drawn from this study.

Study Findings

The first and most important finding of the study has to do with commitment. Effortless high performers operate at a level of WHOLEHEARTED commitment that is far deeper, more intuitive and longer-lasting than most people ever experience. Most of my later findings actually grew out of my desire to gain a deeper understanding of this phenomenon of WHOLEHEARTED commitment. Once it surfaced as the central issue of my quest, I also began to experience a profound deepening of my own personal commitment. I vowed to become the world's leading expert in the area of commitment. I wanted to know what causes it—in its healthiest, least stressful and yet most highly productive form.

Another key factor shared by those who experienced this unusually deep form of commitment was a clear sense of purpose. Somehow, each had an ability to keep their actions and behaviors in alignment with their purpose in life. This early finding about purpose also played a big role in my decision to choose Clear Purpose Management, Inc. as the name for my consulting practice.

Three issues emerged to demand my attention as I began to explore the relationship between WHOLEHEARTED commitment and being in alignment with our life's purpose. First, each of us already has a definite and unique purpose in life. Purpose, therefore, is not something that can be "invented" or decided upon intellectually. It is something we already know—even though it may be at some intuitive level deep within us—and it waits patiently to be discovered and brought up to a conscious level of awareness. Second, fewer than five out of 100 people have even the remotest clue as to what our purpose in life might be. Third, while some 60% of my clients had at least been exposed to the concept of goals, fewer than 10% of them were able to distinguish the difference between a purpose and a goal. When each of us is clear about this distinction, it makes a major contribution to our ability to achieve our goals as well as elevate our sense of fulfillment. (I do intend to help you make this distinction perfectly clear in your own life.)

Very Different Questions

It has always been my style to search for underlying causes of behaviors I find to be significant. It took several years of searching before the insight emerged that effortless high performers ask very different questions of themselves than do less productive people. These questions are of an intuition-engaging nature, and play an immensely important role in helping those who use them to recognize opportunities where others may see only problems. I now know that the discipline of asking properly framed questions will play a far greater role in allowing us to reach the state of effortless high performance than any other single factor. Therefore, it is my intent to identify and describe as many practices as possible which will allow each of us to master the discipline of asking RIGHT QUESTIONS.

Here is a helpful way to understand the importance of asking the RIGHT QUESTIONS. Can you bring to mind a three-year-old child? It can be one you know currently, or one you can remember knowing in the past. With the child you have brought to mind as a specific reference point, can you now identify four or five key characteristics you might expect to find in nearly every three-year-old you meet? Please give this some quality thought before reading the next paragraph.

Did "fearless" show up on your list? How about "insatiable curiosity?" Can you think of a specific question most three-year-olds might ask? What about their energy level? Is it generally high or low?

Now here is a most interesting observation. People who operate at their best most of the time all exhibit the same boundless energy and insatiable curiosity as a three-year-old child! In other words, both share the same approach to questions and exhibit the same unbounded energy. Could the style with which each asks questions and the resulting surplus energy be linked in a cause-and-effect relationship? In other words, might the unique questions asked by each be the spark that ignites their intuitive insights—which in turn produce their surplus creative energy? The answer is an unequivocal yes, and I will describe how each is using their conscious, rational mind to ask questions so they can only be processed intuitively. And, as a result, additional creative energy is generated every time the intuition sparks a new insight.

15

How does this relate to being fearless? you might ask. Could it be that the three-year-old child and the visionary leader each experience less fear than the average person? This is certainly what I observe. And, along with reduced fear comes a willingness to ask more intuition-engaging questions—which further strengthens the cycle.

As we all know, most three-year-old children enjoy a built-in surplus of creative energy. It's as if they're plugged directly into Hoover Dam. This has a dramatic effect on their view of the world, too—which is clearly one of surplus and abundance. Unfortunately, as adults fewer than five percent of us are still framing our questions in the natural, energy-generating style of a three-year-old. Somewhere between the ages of three and ten, we get "penalized" out of the natural way of asking questions we practiced at age three. Most of us became culturally and educationally conditioned to ask self-protective questions which deplete our energy. As with the three-year-old, this also has a dramatic effect on our world view—only in this case we come to expect nothing from life but depletion and shortage. The energy-depleting effect of this is like being unplugged from Hoover Dam and having to switch to a battery as our source of energy. But a battery never gets beyond full and is always depleted by use. When we're plugged into Hoover Dam, we never have to think about running out of energy. When we switch to a battery, we always have to be concerned about running out.

A world view of depletion and shortage is not the truth. It is pure illusion, but an illusion that nevertheless for most people seems very real. The three-year-old child's world view of surplus and abundance is the truth. It is a truth all of us were connected with as young children. And it is a truth all spiritually evolved persons as well as visionary leaders and effortless high performers will verify as being consistent with their experience.

Fear is a key by-product of the illusory world view of depletion and shortage. Love, trust and anticipation of joy is the by-product of the world view of surplus and abundance. The question we must ask ourselves is, "How do we switch from a world view of depletion and shortage to one of surplus and abundance?" Again, welcome to the purpose of this book.

Desired Outcomes

It is now time to reflect on some of the challenges I faced in putting this material in writing. As the book's subtitle implies, it *is* possible to remove obstacles to effortless high performance. In attempting to do so, however, we face a paradox. Obstacles cannot be removed by putting our attention on them. This brings up a significant finding from my study. Problems will disappear faster than we could ever solve them, once we get our thinking right. Obstacles are the things we see when we take our eyes off our goal, and you will learn why it is so much more effective to deliberately and systematically abandon obstacles than attempt to overcome them.

I would much prefer for you to be with me in person right now, as this is where most of my experience with mentor-coaching lies. Even though this is not exactly the case, I am choosing to operate throughout the book as if we are enjoying ourselves on the patio of my home in the paradise island of Maui. As we sip iced tea and look out from our padded, rocking, swiveling patio chairs, the scene in front of us includes the southwest ridge of beautiful Mount Haleakala on our left and an inspiring view of the Pacific and two neighboring islands on our right. I now offer you a menu of desired outcomes from our interaction and ask you to pick one or more items you feel hold the most promise for helping you be more effective. Once you make your selection, I ask you describe a couple of key situations in either your personal or work life where you would most like to see changes occur as a result of putting into practice any items chosen. Throughout our dialogue I pay close attention to your specific needs and also attempt to enrich your picture of the anticipated benefits from our dialogue. It is my desire and intent to have you see yourself using your new understanding and skills to begin making desired changes in your life circumstances.

My intent in engaging you in this dialogue is to enable you to move out of the observer role and take active ownership of the desired outcome of reading this book. A great description of my model for this learning process can be found in the book, *The Path of Least Resistance*, by Robert Fritz. His explanation of this process is the clearest I have ever found, and my experience has repeatedly confirmed its accuracy. In his book, Fritz describes what takes place in our minds when we hold a clear vision of an ideal in juxtaposition to an equally clear and non-judgmental perception of "current reality." When these conditions are properly met, Fritz says the true path of least resistance is for current reality to "merge" with our clearly held vision of the ideal. There are many challenges involved in successfully bringing this about, of course, and I will attempt to address every one I have identified. Most importantly, my approach is to put my findings to work first, then set about to expand our understanding of those findings once we have experienced their benefits in practice.

So let's proceed as if we are actually face-to-face, and are about to look over a menu of ten possible outcomes available from our discussion. By selecting one or more of the items as a goal, we improve our chances for the subsequent discussion to be useful.

1. We could learn to master a new style of asking the RIGHT QUESTIONS to build trust, improve communications and make all of our interactions with others more meaningful and productive.

2. We could learn to be more disciplined in the use of our intuition, which could help reduce or even eliminate undesired stress in our lives and allow us to enjoy greater comfort and confidence in our everyday decision making.

3. We could gain more insight into the process of dissolving communication barriers. This in turn could give us more skill at building commitment and obtaining enthusiastic cooperation from everyone around us.

4. We could learn how to have more control over our own attitude. This would bring us more peace of mind, as well as allow us to have a more constructive influence on everyone with whom we come in contact.

5. We could learn to shift our focus away from avoiding the downside of life's experiences and thus feel empowered to take more responsibility and initiative.

6. We could learn to reflect from within ourselves a stronger spirit of teamwork and commitment, and use it to put ourselves and others around us ahead of the curve and on a roll.

7. We could learn how to convert energies now being wasted on resistance to change into a performance improvement advantage for ourselves and others around us.

8. We could reduce the amount of stress in our lives by developing new habits to consistently bring out the best in ourselves as well as others around us.

9. We could identify or confirm our own life's purpose and learn to stay more in tune with it. This would assure more energy, creativity and fulfillment in our personal and work lives.

10. We could learn all the steps of building our own strategic life plans and how to master the use of each step in order to reach optimum levels of personal accomplishment and contribution in our lives.

Which one or more of the above items has the most appeal as a desired outcome for our discussion? All are available, of course, and if you pick more than one, it may be helpful to go back and prioritize what you've chosen. Now I'd like to elaborate on each one a bit and give you a preliminary glimpse of how we'll go about accomplishing them.

Asking the RIGHT QUESTIONS

If you happened to pick Item 1, I must first applaud your astuteness, and then commend you for paying close attention so far. Asking properly framed questions is truly the key skill which leads to effortless high performance—and ultimately nearly every other desired outcome on the list as well. I often introduce Clear Purpose Management as an intuition-based system of management. My emphasis here is on both the words "system" and "intuition-based." I do not find it useful to think of someone as being either analytical or intuitive. That misses the point entirely. Effortless high performance is not a matter of being one *or* the other. It is a matter of learning to use *both* the analytical and intuitive aspects of ourselves correctly *in relation to* each other. To be even more specific, we must learn to use our intellects—our conscious, rational minds—to frame questions so they *cannot* be processed rationally. When we do this correctly, the processing of our questions is shifted by default to our intuitive minds.

Our analytical minds are known to use a deductive reasoning process that depletes our energy, while our intuitive minds use an inductive reasoning process that generates fresh, new supplies of creative energy. (i.e., our earlier reference to the three-year-old child.) It is also known that all questions are framed by our conscious, rational minds. Here is where I offer an important new insight: Whenever we ask any kind of a WHAT'S WRONG question, it is both framed and processed in our rational mind. In other words, the way the question is framed allows our rational mind to use its deductive, dismantling way of processing to break down the whole into pieces. And, while there is certainly a time and place for it, deductive reasoning always depletes our stores of creative energy and leaves us tired.

Rational thought, however, has a far more significant limitation than depleting our energy. When completely disconnected from our intuitive minds, our rational minds have been proven totally incapable of distinguishing truth from fiction. This startling discovery comes from the clinical medical research which earned Dr. Roger Sperry the 1981 Nobel Prize for Medicine.

When we ask any kind of a WHAT'S RIGHT question, on the other hand, our rational mind hasn't a clue about how to process the question on its own. As a result, our WHAT'S RIGHT questions are deferred to our less assertive but far more powerful intuition—where they are processed in a manner that generates energy. By "more powerful," I mean that our intuition processes somewhere between 1,000 and 10,000 times as fast as our rational mind. In addition, we know it synthesizes parts into a unified whole, generates creative energy in the process and also cannot be deceived. This means we can tell where our questions are being processed by monitoring our energy levels. This area of inquiry will obviously require lots more attention as we move along in our discussion.

Here is where I'm glad we're together on the patio. It allows me to immediately demonstrate the WHAT'S RIGHT form of questions. *Of the brief information I've just offered about learning to ask properly framed questions, what do you find most intriguing?* After listening carefully to your response, and perhaps answering a question or two, I inquire further, "Can you be even more specific about what intrigues you about the piece you've mentioned?" My intent in asking you such questions is to provide a direct experience of responding to questions which are difficult to process logically, and therefore have a good chance of being processed intuitively.

Confidence in our Intuition

Now, if Item 2 is included in your selection from the list of desired outcomes, I will call your attention to the word "discipline." How does discipline relate to intuition? First, it is important to understand that we have no direct control over our intuition. Therefore, being able to access it properly requires a form of discipline of our rational mind which is entirely different from that which we are taught in school. We have direct control only over the rational part of our mind. Mastering the disciplines required to exercise this control correctly is simply the only way any of us can become effectively guided by our intuition. It is also the only way we can reach and enjoy the state of effortless high performance, or even feel totally comfortable and confident in our everyday decision-making. Gaining full, complete access to our intuitive power is paradoxical. It is entirely dependent on our ability to discipline our rational mind correctly. Only in this way can we become free of stress and enter the state of effortless high performance.

"How do we do this," you ask? Anyone who is consistently able to operate in this state can point to being influenced by a very special mentor-coaching relationship, the structure of which we will explore thoroughly. As you might have already guessed, a big key to the success of such a relationship is someone who asks us properly framed questions rather than presuming to give us "good advice."

How does all of this relate to reducing stress and increasing your feeling of comfort and confidence in everyday decision-making? First of all, there is simply no way to ever enjoy true confidence without learning to honor and gain full access to the intuitive part of ourselves. Second, I propose there is no better way to do this than to find a mentor-coach who will supply us with properly framed questions. In Chapters 7 & 8, I will provide clear guidelines for developing such a relationship.

Incidentally, are you starting to feel any of the discomfort I promised? My goal here is for you to begin developing your own set of unanswered questions, as well as kindle a desire for additional understanding. It is *not* to furnish answers that close down this desire! In order to model good mentorship, I must also ask you to take a moment now to reflect on the ideas set forth in the last three paragraphs. Perhaps you will want to make a note or two to yourself about what special questions have been raised for you, and also what aspect you find most intriguing. It might be even more beneficial for you to reflect on where you stand about honoring your own intuition and any feelings brought up by the information supplied so far. The more time you take here to practice putting your feelings into words, the better prepared you will be to reach and sustain the state of effortless high performance in your life.

Communication Barriers

Let's now take a look at Item 3 on our list of possible outcomes. If you picked this item about dissolving communication barriers, is your focus on those frustrating barriers which seem to exist in others, or is it on barriers found inside yourself? Have you noticed how in our culture we seem to associate the word "communication" more with sending information than with receiving it. I like to characterize this as a John Wayne approach to communications, where we see ourselves riding into town on a big white horse with all the answers. This is in pretty stark contrast to our findings about the communication environment found consistently in the backgrounds of effortless high performers, where a far greater emphasis was placed on questions than on answers.

In my view, the biggest communication barrier any of us will ever address is the one inside ourselves between our head and our heart, or between our intellect and our intuition. This would suggest that the best way to learn how to deal with communication barriers in others is to learn how to dissolve our own. This also takes our discussion out of the realm of theory and makes it immensely practical. It puts us to work on the only area over which we have total control.

My favorite way to begin this process is to share the insightful poem entitled, "Don't Be Fooled By Me."

Don't be fooled by me.
Don't be fooled by the face I wear.
For I wear a thousand masks, masks that I'm afraid to take off, and none of them are me.
Pretending is an art that's second nature with me, but don't be fooled, for God's sake, don't be fooled.
I give the impression that I'm secure, that all is sunny and unruffled with me, within as well as without; that confidence is my name and coolness my game; that the water's calm and I'm in command, and that I need no one.
But don't believe me. Please.
My surface may seem smooth, but my surface is my mask.
Beneath lies no complacence.
Beneath dwells the real me in confusion, in fear and aloneness.
But I hide this. I don't want anybody to know it.
I panic at the thought of my weakness, and fear of being exposed.

That's why I frantically create a mask to hide behind, a nonchalant,
sophisticated facade, to help me pretend, to shield me from the
glance that knows.
But such a glance is precisely my salvation, my only salvation, and
I know it!
That is if it's followed by acceptance, if it's followed by love.
It's the only thing that will assure me of what I cannot assure my-
self—that I am worth something.
But I don't tell you this; I don't dare. I'm afraid to.
I'm afraid your glance will not be followed by acceptance and love.
I'm afraid that deep down I am nothing, that I'm no good, and
that you will see this and reject me.
So I play my game, my desperate game, with a facade of assurance
without, and a trembling child within.
So begins the parade of masks, and my life becomes a front.
Who am I, you may wonder? I am someone you know very well.
For I am every man you meet and I am every woman you meet."

- Author Unknown

I still remember how deeply and painfully I resonated with every one of those words when I first memorized this poem 27 years ago. I now know that the vast majority of us deal every day with the kind of inhibiting emotions it expresses so clearly. Is there any wonder, then, why our communications with others can at times be so challenging?

Here's some good news. Effortless high performers are simply not inhibited by such inner emotions. This presents us with two questions. First, might it be possible for any of us to actually free ourselves from having such inhibiting inner emotions? Second, if it is possible, how do we go about doing so? The answer, of course, is yes, it is possible, and a most important clue for how to gain this freedom lies in the poem, where it refers to "the glance that knows" that is "followed by acceptance and love." The mentor-coaching guidelines offered in Chapter 8, as well as all practices offered throughout the book, are firmly based on such a philosophy.

To continue modeling the mentor-coaching process, I will now ask you to reflect for a moment on whatever might have struck you the most in anything I expressed around communication barriers. The real question is, *Why might it be important for you to learn more about this?* If you will take a moment and jot down a note or two about your observations, you will have again taken advantage of an opportunity to gain more skill at putting your feelings into words. It would be far better, of course, if someone else who is capable of listening with unconditional acceptance were present to hear you put your observations into words.

Attitude Control

Item 4 of possible outcomes from reading this book is improved attitude control, and this could also bring you more peace of mind and a stronger influence over others. Let's say that you picked this item in a different setting where I can use your choice to trigger some dialogue with you and a group of your peers. I will first ask for further clarification about what improved attitude control will do for you. If I conclude from the group's responses that the following example is appropriate, I will invite you to help me develop a list of character traits that most of us would admire in others and desire for ourselves. Typical responses usually include such traits as honesty, integrity, vision, persistence, trust-worthiness, caring, ambition and charisma, as well as ability to lead, organize, delegate, communicate, etc. After listing 15 to 20 suggestions on a blackboard or flip chart, I then ask for a group consensus on each item as to whether it could be considered a skill or an attitude.

Now here is a key question. Imagine you have divided the above traits into the categories of skills and attitudes, with at least one trait that is listed in both categories. Now, over which category of traits do you have the most immediate control? Is it skills or attitudes? It's attitudes, of course. It isn't a matter of whether or not we have control over our attitude. It's a matter of whether or not we know how to exercise to our greatest advantage the control we actually do have.

Learning to put ourselves in a state of effortless high performance does require a good bit of attitude control. Fortunately, a simple and effective way to maintain control over our attitude is the discipline of approaching every person, issue or situation we encounter with a WHAT'S RIGHT mode of inquiry rather than WHAT'S WRONG. This is often much easier said than done, of course, and in the early stages of exploring this discipline it can also seem like we are using this approach to avoid confronting the "obvious" negatives right in front of us. I can assure you right now, this is not our intent whatsoever. Once you have completed your own full examination of this discipline, and in fact put it to work in your life for a few weeks, you will no doubt wonder how you ever survived without it. *Speaking of* WHAT'S RIGHT *questions, what are you finding to be most appealing about the picture I am unfolding before you? Is there any special part of it that somehow "rings true" for you? What is happening to your desire to learn more?*

Taking the Initiative

Item 5 addresses the need to shift our focus away from avoiding the downside of life's experiences. As I sit here searching for the right words to describe this item, I am feeling an urgent need to convey its importance. Very few of us are aware of the degree to which we *create* our own negative life experiences out of the very energy we expend in trying to *avoid* or *prevent* them. It's another of those paradoxes we find so often in the arena of effortless high performance. Perhaps you have heard it said that what we resist persists. I could simply add that what we try to avoid appears—as surely as night follows day. How would you like to instead tap into the very same power and use it to bring your visions of the "ideal" rather than your fears directly into current reality?

At least two areas must be addressed here in order to do that. First, we must understand energy and how our thoughts affect it. Here is the basic concept. Whenever we focus our attention on something—give our energy to it—we can be certain it will expand. In other words, whenever we focus our attention on a negative or undesired aspect of our life, it expands. Whenever we keep our attention focused on a desired goal or positive aspect of our life, it too expands. The issue is it's our choice. It's as simple as that.

A friend of mine got a real insight from this idea of where we put our attention. While he tried to treat his two children equally in regard to financial support he gave them, he found that one kept track of bills and the other kept track of money. Over time, he watched one attract a mountain of debts, and the other a healthy bank account with no debts.

The second area we want to address has to do with the effect of fear on our rational mind's ability to carry out its intended role in our life. Any time our rational mind is focused on avoiding what it fears—or judges to be negative—it simply cannot generate the questions needed to properly engage our intuition. Throughout this book we address both issues quite thoroughly. Our ultimate goal is to enable you to develop the same kind of "can't-lose" perspective on life found in every one of the effortless high performers we studied.

As you can imagine, this is a complex issue. I have seen at least eight approaches to it in practice. What works for one person may not work for another. The end result of having your own personal "can't-lose" perspective is extremely empowering, however, so I will do all I can to help you establish your own path to getting there. For now, I will simply invite you to dream a little about what it might be like for you to be fully empowered to take up the initiative and assume total responsibility for exercising all of your strengths.

Wow! That's quite a bit to reflect on, isn't it? *What aspect of the picture I've just painted about Item 5 is most appealing to you? Are there any surprises for you in this area? How do you see yourself applying and reaping the benefits from the development of your own "can't-lose" approach to life? If there were no potential "downsides" to distract you, how would your actions be different?*

Teamwork and Commitment

Item 6 addresses teamwork and commitment. If you included this item in your choice of desired outcomes, can I guess that your interest in improved teamwork is primarily focused on your relationships with others? If so, perhaps we have a surprise in store. Teamwork difficulties encountered between ourselves and others are often direct reflections of insufficient teamwork taking place internally—between our head and our heart. Therefore, by far the most effective way to address teamwork issues we might have with others is to strengthen our internal sense of teamwork between our rational and intuitive capabilities— between our head and our heart.

For a quick look at a key factor involved in this issue, let's look at some of the misunderstandings we have around the issue of feelings and emotions. Most of us have been taught correctly that emotions aren't okay in business. What we fail to realize, of course, is that a vast difference exists between feelings and emotions. Emotions such as anger,

29

fear, jealousy, hatred, desire and greed are unhealthy residues or debris resulting from our judging things to be good or bad, right or wrong. It is therefore quite appropriate for us not to trust our emotions. Feelings, on the other hand, are one of our intuition's three primary languages, and they are vitally important to our success. The two most important feelings are comfort with things which intuitively "fit" and discomfort with things which don't. Feelings are also the "glue" of teamwork and commitment. Learning to honor our feelings and grasp the full meaning of the messages they are trying to bring us is of utmost importance. The difficulty arises when we fail to make a distinction between feelings and emotions and end up throwing the baby out with the bath water. That certainly raises some interesting questions, doesn't it?

Speaking of teamwork, let's focus for a moment specifically on the intended ideal of teamwork between you, the reader, and me, the writer. Through questions I ask after expanding upon each of the ten desired outcomes, I am attempting to demonstrate many subtle aspects of the ideal mentor-coaching relationship. One aspect is actions I take to help you create in your mind a meaningful picture of each piece of the desired outcome as well as its whole. Each time it becomes a bit clearer, and at the same time more appealing, your picture of the desired outcome becomes that much more likely to transform itself into your current reality. Another aspect lies in your willingness to reflect as deeply as you are now capable on the questions I ask. These reflections are important action steps on your part. They work to strengthen teamwork between your head and your heart as well as between the two of us. In other words, your internal practice expands your external teamwork capability, just as external practice enhances your internal teamwork capability.

At this point, I am prompted to acknowledge a common reaction I get from people being exposed to some of this for the first time: "Boy, is this stuff deep! I'm not sure I'm ready for this." If you should be having even a hint of such feelings, let me offer some encouragement. In her book, *Drawing on the Right Side of the Brain*, Betty Edwards teaches us a way to distract our rational mind and stop it from interfering with our intuitive mind's natural ability to draw. Her approach is to give our rational mind a task too complex for it to handle. When done in an environment free from threat, this can allow our rational mind to throw up its hands, step out of the way and let our intuition step in and handle the challenge.

Here is another paradox. If I were to present this material so your intellect could easily grasp everything being said, I would risk complete failure in my efforts to equip you to become a practicing effortless high performer in your own right. In its outer-directed, self-protective role, the intellect takes great pride in being able to show that it understands. Effortless high performance, however, is inner-directed, and requires an entirely different level of involvement from the intellect than mastery of concepts. At the same time, if you were to judge yourself to be "deficient," or choose to feel threatened because you do not understand everything as quickly and perfectly as you'd like, I would risk failure of my efforts, too. Perhaps it would be good to remind you of the book's title. This idea of needing to understand everything intellectually is just one of the "rules" we're setting out to break. Are we having fun yet?

As our picture of the desired outcomes continues to unfold, are any changes taking place in your expectations for reading this book? If so, how would you describe these changes? What is the most useful insight you have gained from our ideas about teamwork? What is the most powerful unanswered question it raises in your mind?

Resistance to Change

Item 7 addresses the need to learn how to convert energies now being wasted on resistance to change into a performance improvement advantage for yourself and everyone around you. Before I continue, I must first check to see if any interest you might have in this area is focused on dealing with your own resistance, or if it is instead focused on dealing with resistance found in others. This is actually a trick question, because for us to presume to deal with resistance to change in others would be dealing in theory. Hopefully you have some of your own resistance left to be addressed, for if you have none of your own from which to learn, you will find it nearly impossible to learn how to deal with resistance to change in others.

Let's begin by calling attention to common sources of resistance to change. First, rather than moving forward through life in pursuit of a clear vision of an ideal, most of us are paying too much attention to past negatives and working particularly hard to "avoid mistakes." It's as if we are "backing" through life, pulling along a little box of secret hang-ups as we go. Our little box is filled with painful memories of emotions we've felt in the past and never ever wish to feel again. Now imagine the energy it takes to keep the lid on that box so none of those painful emotions can pop out and hurt us again.

To illustrate another source of resistance to change, please note I have chosen to use the word "convert" rather than "overcome," which is the word much more often linked to resistance to change. In order to convert or transform this energy, my intent is to find its inherent value rather than take a negative view and see it as a problem. This calls our attention to a huge issue in our culture. By approaching issues, people or situations as problems or negatives, we drain our energy as well as block the potential for insights we could be gaining from our intuition.

Effortless high performers enjoy an immense contribution of both energy and insights from their intuition. This occurs as a result of their discipline to search for the inherent value or opportunity in everything. A good way to summarize my observations about resistance to change is to reiterate what I said earlier in this chapter: what we embrace expands, and what we resist persists.

Now, for more of our mentoring questions. *What idea or concept struck you the most from the last three paragraphs about resistance to change? Have any special "lightbulbs" gone on for you as a result? How would you describe a key benefit you hope to gain in the area of dealing with resistance to change?*

A Fresh Look at Stress

With Item 8 we get to address some fun new ways to deal with stress. By now you are surely beginning to see at least one common theme present in several of these items. Suppressing the worst simply doesn't work. Attempting to do so causes a lot of stress. Presuming we could actually succeed at suppressing the worst is a rule in serious need of being broken. Looking for the good in ourselves and others, counting our blessings, bringing out the best and building on strengths are wonderful habits each of us could well afford to practice on a much more frequent basis.

Now, about stress. First of all, it's time for everyone to realize all stress is self-induced. No more excuses. It is not possible for any of us to have any stress which we ourselves do not cause. Unfortunately, many people do not yet realize this. Look at the stress management courses, for example. All of them attempt to show us how to deal with stress after we have it. How typical of our symptom-focused culture! Our approach here is to remove the causes of stress—at least the form of stress all of us would be happy to do without. The technical word for this form of stress is "distress." The more desirable form of stress—the form we will want to know more about how to generate by our own choice—is called "u-stress." (U-stress is the form of stress which keeps us acting in ways which support the achievement of our goals.)

So how do we manage to cause our own stress? We do it by assigning positive or negative value to facts. It's as simple as that. Now, if you are serious about putting into practice the principles and tools offered here, you can soon expect to be relatively free from stress. What else would you expect from effortless high performance?

Surely something must have struck you in the last two paragraphs on stress. *Can you put a finger on any area in your own life where you are causing yourself more stress than you need? What is the most useful insight you have gained in this area?* I invite you to set the book aside for a few moments and take time to reflect on any feelings you may be having in this area. Writing your feelings down on paper is also a good way to improve your skills at putting them into words.

Defining Purpose

Item 9 on our list of desired outcomes hints at significant benefits we can enjoy when we understand our own life purpose and learn to bring our actions into alignment with it. Our purpose answers the question of *why* we are here. As such, it is a very different concept than a goal. I mention the distinction because, when first introduced to the concept of purpose, 90% of Americans are unable to distinguish the difference between purpose and goals. Purpose is far more subtle than a goal. Purpose works very much like a radar beacon in an airplane. When we're on the intangible "beam" of our purpose, life just sings. When we fall off this beam, our life "squawks," typically in the form of "problems." I see problems as having only one reason to show up in our life: to tell us we are out of alignment with our purpose. As a result, whenever a problem shows up in my life, I am far more intent on getting the "message" than on solving the problem. I have learned this the hard way. If a little problem shows up and I "successfully" solve it while failing to get its message, I have unintentionally set myself up for an even larger problem. Have you ever noticed how some people seem to keep attracting larger and larger problems and never seem to get the message? Can you imagine how far off track they must be from their purpose? How much simpler life can be when we get our messages from the *little* problems!

As I mentioned earlier, each of us already has an inherent purpose in our life. Yet, isn't it amazing that fewer than five out of 100 of us have even the remotest clue as to what ours might be? (Where do you fit in this?) In addition, while some 60% of us have a relatively good grasp of the concept of goals, 90% are unable to distinguish the difference between a purpose and a goal. I believe this discrepancy is related to the dominance of WHAT'S WRONG questions in our lives. This is one reason why both in my consulting work and throughout this book I place a strong emphasis on mastering the discipline of asking intuition-engaging questions. I intend for you to be fully equipped to either identify or confirm your life's purpose as a result of participating in the exercises presented here.

Getting your purpose in writing is one thing. It is quite another matter, however, to keep our lives in alignment with that purpose. Only after we strengthen our connection with our intuition can we expect to keep our lives in full alignment with our purpose, and do so with little effort. This is the essence of effortless high performance, and it is high among my reasons for putting this material into writing.

From my added observations about the issue of purpose, what are you finding most intriguing? *If you were to put at least part of your life's purpose in writing right now, what would it look like? How would you describe your level of confidence that you have correctly captured the parts of it you are able to identify? On a one to ten scale, where would you place your interest level in having a complete grasp of your purpose in life? What do you now sense would be the biggest benefit of that? What additional insights are you getting about yourself from reflecting on your answers to these questions? If your interest in this is high, what is the primary benefit you see from taking time out to reflect on every mentor-coaching question I ask?*

A Strategic Life Plan

Finally we come to Item 10 on our list of possible outcomes you can anticipate from reading this book. This one offers to teach all of the steps in the planning and tracking structure used to draw everything we've mentioned so far into a coherent whole. Those who share my enthusiasm for cross-applying all of these principles to organizational entities will be particularly delighted with our structure.

The strategic life plan used to reach and sustain the on-a-roll state of being is made up of five elements. As I introduce each, be sure to examine it with an intuition-engaging question such as, *"How could personal mastery of this element enhance my overall state of being?"* Do the same at the end with the elements as a whole.

The first element is to have a clearly defined statement of purpose for our lives. This vitally important element supplies the intuitive driving-force energy used by effortless high performers to sustain their commitment. The words of the purpose statement are not important. They serve merely as symbols to collect and represent the intangible energy of our actual purpose.

The second element is to have a set of long-range goals to serve as a distant focal point chosen to optimize fulfillment of our purpose. A keen observer will note the second element is purely analytical, while the first is purely intuitive. It is always tempting for the second, analytical element to be the "master" over the intuitive, but for the entire process to succeed, the element of goals must always be in service to purpose.

The third element of our personal strategic life plan is to be perfectly clear on our short-range action plans. Nothing new here except most people bridge from the short-range to mid-range to long-range goals without ever tapping into the energy of purpose for use in sustaining WHOLEHEARTED commitment. Action plans are the tactical what, when and how-to steps which ultimately transform our distant visions into current reality.

The fourth element may well come as a surprise to those who recognize the contribution of Peter Drucker in the first three elements. I, too, overlooked it in my earlier years, but later realized all effortless high performers make a practice of keeping track of what they are doing right. This continuous monitoring of progress toward desired end results keeps generating fresh supplies of creative energy needed to make high performance appear to be so effortless.

The fifth and final element has been repeatedly and eloquently addressed by Drucker, yet its awesome potential remains untapped by most people. This element calls our attention to the vitally important discipline of continually identifying and building upon our strengths. It shows the benefits of relentless, disciplined use of WHAT'S RIGHT questions, and enables us to fully comprehend all aspects of our strengths —so we can use them as building blocks to create our ideal future.

This fifth element holds the key for unlocking the entire plan. I see more than 90% of us operating in a "find-what's-wrong-and-fix-it" mode. This is directly opposed to the mode required to activate this plan. Only after we reverse this mode of thinking and begin to master the key discipline of identifying and building upon our strengths can we expect to begin accessing the power of our purpose. It is almost as if the fifth element needs to be first, yet it also clearly belongs at the end (where it is now). Perhaps if we saw all five elements in a circle, we might have an even better appreciation for the vitally important role this discipline plays in continually intensifying the power of the full model.

I cannot overemphasize how important it is for us to get fully grounded in this discipline of building on strengths. At least three-quarters of our time and effort in the typical 18-hour time frame of each of the several hundred team dialogues we have conducted has been devoted to this agenda. This book will be no different. Once we gain full mastery of this discipline, the other four elements will fall into place with very little effort. I suppose it is like any other field of endeavor. Master the basics and the game virtually plays itself. This is certainly the case here.

Transforming Knowledge Into Wisdom

I shall now get back to modeling the mentor-coaching questions to enable you to continue transforming the ideas set forth in this chapter into some truly useful wisdom. *I'll begin by asking you what two or three ideas from this chapter have impacted you the most? What makes each of these ideas stand out in your mind at this moment? Does one or more of them resonate with what you already know at a deeper level, but hadn't thought about? What idea appears to offer the greatest promise for getting you on a roll and keeping you there? Of all the desired outcomes explored here, which one now holds the greatest appeal to you?*

Chapter Three

The Structure of WHAT'S RIGHT Questions

WHAT'S RIGHT Questions

This is a perfect time to introduce my "cascading hierarchy" of WHAT'S RIGHT questions asked by all visionary leaders and effortless high performers. In many ways this model offers an extended look at how building on strengths really works in practice. I shall never forget the personal thrill of describing this thought process to Fred Smith, chairman and founder of Federal Express, and having him remark afterwards, "This is the first time in my life I have ever had anyone describe to me the exact thought process I used to build this company."

I think it would work best to start with a bare-bones framework and then expand it.

❖ The initial question is simply "WHAT'S RIGHT?" or "WHAT'S WORKING?

❖ Next, "What makes it RIGHT?" or "Why does it WORK?"

❖ Third, "What would be ideally RIGHT?" or "What would WORK ideally?"

❖ Fourth, "What's not yet quite RIGHT?"

❖ Last, "What resources can I find to make it RIGHT?"

39

Now let's expand on each. The first question is an agenda-setting question. Its intent is to help us identify something that is working so well it deserves further study. Even though I use the word RIGHT in all of these questions—mostly because of its "slogan" or memory potential—this is definitely not a right/wrong form of RIGHT. Instead, it's a WHAT'S WORKING form of RIGHT. Regardless of how the question is framed, however, some 90 to 95% of the population prefers to use it as a dismissal question. From the depletion/shortage point of view, if something is working, why waste energy thinking about it? We will go into this in more detail in Chapter 7, but those who see the world from this perspective typically consider thinking to be an energy-cost item. I even find it useful to characterize some of these people as looking frantically under every rock for a way to not think. In this case, they will set aside whatever is working in order to remain alert to where they may be vulnerable.

Once the effortless high performer has identified something deserving of further inquiry, their next step is to begin wondering, "What is it that makes this RIGHT?" or "What makes this WORK?" This is really the three-year-old's *why* question. It's a wonderful, intuition-engaging, insight-producing, energy-generating question. I cannot begin to overemphasize the importance of asking this question. Among other things, it works to transform knowledge into wisdom. I like to imagine millions of little data bits being accumulated in our intuition from our life experience. In response to our probing *"Why?"* question, they begin to swirl about looking for ways to inter-link with other data.

Watch now as two of these unconnected data bits come into proximity of each other and discover, "Oh, look! We fit. We belong together." The joining I have just described is an attempt to characterize the "eureka" moment, often symbolized by a light bulb, when two disparate pieces of knowledge are joined together and thus transformed into wisdom. Whenever this occurs, a permanent node of energy is always created. Then, as tiny chunks of wisdom are brought into proximity with other pieces of knowledge or wisdom, subsequent eureka moments continue to build larger and larger chunks of wisdom. At the same time this process generates greater and greater stores of creative energy. To interact with someone who has done this for years is truly a wonder to behold. It is as if they have transformed the entire accumulation of data or knowledge from their life experience into a rich fabric of wisdom. It's tremendously inspiring!

The third question, "What can I imagine might be ideally RIGHT?" is a vision-building question actually processed by the analytical mind. Since this is true, the process of developing a vision is known to consume a vast amount of creative energy. It requires so much energy, in fact, that the 90% of our population which operates in the depletion/shortage mode will not even dare to consider it. I like to portray the vision-building process by putting my hands together in front of me and shoving a big wedge out into space and prying open a vacuum. It takes a great deal of energy to shove my wedge out into space, and even more energy to pry open the vacuum. Only those who have built up ample reserves of creative energy through their use of Question 2 are capable of processing Question 3. Then, as the vacuum grows, a powerful feeling known as creative tension develops around its outer edge. After watching this powerful feeling at work for several years, I suspect it could easily be the most powerful motivating force in the entire universe. It is as if this feeling of creative tension sends out a telegraph message to the universe inviting the perfect resources to come and fill the void created by the question, "What would the ideal (_____) look like?"

41

Running continually on this level-three WHAT'S RIGHT QUESTION is the ultimate secret of effortless high performance. It is the central theme in the life of every visionary leader I have studied. Knowing the contribution it makes to the lives of individual effortless high performers is what inspired me to use it as my model for the challenging software development project described in Chapter 1. In Chapter 9 I cite another example of its use, and relate even more details about how this level-three question can be applied to produce dramatic improvements in business performance.

I must also mention a big caution flag at this point. The feeling of emptiness that develops around the vacuum—the feeling of not having the answer—has an extremely close resemblance to pain. As a result, any of us in the depletion/shortage mode will tend to run *from* it like the plague. Those of us who are "pain avoiders" will even scramble like crazy to find anything available to fill the void and shut down the feeling of not knowing. Effortless high performers, on the other hand, run *on* the feeling—as if it were a radar beacon. Somehow they are able to rely on the feeling as if it were an announcement mechanism to pinpoint the location of the next eureka event.

The fourth question in this cascading hierarchy is, "What, then, is not yet quite right?" This is the true motivating question for visionary leaders and other effortless high performers. As the ultimate intuition-engaging question, it further defines the edges of the "holes" in an evolving vision of the ideal. It thereby gives the resulting vacuum even more power to attract the perfect resources to fill the ever more clearly defined hole in their vision. We need to realize that a vision of an ideal is like Swiss cheese. It is filled with holes. The holes, in fact, are what give the vision its power. A vision resides in our conscious, rational mind, and its holes furnish our intuitive mind with an endless supply of un-articulated WHAT'S RIGHT QUESTIONS to keep it fully engaged and productive. This point will be discussed in more detail on several occasions throughout the book.

Incidentally, visionary leaders and other effortless high performers rarely articulate Question 4 as I have above. Invariably they have been processing Questions 1, 2 and 3 for a long time. Rarely are the first three levels of WHAT'S RIGHT questions visible to anyone around them, however. This means the only question visible to the rest of us is #4— and seldom is it verbalized as "What's not yet quite right?" Since people frequently choose the shortcut wording of WHAT'S WRONG, visionaries are often seen by others around them as being oppressively negative. However, even when they verbalize Question 4 as "WHAT'S WRONG?" it is emphatically not the normal WHAT'S WRONG question. Instead, it is an attempt to more precisely define the edges of the unknown in a way that gives it more power to attract the perfect solution to fill in the hole so defined.

Question 5 is simply, "What resources can I find to fill in the gap?" As a natural follow-on question, it hardly needs explanation. It serves, however, as a marvelous focusing question to guide constructive action.

> # What do I know is already *RIGHT?*
> ### The agenda setting question
> # **What is it that makes it *RIGHT?***
> ### **The energy generating question**
> # What would be ideally *RIGHT?*
> ### The vision-building question
> # What's not yet quite *RIGHT?*
> ### The gap-defining question
> # What resources can I find to make it *RIGHT?*
> ### The action-engaging question

It is now time for me to slip back into my mentor-coaching role and model Questions 1 and 2 for you. (Every visionary leader and effortless high performer I have studied can tell us who filled this vitally important role in their life.) *How would you describe the two or three most useful insights you gained from the above description of my five-level cascading hierarchy of* WHAT'S RIGHT *questions? Since this is such a significant piece, it could be well worth your time to grab a notebook and jot down several ideas which may have crossed your mind while reading this information. Does the sequence describe an experience common for you? If so, what piece do you now understand more clearly? How might you benefit from this additional understanding?*

What aspect of using the five levels of right questions is not yet a common experience for you? What aspect of this thought process is most appealing? How would you describe what is most appealing about it? Does the description give you any special insights into others you know? In what way do you see yourself benefiting from these additional insights? How would you describe the major appeal that learning to master this mode of asking questions would have for you? What would be the single biggest benefit you could imagine from learning how to ask these questions?

Hypothetical Extremes

Just for fun, I will now bring Chapter 3 to a close by describing behavioral traits found in two types of individuals who represent the hypothetical extremes of those who fail to ask RIGHT QUESTIONS. This is followed by descriptions of parallel behavioral traits for two types of individuals who represent the hypothetical extremes of those who succeed at asking RIGHT QUESTIONS.

First, we look at those who fail to ask RIGHT QUESTIONS. Type 1 is the characterization of someone who asks all the WRONG QUESTIONS.

He or she is hard and coldly logical and drives to get the facts. In the extreme, this person uses up the energy and talent of others, then discards them. These people are self-centered, controlling and overly conscious of their image. They diligently collect data with which to claim credit or shift blame. They pick subordinates who can be intimidated, and cause others to waste lots of energy on flank-guarding and stress.

Type 2 is the characterization of someone who is dependent on others for questions. He or she is soft and overly sensitive to other people's feelings. In the extreme, these people find it easy to inspire others, but fail to direct their efforts. They are defensive and vulnerable to negative influences from others. They are short on follow-through and thus deliver unpredictable performance. They pick subordinates who are non-confrontive and un-threatening. They also tend to over-trust and get burned.

Next, we look at those who profit from asking RIGHT QUESTIONS. Type 3 is one who asks himself or herself all the RIGHT QUESTIONS. These people absorb information from the environment very rapidly. In the extreme, they are purpose-driven and can easily become impatient with others who lack commitment. They are results-oriented and are not inhibited by obstacles. They deliver consistently outstanding individual performance. They prefer subordinates who are equally competent. They also find it difficult to inspire teamwork and commitment.

Type 4 is one who asks RIGHT QUESTIONS of others. He or she fosters a high-trust environment and typically uses questions within that environment to create a shared vision. These people are strongly results-oriented and develop a strong team commitment. They produce steady improvement in performance through teamwork. They bring out the best in all types of subordinates. As you can imagine, they build a cohesive and highly effective team on which any of us would gladly participate.

As you reflect on the above four character types, what stands out to you the most? Which one has the most to teach you? What are you learning about yourself from reviewing these four types? Remember, we deliberately set these up as hypothetical extremes. Keeping that in mind, *if you could choose to adopt any one of these styles as your own, which would it be? Is that a different style from where you see yourself today? If so, what is preventing you from making that change immediately? To approach this from another angle, what level of control do you feel you have today over the style you utilize? In what way might you find yourself dependent on circumstances to determine the style you use?*

Lots of insights are available from examining these four types. Let's now see if we can generate some additional insights by shining more light on each type. First of all, Type 1 exemplifies someone whose development is skewed to the analytical, while Type 2 exemplifies someone whose development is skewed to the intuitive. Hopefully none of us find ourselves operating at either of these two extremes, but they certainly are instructive. Using the hypothetical extreme of Type 1 allows us to characterize someone who is totally analytical and thus by definition lives completely in a world of illusion. (Remember, the rational mind by itself is completely incapable of distinguishing truth from fiction.) This is why we can cast the motivation for Type 1 as purely to build a "case" with which to claim credit or shift blame.

Examining Type 2 can be equally instructive, as this hypothetical extreme allows us to characterize someone who is totally intuitive and thus by definition is completely dependent on others for activating or motivating questions. Yes, they're connected to their intuition's awesome source of power, but of what use is it without the means to generate the questions to put it to work? Notice how Type 1 is directive while Type 2 is responsive. It is characteristic of Type 1's to operate under the illusion they can be the master over the "powerless" intuitive. Type 2's are in need of a properly disciplined rational mind to support them as a servant.

By the way, there is another fun way to contrast differences between those whose development is skewed far over to the analytical compared to those whose development is skewed far over to the intuitive. At the analytical extreme we see people who can explain everything—if they could only feel it. At the intuitive extreme we see people who can feel everything—if they could only explain it. We will cover this in more detail in Chapter 6.

The primary difference between Types 3 and 4 is where the questions are directed. In Type 3 they are directed internally, while in Type 4 they are supplied to others. Given the choice, most of us would like to have as many Type 4 traits as possible. We find the only way to get there, however, is to master everything it takes to be a successful Type 3. Actually, I would expect a high proportion of those who read this book will already be operating primarily as a Type 3. If this is the case for you, all we have to do is thoroughly and explicitly validate what you are already doing right internally so you can simply externalize those same actions.

I have good news, too, for anyone whose operating style leans more toward Type 1. If this is the case for you, I can confirm that your greatest strength is mental discipline. There is a good chance you have developed this discipline out of a perceived need to keep control over all the possible ways you could lose in order to protect yourself from being hurt. I cannot say the solution for you will be easy, but it certainly is simple. All you have to do is convert your WHAT'S WRONG questions into WHAT'S RIGHT questions and, because of your discipline strength, you could end up effortlessly outperforming all of us.

I only wish it were such a simple matter to transform someone with a Type 2 style into an effortless high performer. If you lean toward a

Type 2 style, you already know how "tuned in" you are to a far deeper level of knowing than most. There is also a good chance you have been intimidated into not trusting your "knowing" by those who are good at explaining the things they have only been told, but now think they know. Perhaps you have noticed how much of the world we live in is geared to reward those who are good at explaining things, rather than those who truly "know." This leaves you in a motivational quandary. In order to achieve success, you must develop a much better set of analytical disciplines. But why would you ever want to start from scratch and build a mere PC—i.e., develop your analytical disciplines—if you are already plugged directly into the mainframe of greater intuitive knowing? It's simply because the world we live in writes its biggest checks to those who have excellent use of their PC—and can thus explain with their analytical mind what they have been told by others. Incidently, a remarkably simple and effective way to begin developing the needed disciplines is to practice reading out loud for about 20 minutes a day.

So regardless of where of you are today, in the pages that follow we'll put most of our attention on developing explicit mastery of the Type 3 style. We will do so because we see this as the surest path for us to evolve into a natural Type 4 style.

It is now time for some more mentor-coaching questions. *What description impacted you the most from the four hypothetical extremes? Does thinking about one or more of them trigger insights about your own personal style? Did anything make you look at a "rule" about how you think something "should" work and realize it no longer serves you? If you were to send me a brief note or e-mail message right now, what two thoughts or feelings would you most want to express? What is your greatest hope in continuing to read this book?*

Chapter Four

CHANGING PERCEPTIONS

Developing a Strengths Awareness

Now the fun begins. Here we get to roll up our sleeves and jump right into our project of constructing a fully operational "build on strengths" mind set. Let's begin with a simple exercise that asks you to jot down on a sheet of paper what you consider to be six of your greatest personal strengths and six of your most bothersome personal weaknesses. It might be helpful to list them in two side-by-side columns, but that is not essential. Do your best to list six of each, noting that the entire success of the exercise is dependent on having you pay careful attention to any and all feelings you may have while you jot down each item on your list. What you write down on your list is nobody's business, so please don't think you will need to show it to anyone. You must write the six items down in each category, however, if you wish to enjoy any of the marvelous insights available from this exercise. And, while you may think you have done this before and thus want to keep right on reading, it is doubtful you have done it with our special focus on the feelings associated with the process. I believe this aspect of the exercise

49

is necessary if we are each to gain all the insights available as it unfolds. Therefore, please set aside this book and make your two lists. **PAUSE**

Here are some questions I would like you to reflect on once your two lists are complete. Which of the two lists do you have the strongest feelings about right now as you read them over again—your strengths or your weaknesses? What words would you use to describe your sense of enjoyment or appreciation of such introspective exercises as this, where you are asked to examine your strengths and weaknesses? Is it pleasure? Pain? Or are your feelings rather neutral?

Please go back to your two lists now and place a check mark (√) by as many as five of the characteristics on your list you would most like to see changed over the next 12 months. **PAUSE** We are now ready to explore some of the additional feelings you may have noticed so far in this exercise. First of all, which column did you choose to start making your list—your strengths or your weaknesses? It's fascinating to be a mouse in the corner and watch people do this when we are working with a group of 12 to 16 team members. We never look at what people list as their strengths or weaknesses, but we do notice some who list all six strengths quite easily and then labor over listing four or five weaknesses. It works the same way in reverse sometimes, too. Some people quickly list six weaknesses and then labor over listing their strengths. Then occasionally we notice someone who lists one strength, one weakness, a second strength and second weakness, etc. The point of this is to simply wonder together, what feelings must be guiding all those choices? Quite often we also find people listing the same character trait on both lists. What feelings do you suppose might be prompting all of these fascinating choices? None of these feelings are either good or bad, you understand, it is just extremely useful to raise our awareness of how powerfully we are being guided by them.

Speaking of being guided by feelings, let's try this one. Notice which character traits you placed your check marks beside to indicate those you would most wish to see changed in the next year. We have a special way of scoring your check marks. For each one you placed beside a strength you wish to build up, please give yourself a score of minus one (–1). Then, for each mark you placed beside a weakness you would like to correct, please give yourself a score of plus one (+1). Total your net score (your possible range is between a –5 if you checked all five strengths and a +5 if you checked all five weaknesses) and make note of it where we can refer back to it during a later exercise. PAUSE

Lots of us will notice another feeling when we have perhaps two or three character traits left to jot down on one side or the other and can't think of any more to add. What should we do about our list not being complete, we wonder? Is it a stab of guilt we feel? After all, we "should" complete the assignment, shouldn't we? Fascinating how powerfully we are guided by our feelings, isn't it?

Perhaps the most important feeling we might want to explore is what happens to our energy levels while we are putting attention on our strengths as compared to our weaknesses. How did this work out for you? Did you feel your energy level going up or down while you were focused on preparing your list of strengths? What about when you were listing your weaknesses? What insights are you gaining from your answers? Remember, feelings are a major message medium for our intuition. Most of us could use a good deal more practice at putting our feelings into words before we will have any real confidence in reading the messages our intuition wishes to send us. Out of nearly 10,000 people with whom we have interacted around this specific set of questions, I can assure you a clear majority actually feels the energy level rise while they are putting attention on their strengths and then fall while atten-

51

tion is being put on their weaknesses. We happen to think this is highly significant. It also relates directly to the energy we must all learn to generate if we are to reach the state of effortless high performance. What is your intuition telling you about this right now?

Finally, someone nearly always brings up the frustrating point about the items on their list of weaknesses being exactly the same as those listed five years, ten years or sometimes even 15 years ago. Now what is this telling us? No puzzle here! Clearly the approach we have all learned to use for correcting our weaknesses is failing miserably everywhere we turn. I can promise you, the old approach for dealing with weaknesses is one of the most important practices we expect you will wish to change as a result of reading this book. In fact, we are working on that change in this very chapter.

Before we move on, however, I'd better not forget to ask at least a couple of my mentor-coaching questions. I myself am feeling rather delighted at the moment over having captured the above material in writing for the very first time. I have worked with it verbally hundreds of times in my team dialogues, but have never before attempted to capture the enlightening power of the experience in writing. This also reminds me of an experience from years ago when I was invited to conduct one of our team dialogues for a group of insurance company managers in Bogota, Colombia. I was told everyone would be able to speak English. As it turned out, 15 of the 18 participants did, in fact, speak English. About two hours into the dialogue, however, it suddenly occurred to me that while most of them spoke reasonable English, I was the only one in the room who "thought" in English.

From that moment on, I continued to ask my questions in English, but encouraged everyone to respond in Spanish. I realized it was not important for me to understand their answers. It was important for them to experience success after success at putting their feelings into words. A bit like the experience I am having right now as I furnish you with questions, but don't have the direct pleasure of seeing the insights you are gaining as you express your feelings back in return. Perhaps it would be good for all of us to remind ourselves from time to time of what I learned in Bogota. It was amazing how the language difference prevented my ego from interfering with their learning.

So what are the two most useful insights you have gained from exploring your own feelings around your strengths and weaknesses? In what special ways did you benefit from being given a peek at the wide variety of different feelings other people have expressed around their feelings in this area? Have you noticed any changes beginning to occur in how you view your own strengths and weaknesses? If so, what might those changes look like?

Mission Control

For our next step we'll need to apply some imagination. Let's pretend we're sitting in the mission control center of our personality. Before us (see next page) lies a bank of gauges which allow us to take an accurate reading of the relative value of our strengths in each of a dozen personal productivity areas. Each gauge represents a personality trait or characteristic normally associated with being a highly productive, successful person.

Please take a few moments right now and use a pencil or pen to position a needle on each gauge to signify where you would intuitively rate yourself in each area at this time. Since it is not intended for anyone else to ever see your answers, please make a concerted effort to be as totally honest with yourself as you are capable of being. Remember, too, your first answer is usually best. The insights that are available later for those who complete this exercise can be quite profound. PAUSE

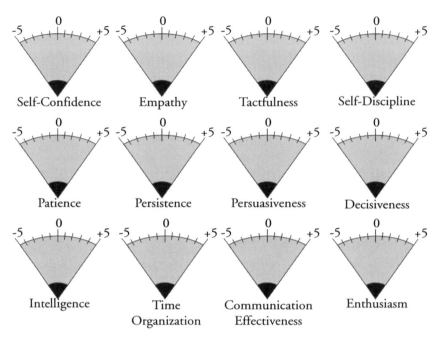

As I prepare to walk alongside of you through our next exercise, I am especially aware of the limitations of not being there with you in person. Perhaps we can offset some of those limitations if you will make an extra-special effort to follow my directions exactly. Let's imagine I'm either sitting beside you with a pad of paper and a pencil, or standing beside a flip chart in front of you and a small group of your peers. I now proceed to give you a careful set of instructions before I begin writing on the pad. My instructions are as follows. Please pay very close attention to what I am about to do. I am going to put some numbers on the pad. If you see anything you agree with, please speak up and tell me about it . . . or if you disagree. I then proceed to write the following numbers on my pad, expressing each one out loud as I go along: "4 plus 6 equals 10, 11 plus 8 equals 19, 6 plus 3 equals 9, 7 plus 11 equals 16, 3 plus. . ." and about then either you or someone else will speak up to stop me, saying, "Oops! 7 plus 11 is not 16."

4	11	6	7	3
+6	+8	+3	+11	+9
10	19	9	16	12

At this point I will look puzzled and ask, "What about the rest of these?" Without a moment's hesitation I then add with a fair amount of intensity, "Why is it that the only thing you have told me about is what I did wrong? Didn't I ask you to pay very close attention to what I do, and if you see anything you *agree* with, please speak up and tell me about it?" As you might guess, this usually triggers a fair amount of rationalizing—with which we can also have some fun. Sometimes it is even helpful to ask the person doing the rationalizing to check their feelings to see what is driving the rationalizations.

I must mention here that I have personally conducted this exercise one-on-one more than 1,000 times during the past 20 years, and hundreds of times in small groups, too. In all that time, I have seen only 24 occasions when someone spoke up immediately after I put up the first set of numbers and said out loud, "I agree." This certainly points out how focused we are as a culture on WHAT'S WRONG, doesn't it?

One more very powerful lesson remains to be learned from this experience. Perhaps more than anything, this exercise makes it abundantly clear that the vast majority of us are negatively motivated. To be more precise, most of us are motivated to avoid pain. And the pain we most want to avoid is having to feel, once again, a negative emotion we've felt before and never, ever want to *ever* feel again. (Didn't you think all those never ever's did a great job of demonstrating the intensity of this desire we have to avoid pain?) We are only kidding ourselves, however, if we think this approach is helping us. This is because in our efforts to avoid negatives, we mistakenly keep ourselves on high alert to spot any and all negatives we might wish to avoid. And, in case you missed it, this is negative motivation, pure and simple. It is a compulsive focus on the negative, and all of the attention we put on the negative does more to create negatives in our lives than most of us would ever imagine. You can be sure this is one of the practices we will soon be changing with this book.

A Look at Self-Image

For our next exercise I will ask you to picture a simple round circle in front of you. The circle symbolizes our self-image. In other words, it represents both how we see ourselves and how we imagine other people see us. From another perspective it will also represent a mixture of every one of our many strengths and weaknesses. To illustrate the relationship between our strengths and weaknesses, let's draw a tiny little wedge in the left portion of the circle and give it a darker shade to represent our weaknesses. We can then give the entire remainder of the circle a lighter shade and have it represent our strengths, as shown in the diagram.

Does this diagram offer a reasonably accurate representation of strengths and weaknesses present in your own self-image? What's your rational mind wanting you to say right now about your reactions to this picture? What kind of a feeling message is your intuition trying to give you about it? Are you able to distinguish the difference?

Since 1975 when I first developed this illustration, I have shared it over 1,000 times in one-on-one discussions and more than 500 times in front of small or large groups. Nearly all participants respond by telling me I have drawn the wedge of weakness too small. Occasionally while sharing it in a personal discussion, and almost always while sharing it with a group, someone will speak up and say, "I think they should be flip-flopped." Lots of people have responded by suggesting they would be more comfortable drawing a vertical line down the center to make it half and half. Isn't all of this a fascinating commentary on our self-images?

But let's take a deeper look at this for a moment. To think we could really make any kind of an accurate assessment of the relative balance between our strengths and weaknesses would actually be quite challenging, wouldn't it? When we note the actual energy expended in thinking about our weaknesses, as compared to what we expend on our strengths, however, most of us would say the above diagram misses the mark completely. Would you agree that the energy and effort most of us put into our perceived weaknesses is far greater than the energy invested by most of us in our strengths?

Energy Flow

It really is an energy issue, isn't it? Speaking of energy, do you know what a physicist would tell us about the flow of electrical energy? It causes a magnetic field to develop around that flow. Isn't it interesting how few people have thought about the way human emotional energy has a similar effect. Energy we focus on our weaknesses—whether to shield them from other people's view or to go in and dig them out by their roots—sets up a powerful "magnet like" attraction for problems, obstacles, mistakes and failure. Yes, it's true! The energy we focus on negatives in our life creates the magnetic effect of attracting the very undesired consequences we think we are trying to protect ourselves against. This is particularly true when our energy is focused on trying to keep our weaknesses from being exposed. It is equally true, however, when our efforts are focused on trying to "fix" our weaknesses so they are no longer a source of concern. Wow! Did you get that? Could our notion of trying to find WHAT'S WRONG and fix it be WHAT'S WRONG and we've found it? You got it. Not only that, but it can't be fixed! Just think of how wonderful it will be to abandon this self-limiting illusion and discover an alternative that actually works!

How about all the energy we focus on our strengths? You guessed it again. This has the wonderful, effect of magnetically and effortlessly attracting to us the results we desire. This magnetic effect means those of us who master the discipline of identifying and building on our strengths will find ourselves achieving results we desire with far less effort than we would normally expect. Are you beginning to see the foundations being put in place to enable each of us to reach and sustain the wonderful state of effortless high performance? Do you also see, as mentioned above, how the whole notion of "find-what's-wrong-and-fix-it" may be precisely WHAT'S WRONG, and that we have actually found it? Reminds me of that fun statement from Pogo, "We have found the

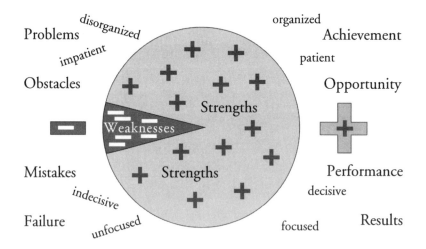

enemy and it is us!" As you review the diagram on the next page, please remember effortless high performance is much more a by-product of energy management than of fact management.

Defensiveness

Before we begin this next section on defensiveness, I must ask you to return to page 51 and retrieve the score you gave yourself around the traits you would most like to see changed over the next year. If you recall, you were asked to give yourself a negative score for every strength you checked, and a positive score for every weakness you checked. The resulting net score is your defensiveness rating. A score of –5 would mean you are entirely free from defensiveness and are putting all of your attention on building up your strengths. If you gave yourself a plus score, it means you put more attention on your weaknesses than strengths and may be experiencing some defensiveness. If you happened to check all five weaknesses and have thus ended up with a +5 score, this suggests you may want to take a serious look at what defensiveness is costing you and how you can go about changing that.

Defensiveness is a phenomenon we associate with energy we put into our weaknesses. It is largely an unconscious, involuntary mental reaction. Its role is to protect us from the anticipated feelings of anxiety, discomfort, or pain associated with having our weaknesses, shortcomings or other undesirable attributes exposed to others. All defensiveness is self-induced. We trigger defensive reactions in ourselves whenever we decide, after quickly analyzing a situation in front of us, that we are at risk of "losing face," or that our competence or some other aspect of our self-worth is in doubt or about to be criticized.

One example of defensiveness we can all identify with is the feeling we get whenever we are introduced to someone and immediately forget their name. How many of us will spend the next few minutes trying in vain to pay attention to the conversation while at the same time trying to keep from looking ridiculous because we simply cannot remember the person's name? What prevents us from simply admitting we have forgotten the person's name and asking for it to be repeated? Is it concern over our image? What about lack of confidence? Yes, defensiveness is clearly a symptom of low self-confidence—which I define as being unable to separate our doubts about our worth and value as a person from our need to meet perfectly all of society's wonderful "shoulds" and expectations.

What is the price we pay for being defensive? It certainly makes it more difficult to get fully committed, to accept criticism, to resolve conflicts, to deal with adversity, to accept responsibility and to bring about desired changes in our attitudes. Defensiveness also keeps us from reaching the state of effortless high performance. Several common but sometimes unrecognized forms of defensiveness are shown below:

Resistance to change	Temper	Nervousness
Role-playing	Poor communication	Jealousy
Political posturing	Overcompensating	Prejudgment
Intellectualizing	Empire-building	Rationalization
Sensitivity to criticism	Turf-guarding	Authoritarianism
Lack of initiative	Procrastination	Resentment

One additional form of defensiveness is particularly difficult to identify. It shows up frequently in a person who gives all outward appearances of being super-confident, yet is quite insecure internally and uses an overbearing form of pseudo-confidence or bravado to cover up those private, hidden feelings of insecurity.

As you might imagine, defensiveness in any form is a self-defeating behavior. It is also a major impediment to performance improvement. Defensiveness actually defeats itself by magnetically attracting the very undesired consequences against which we think we are protecting ourselves. "Self-fulfilling prophecy" is the label often given to this phenomenon. What do you suppose could happen if we all understood how a prolonged focus of our energy on protecting ourselves against negatives might just have the actual effect of setting up a powerful magnetic force that attracts to us the very negatives we are trying to avoid?

How Defensiveness is Caused

All defensiveness begins the moment we assign negative value to facts. In and of themselves, facts are neither positive nor negative. It is we who attach a positive or negative value to them, and in so doing, cause all our own defensiveness. Yes, it's true. By being critical of ourselves, by finding fault with ourselves or others or by judging things negatively in any way, we set in motion a chain of events which causes every single bit of our own defensiveness—along with all of its undesired, self-limiting consequences. In other words, the negative judgments we make, which in turn trigger our own defensiveness, are a key set of obstacles serving to limit our growth and development.

This means whenever we try to be the analytical expert on what's wrong with something, each of us can be held personally responsible for blocking our own growth. Also, whenever our defensiveness does get triggered, we shift into a costly "protect" mode that depletes our supply of creative energy. Perhaps we can think of one or more personal examples to illustrate this. Can you recall a time, for example, when you might have felt emotionally drained immediately after an experience of having been in the defensive mode?

Notice how difficult it can be to think objectively or be productive for some period of time after such an experience! Have you noticed how important it is to give yourself extra time to replenish creative energy lost through defensiveness? How does one go about doing this?

Is there a personal example you can think of right now? Perhaps you can think of an example where defensiveness may have resulted in an identifiable loss of time, energy or money; or even damaged a relationship in your life. Are there others around you who could participate in a discussion with you about your thoughts and feelings about what you have just read?

Freedom from Defensiveness

We are now ready to address our vital first step in the process of learning to free ourselves from defensiveness. Can we first agree that all defensiveness is related to the energy we put into our weaknesses—whether we are trying to shield those weaknesses from view or dig them out by their roots? If we can agree on this, it is then clear we must find a better way to deal with our weaknesses.

One fun way to expand our perspectives around weakness is to ask if you could show me a way to measure darkness. After giving this a few moments of thought, you might very well respond with some kind of a suggestion involving the measurement of light. It would then be my job to quickly point out this was not my question. I specifically asked to be shown a way to measure darkness, not light. After a bit of additional time, it will probably dawn on you that there is actually no way to measure darkness. It is only possible to measure light in degrees up from none, or zero.

My next question is to ask you to show me a way to measure cold. Again, most of those who have participated in this exercise with me have responded with some kind of a suggestion requiring the measurement of heat. After reminding them that my question did not address the measurement of heat, but rather asked for a way to measure cold, the awareness dawns more quickly that it is no more possible to measure cold than it is to measure darkness. We can measure the amount of heat in degrees up from absolute zero, but in no way can we actually measure the amount of cold.

Weaknesses Do Not Exist

The obvious question we must now ask is, "If we can't measure darkness or cold, then how do we propose to measure weakness?" The same principle has to apply, doesn't it? In other words, if there is nothing less than zero, there can be *no such thing* as a weakness. As soon as we begin to make this rather profound leap in our understanding, we also begin to make a shift in where we put our attention—away from what used to be our weaknesses and self-doubts and onto our strengths. How would our lives be different if we could accept the powerful reality that there is no such thing as a weakness? What a wonderful breath of fresh air this could bring into our lives! Can you feel the warm breeze?

The concept of weakness is an imaginary construct of the human mind. In reality weaknesses cannot and do not exist! We must learn to recognize the truth that reality consists only of degrees of strength. This principle is illustrated by the scale below. Note how each of our strengths can best be measured on a scale from 0 to some X point, which we will call 10.

When we stop to think about it, just how could it be possible for anyone to have less than a zero level of any given strength! But just imagine all of the painful and unnecessary difficulties we create for ourselves when, in response to negative feedback in our lives, we "choose" to install an artificial zero point well above true zero on our own personal scale. For example, let's imagine we have imposed an artificial zero point on the scale above at about 8. Given this imaginary rule, we find ourselves judging any strength falling below the new artificial zero point (8) to be a weakness. In other words, a true level-six strength is judged to be a –2 level weakness. Look at what just happened. We set up our own defensiveness by choosing to view a level-six strength as a –2 weakness.

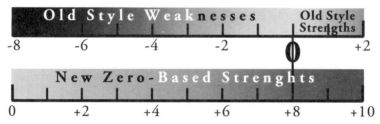

Unfortunately, all of our self-imposed negative judgments, as well as those imposed on us by others, can too easily trigger defensive reactions around any and all strengths we judge to fall below the artificial zero point. An actual two-level strength, for example, is now judged to be a –6 level weakness and a defensive reaction is as sure to follow as night follows day.

Re-calibrating Our Gauges

To illustrate this point a bit further, turn back to the mission control page earlier in this chapter where we rated a dozen of our personal productivity characteristics. What happens to our energy level and our sense of self-esteem as we review our previous assessments from the standpoint of this new zero-based input? Notice the changes we must now make to the calibration of each gauge. What was initially a –5 now becomes a zero, a former zero now becomes a +5 and the former +5 becomes a +10. As you can see by the re-calibrated gauge shown here, a former reading of –3 now becomes a +2. Please go back and review your strengths using this new viewpoint. As you do so, I invite you to reflect on the question, which is truly the more honest way of actually seeing your- self? While doing so, please recall how the initial instructions were quite explicit in asking you be as honest with yourself as you are capable of being. Opens up a lot of questions, doesn't it, about our ability or inability to be truly honest with ourselves? **PAUSE**

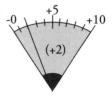

This is a perfect time for some more mentor-coaching questions to help crystallize additional insights from this powerful set of examples. *What would you say is the most significant adjustment beginning to take place in your thinking since reading the past few pages? What area of your life do you suspect will be the first to be impacted by any changes that may be taking place in your outlook? Were you able to identify any ways in which defensiveness might have been inhibiting your effectiveness more than you realized? What do you think will be the biggest benefit from this expanded awareness? What progress are you making toward accepting our proposal that we each cause all of our own defensiveness? If you have not yet fully embraced this idea, can you put a finger on what might be holding you back? If you were to fully accept our observation that defensiveness can only occur after we have assigned negative value to a fact, what immediate changes might take place in your life? Who around you might be most threatened by such changes? What kind of extra support might be most useful to you in moving forward with any changes you would desire to make?*

While we are at it, let's now take this question of whether or not we know how to be honest with ourselves about our strengths to a new level. Did you happen to mark any of the 12 strength areas in mission control as a minus on the first go-around? Hopefully you did, because those negative self-assessments can give us major clues for helping to identify your greatest single strength. Here is how it works. Whichever item you marked the lowest—if it fell below zero before the gauges were re-calibrated—will typically be enough of a clue to enable us both to identify your greatest single strength. Let's try some examples.

Seeing Our Little Strengths In a New Light

If you happened to rate self-confidence as the lowest of all your strengths, I would be delighted to inform you that your self-confidence is positioned to eventually become your greatest single strength. Here is how this one works. I have found that anyone who rates their own self-confidence to be unusually low often places such a high value on the trait that they place anyone with an abundance of confidence on a pedestal. It is as if they rate the highly confident person as being a 16 on a 10-point scale. They then rate themselves as being a –8 by comparison, which actually puts them at about an honest 8. In other words, such a person already possesses far more inherent confidence than they give themselves credit for. Not only that, but their desire to be a confident person is often so great it will inevitably lift the person into the desired level of confidence. It is particularly fun to point all of this out to some-one while they are discovering it for the first time among a group of peers. The admission of low self-confidence always triggers looks of astonishment from those peers. In other words, when someone holds a view of their own confidence as being low, that view is seldom shared by others around them.

A similar set of circumstances is typically associated with those who choose either enthusiasm, persuasiveness or communication effectiveness as the lowest of your strengths. We again see similar patterns of people placing an unusually high value on the traits and as a result comparing themselves against a distorted perception of others. Similar reflections of surprise from peers will usually show up here, too.

If you happened to rate patience as the lowest of all your strengths, it is a sure sign that your greatest strength is the speed with which you grasp the big picture. The trouble with this strength lies with one little item which often fails to show up in the big picture which you typically see so quickly. Since each of us sees the world through our own set of eyes, it seldom occurs to us how others may simply be unable to see the big picture as quickly as we can. Watch our patience soar as we deliberately add this overlooked awareness item to the big picture we see so quickly.

If you rated either time organization or self-discipline as the lowest of all your strengths, your greatest strength is sure to be capacity for commitment. This is not to say you have mastered the ability to exercise your capacity for commitment, but it definitely is your greatest strength. Now imagine what would happen to either your time organization or self-discipline strength if you successfully applied your capacity for commitment to those areas. Either one could be quickly transformed into a dominant strength if you were to do so.

Whenever someone judges tactfulness to be their lowest, I find it a most rewarding situation to work with. Inevitably the person's greatest strength will be how deeply they care. And, since they do care so deeply, they are always touched when the truth of their strength is brought into the open. What a wonderful experience it is to share this with someone where it fits. As I'm sure you know, we live in a world where most people haven't a clue about how to deal with someone who cares so deeply. I have seen time and again where such people have a history of being repeatedly burned while attempting to express their caring. The natural response, of course, is to pull back and withdraw their caring from people around them and invest it instead in ideas that capture their interest. This is where tactfulness can become an issue. It is clearly related to the force of unexpressed caring that lies hidden behind their ideas. This often causes those ideas to be poured out too forcefully onto others who can be overwhelmed by the intensity with which they are expressed. Fortunately, a simple solution is available. We must face the fact that caring truly is our greatest strength. We must then learn how to shift the focus of our caring back onto the people receiving our messages instead of allowing all that suppressed energy to remain focused on our ideas. Everything we cover about learning to put our feelings into words will be immensely helpful in reducing the pressure, too.

Decisiveness is also an interesting trait to work with whenever someone judges it to be their lowest. If you happened to pick it as your lowest, this would typically point to empathy as your greatest strength. Here is how it works: If decisiveness is a concern for you, take a quick look at the tremendous amount of feeling you have for the potential value of each of the options or alternatives you are considering. This is called empathy. It gets kind of challenging to make clear decisions when you have this much feeling for each option, doesn't it? What would happen instead, if you were to go out at least ten years from today and use this empathy to create a picture of the ideal future for yourself and your family? You could then use your empathy strength to develop powerful feelings for several aspects of the picture. Can you now feel how this process could quickly transform your perceived low level of decisiveness into a dominant strength? Fascinating, wouldn't you say?

If you happened to pick empathy as your lowest strength, we are facing a paradox. Even though you may have picked it as your lowest, my experience with others who have done so suggests it may be your highest. As a result, many who know you well may see empathy as one of your greatest strengths and if so, might be quite surprised by your choice. One possible explanation could be that your high awareness of feelings makes you also aware of how much you can *not* feel. This may seem confusing to many readers, but will be crystal clear if it fits you.

The only mission control item we have left to cover is intelligence. First of all, it is rarely picked as someone's lowest. Second, later in the book we will introduce some profound new insights about the effects of high intelligence on motivation and performance. These insights are based on our discovery in 1978 of a direct correlation between our level of mental capacity and our emotional intensity. I certainly do look forward to sharing them with you.

So, what has been the biggest benefit to you from our efforts to give you quite a different perspective on weaknesses? Were you able to identify with any of the "little strengths" for which I was able to point out a corresponding dominant strength? Were there any special surprises in this for you? Did it raise any new questions for you?

In Summary

To summarize this chapter, we've learned how our negative self-image is created by aspects of ourselves we see as falling below an artificially imposed zero point on our scale of strengths. These "smaller strengths" are those formerly labeled "weaknesses." Thus, whatever forms of low self-esteem we might be wishing to abandon are quite likely caused by these artificial, negative judgments. Any concern we may have felt over our weaknesses, over poor self-image, low self-esteem and any other negative attitudes we may have been struggling to overcome are direct consequences of our own choice to set an artificial or imaginary zero point above true zero on our scale of strengths.

From this moment on, you have a golden opportunity to fully accept and begin enjoying this new awareness that only strengths exist. This requires simply moving your zero point from wherever you might have arbitrarily set it to the new point where it can be permanently anchored at true zero. As soon as this is accomplished, you will have gained a new freedom from wasting emotional energy on defensive actions. I cannot say it is easy to make this change. I can only point out its utter simplicity and encourage you to invest the time, self-discipline and patience required to make it fully operational in your life.

Are you ready to make the commitment right now to begin shifting those arbitrary zero points on your scale to the more powerful and functional true zero point? For many of us, this could easily qualify as the highest priority short-term objective in our life! We must always remember that the nurturing of weaknesses grows weaknesses, and that mastery of the zero-based strengths perspective can be a giant step in building the disciplines required to manage our own growth and move toward that wonderful state of effortless high performance. The next seven chapters are focused on ways to make this shift a permanent reality in our lives.

Chapter Five

Praise, Self-Esteem & Charisma

Identifying Strengths in Others

Now we are ready to take a second giant step in our project of constructing a fully operational build-on-strengths mind set. Our goal in this chapter is to strongly reinforce the shift to zero-based strengths that was introduced in the last chapter. We will begin with another simple exercise that asks you to get out a new sheet of paper and be ready to jot down some more strengths. In this case, however, we will focus on improving our skill at identifying strengths we see in others. No doubt you will find the practice we are introducing here to be quite effective at bringing about a permanent shift in your attention—away from your "lesser" strengths and onto your "greater" strengths.

We begin this important exercise by asking you to bring to mind two individuals (other than your parents) for whom you have a great amount of admiration and/or respect. Take a few moments right now to reflect on why these two people would come to mind in response to this question. Begin to reflect on some of the more desirable qualities, attributes or character traits that are so evident in the two people you have selected, and that allow them to hold your admiration and respect as they do. Now jot down on a sheet of paper at least five admired or respected traits for each of the two people you have brought to mind. I can assure you that as this exercise unfolds, you will be glad you didn't skip over this request, so put aside the book right now and make your notes before coming back to continue reading. PAUSE

To continue this exercise, I will ask you to reflect on a similar question with respect to each of your parents. In this case I will ask you to also identify one or two traits in each that you might have found most irritating or bothersome. It is now time to go back to your sheet of paper and jot down for each parent at least three admired or respected traits and one or two that you found most irritating. I will be waiting here ready to continue when you return. PAUSE

Psychocybernetics

By way of background for our next concept, I would like to introduce a very important contribution made to the field of self-image psychology by Dr. Maxwell Maltz. Dr. Maltz is a famous plastic surgeon whose insightful book, *Psychocybernetics*, was first published in 1960. The findings presented in his book had a huge impact on my thinking when I first read them in early 1971. They have also stood the test of time. They are every bit as useful to me today as when I first encountered them. Dr. Maltz did facelifts. Over the years he began to notice that out of every 20 people who came to him for a face lift, 19 would also undergo a significant change for the better in their personality to accompany their change in physical appearance. This in itself might not have been such a big deal if it were not for the fact that one person out of every 20 consistently showed no change in personality at all, even though their physical appearance had clearly changed for the better. Dr. Maltz puzzled over this difference until his RIGHT QUESTIONS led him to a wonderful breakthrough discovery in the field of self-image psychology.

Dr. Maltz discovered that the human personality is cybernetic in nature, which simply means its nature is automatically that of a goal-seeking instrument. His use of the term "psychocybernetics" thus introduces us to the psyche's goal seeking nature, which I propose is perfectly illustrated by the inner workings of a thermostat. To use my words, then, Dr. Maltz discovered that our personalities run on a set of thermostats. For example, when we set the thermostat in our home at a certain temperature, that becomes the goal it seeks. If the room temperature falls below that setting, the thermostat sends a message to the furnace, calling for heat to bring the room temperature back up into alignment with that setting. This out-of-alignment state is called stress. If the room temperature rises above that setting, the thermostat sends a message to the air conditioner, calling for cooled air to bring the room temperature back into alignment with that setting again.

Here is how this applies to the facelift patients in particular, and ultimately to each of us as members of the human race. For the sake of simplicity, let's imagine each patient who comes to Dr. Maltz for a facelift has the thermostat of their personality set on "I'm ugly." This is undoubtedly seen by each of them as a clear negative. Therefore, each time their behaviors move out of alignment with how they perceive that an ugly person acts, their psyches will call forth adjustments to bring their behaviors back into alignment with their picture of ugly. We also know each patient has sought help from plastic surgery to get rid of their "I'm ugly" thermostatic setting. We can safely imagine, therefore, that each must have been relying upon some kind of a "I'm not ugly" mechanism to help suppress their "I'm ugly" self-image. If we look carefully at the above scenario, however, we see how it describes a situation where two negatives are attempting to out-negate each other. "I'm not ugly" is trying to negate "I'm ugly." This cannot succeed. It is, however, precisely why so many of us notice that our list of weaknesses has not changed in the last five, ten and often 15 years or more.

Let's go back to our room temperature example to clarify this further. It is as if our thermostat has somehow been set at 78° Fahrenheit and the minute we come into the room we judge that to be "not okay," or negative. Now, instead of simply going to the thermostat and adjusting it to a more pleasant or positive setting, we rush to the window air conditioner and set its thermostat on "not 78°," or, shall we say, 65°. Do you see the picture I'm attempting to paint? Look at the unresolvable set of stressors we have just created, as in 65° trying to out-negate 78°. Unfortunately this is the state in which most of us find ourselves on a daily basis. We can have dozens of negative thermostats each trying to out-negate the others. Look at the immense amount of energy that's being depleted this way within each of us. This is energy we must learn to redirect if we are to achieve effortless high performance.

It is now time to revisit Dr. Maltz and his 19 patients who use the excuse of their plastic surgery procedure to simply reset their thermostats to "I'm pretty." In spite of a successful plastic surgery procedure, one out of 20 chooses to keep their thermostat set on "I'm ugly." For each of the 19 patients who chooses pretty, we see their lives gradually adjusting to reflect their new setting of pretty. For the one patient out of 20 who chooses to keep the thermostat set on ugly, we see their personality remaining in alignment with their picture of ugly. Here is one of the most important points to take away from this example. The exception of the one who didn't change proves that the wonderful change in personality enjoyed by the other 19 was not dependent upon the surgical procedure at all. Instead, it was purely a matter of choice. Dr. Maltz helps us to realize that each of the 19 made a choice to reset their thermostat to pretty before the bandages were ever removed, while the 20th made a choice also—but in this case it was to keep their thermostat set on ugly.

Our Personalities are Thermostatic

So here are some of the key points we are making. Our personalities are thermostatic in nature. Most of us have both positive and negative thermostats. Negative thermostats deplete our energy and can be the source of considerable stress. Effortless high performance requires that we run on positive thermostatic settings. Now, has it occurred to you that it might be a very good idea to know how to read both the positive and negative thermostatic settings that are presently running your life? Might you then wish to know more about how to strengthen your positive settings? How about any negative settings? Do you think it would be a good idea to figure out how to stop the futile practice of trying to negate negatives? It is my intent to address every one of these questions and more in the next few pages.

We shall begin with an exciting new way to read our positive thermostatic settings—in other words, to identify our true strengths. This is now quite easy, as we just listed as many as 16 or more of them in our last exercise. Each strength we recognize, admire and respect in another is a direct reflection of one of our own greatest strengths. To put it another way, we simply cannot recognize a strength in someone else that we, ourselves, do not already possess. Let's now take some time to reflect on the traits we listed as those we admire in two special people in addition to our parents. This awesome concept is worth expressing again. Qualities we admire and respect the most in others are a direct reflection of our own greatest strengths. We might as well be looking in a mirror when we're paying attention to what we admire in others.

What happens when we reflect on the traits we listed? As we think about each . . . and then shift our attention to ourselves, are we able to see how the trait listed actually represents a healthy self-image component (strength) found in ourselves? Sometimes it can be challenging at first to see and acknowledge this connection, but the more we work with it, the more we see how it is actually true. The longer we work with this concept, the more we will prize it for its amazing accuracy and great potential usefulness to us. It offers a great deal of potential for strengthening our own self-esteem and moving us toward the state of effortless high performance. For some of us, this may be such a revelation that we may just want to close the book and sit with it for a while. From past experience I know it is fully capable of stirring up a lot of new intuitive awareness, and I wouldn't want any of us to miss out on the opportunity to process them.

Meanwhile, I think it might be useful for me to share with you how the discovery of this concept occurred in my life. In 1970, when I first attended the Dale Carnegie Sales Course®, I was introduced to the idea of paying a compliment to my sales prospects as a way of getting my presentation off on the right foot. Somehow this didn't set well with me. Among other things it felt insincere and manipulative. I did see the inherent value in the idea, however, and decided to modify it to fit my personality. Soon after engaging a sales prospect in conversation, I would begin asking questions in an attempt to identify a significant strength of which my prospect might or might not be aware. Sometimes it might take me 20 minutes to find one, but upon doing so, my entire countenance would light up and I would announce, "I've just noticed what a great strength you have in . . . (here I would insert whatever strength I had observed, such as vision, decisiveness or tenacity)." We would then engage in a brief dialogue about that strength, how it was developed and the role it was playing in their current success.

Little did I realize what a powerful impact this discipline was having on my life until one day in the summer of 1975. I was sitting in a coffee shop when suddenly I realized I had been taking on all these strengths I had been praising! They were becoming my own. It was one of those incredible moments when time stood still and the entire framework for understanding the greater implications of Dr. Maltz's work fell in place for me. As you might imagine, I then redoubled my efforts to uncover and praise new strengths in nearly everyone I met, and I suspect my self-esteem rose more in that following year than perhaps it had in the previous five. This is truly an awesome tool, and I can hardly wait to make its power available to everyone.

What are some ways you could learn to use this new discovery to raise your awareness of your own strengths? Can you see its potential for reducing the amount of energy people waste on defensiveness? One of its most promising uses is to build up our smaller strengths—particularly those we may have formerly seen as weaknesses. A very important point to remember from both this and the previous chapter is that we are always free to choose how we wish to see ourselves. And oh, the difference our choices can make! Let's now begin to explore this in more detail.

Praise Has New Meaning

By developing a discipline of studying and praising strengths we find in others, we can provide for ourselves a valuable mirror in which to acknowledge, explore and ultimately develop a deeper understanding of our own strengths. Let's take a look at how this works in practice to raise our self-esteem. First of all, we now have more of an incentive to notice other people's strengths because we now know that any strength we see must mirror one we possess ourselves. This by itself will gradually raise our self-esteem. We can take this a step further, however, by giving more verbal acknowledgment to people about their strengths. Look at the big difference in our intensity of involvement between simply noticing a strength in someone, versus becoming engaged in conversation with them about that strength. The increased intensity speeds up the process of turning one of our smaller strengths into a larger strength.

Let's go back to our thermostat example. Picture the idea of having only a small strength as having only a tiny furnace available to respond to the thermostat's call for additional heat. For example, imagine that I have a decisiveness strength that rates only a one on a ten-point scale. This would be like trying to rely on a 10,000-BTU furnace to heat my big house in the middle of the winter in northern Minnesota where I grew up. Yes, my thermostat may very well be set on decisiveness, but there just isn't enough psychic energy available to keep my actions in alignment with that setting. (In Minnesota one needs at least a 100,000-BTU furnace to be in the game.)

To take our thermostat analogy a step further, every time we verbally acknowledge a strength we see in someone and then engage them in a dialogue about that strength, it is as if we install another 5,000 BTU in our furnace. On the other hand, if we just notice a strength and omit the important step of verbally acknowledging it, the effect is similar to adding 1,000 BTU's to our furnace. Yes, we are still improving our ability to bring our actions into consistent alignment with our thermostatic setting, but the path to mastery will take longer. Any one of our strengths will continue to grow stronger and healthier each time we notice that strength in another and verbally acknowledge our appreciation of it to them. Every time we repeat this process, it in turn allows the healthy self-image we are building to be even more effective at bringing our actions and behaviors into a natural and permanent alignment with those desired character strengths. This high awareness approach to building our own healthy self-esteem through praising others is a matter of consciously equipping our subconscious mind to help us to effortlessly become the person we wish to be.

Freedom from Stress

Will you now indulge me in one more set of understandings that can be gained from our thermostat analogy? We have begun to see that our self-image guides and directs our personality much like an array of little thermostats, each of which work to keep our actions and behaviors in alignment with its own individual aspect. As a result, whenever our actions and behaviors are in full alignment with all aspects of our self-image, we experience the peace of mind and freedom from stress that is essential to reaching the state of effortless high performance. Notice that we are saying peace of mind and freedom from stress can only be achieved when our actions and behaviors are in full alignment with all aspects of our self-image. Each individual aspect of our self-image acts as a subconscious internal guide (thermostatic setting) that continually draws our actions and behaviors into alignment with it. This is true whether the aspect is seen by us as positive or whether it is one we judge to be negative and wish to eliminate.

Whenever any of our actions or behaviors is out of alignment with one or more aspects of our self-image, a certain natural tension develops to bring those actions and behaviors back into alignment. This natural tension process works without prejudice to keep us in alignment with both desired and undesired aspects of our self-image. A major challenge inherent in this process is the amount of inner conflict and stress that can arise when any two or more aspects of our self-image are out of alignment with each other. For example, we can feel as much or more inner conflict and stress when two or more of our positive self-image aspects fail to fully complement each other as we do when we have two negative aspects attempting to out-negate each other. Of course, there will also be inner conflict and stress when a negative aspect is in conflict with a positive one. Fortunately, as we continue to notice an increasing variety of strengths that we admire in others and then take steps to verbally acknowledge those strengths whenever possible, we continue to strengthen the desired aspects of our own self-image. This practice also puts us more and more in contact with our intuition, which is the only part of ourselves that can bring conflicting elements of our self-esteem into our conscious awareness where they can be effectively dealt with.

We've really covered a lot of material here, haven't we? I think it is time to ask some mentor-coaching questions to make sure at least some of it gets more deeply assimilated before we lose its benefit. We have covered two broad categories of information. First, we reviewed the contributions of Dr. Maxwell Maltz to the field of self-image psychology. I wouldn't want anyone to get lost in the technical aspects of this, but I always find it useful to know the underlying causes for things. *What aspect of all that information triggered the most useful insight for you?* For me, I think it's knowing that we can choose how to see ourselves, and that our whole psyche is prepared and equipped to gradually bring whatever picture we set into current reality. *What feelings show up when you think about having that much responsibility for creating your own personality as well as circumstances? Have you always known you had that much control, or is this a new idea for you? What feelings do you have about accepting all of this responsibility? Exhilarating? Threatening? It sure throws into question the whole idea of seeking advice, doesn't it?*

The second category of information we have covered is the new and very practical implications of praise. For most people, the idea of having our own strengths enhanced by recognizing them in others and praising them is pretty new information. An aspect of this I initially left out is that just because we may admire a Level 10 strength in someone doesn't mean our strength is also a Level 10. If it is among the traits we admire most, however, we now have every tool needed to continue strengthening it until that quality or trait reaches a Level 10 in us. *This being the case, what two or three strengths will you be most keenly on the lookout for as you interact with others over the next few weeks? Of all the strengths already present in you, on which type will you be most inclined to place this additional attention? Will you focus on strengths you presently rate as low, or strengths that are already rather high? Does your answer to that last question reflect the kind of build-on-strengths attitude you wish to demonstrate, or does it still reflect a bit too much of the old fix-what's-wrong perspective? These things can get tricky, can't they! Which do you actually believe will give you the quickest payoff, making major strengths even stronger, or building up minor strengths? There surely aren't any right or wrong answers to that question, but a true build-on-strengths attitude would draw us to consider first making our major strengths even stronger. What would you say is the greatest single benefit you have felt from this chapter so far?*

The Payoffs from Praising

Let's now look at a couple of examples and another key concept that will put a nice finishing touch to this chapter. Imagine that you admire highly organized people. From what we've learned here, we can now conclude that being highly organized is a key element of your positive self-image. We also know that as long as your actions are in alignment with that aspect of your self-image, they will not be the source of any inner tension or uneasiness. Should your actions become less organized, however, an inner tension begins to build up in order to bring your actions back into alignment with your picture of organization. This tension will only subside when you feel organized again. The creative tensions thus generated serve as powerful, natural forces inside of us and serve to guide our actions and behaviors into alignment with our chosen ideals.

There are big dividends to be earned when we master this creative discipline of seeing and praising strengths and qualities we admire in other people. It would be nearly impossible to do this without raising both our conscious and subconscious awareness of the attraction we feel toward the strengths we are praising. In turn, this helps raise the intensity and power of our own self-image in these areas. The more creative energy we invest in this process, the more we strengthen the admired qualities inside ourselves. A simple and effective way to take advantage of this new discovery is to find a strength in someone and say to them out loud: "I admire your . . . (quality). Would you please share with me how you developed that quality?" A slightly different approach might be to say, "I admire your . . . (quality). I especially admire that quality because . . ." The more often we practice this discipline, the more quickly we will become comfortable with it. Frequent use will also bring us some of the more subtle and dynamic payoffs enjoyed by those who have a deeply ingrained habit of expressing admiration, appreciation and gratitude.

Gaining Charisma

Perhaps the most impressive quality that develops from a longtime practice of expressing admiration, appreciation and gratitude is the quality of charisma—that intangible force which draws other people to us because they feel good about themselves when they are around us. I define charisma as "other-centeredness" firmly based in self-acceptance. Recognizing and praising a strength found in someone else is being other-centered (the opposite of self-centered). Equipped with this new knowledge about praise, we can hardly be unaware of our own strengths as we verbalize our feelings to others about admired traits we see in them. In the process we cannot help but increase our own self-acceptance. Even if we begin to praise others quite stiffly, deliberately and systematically, the new awareness acquired in this chapter will be helping us to rapidly increase the personal magnetism of our own charisma.

What do you imagine might be your biggest benefit over the next 60 days from having read this material on praise? What do you feel is your biggest incentive for acting on this information? What would be the appeal to you, if any, of having more charisma? What might additional charisma enable you to do that seems out of reach for you today? With whom are you most eager to share this information? What aspect of the information would you want to share first? Is the person you are thinking of someone who "needs it?" Or is it someone for whom the information would be wonderfully reinforcing? If you happened to pick the former, wouldn't that be yet another indicator of how deeply programmed we are to find-what's-wrong-and-fix-it? Hopefully you were focused on reinforcing someone's strength. If not, there will be many more opportunities for me to keep reminding you of the value of making our focus on strengths a habit before we're done.

Speaking of reminders, here is the last one for this chapter. The more we look for strengths in others, the more we bring out strengths in ourselves. The more we look for good in others, the more we bring out the best in ourselves.

83

Chapter Six

The Analytical/Intuitive Relationship

Exploring the Difference Between Analytical and Intuitive Thinking

During my quest to understand what it takes for each of us to be at our best, I've experimented with several conceptual frameworks to help me describe my observations. None comes closer to capturing the essence of my understandings or serves me better than when we explore the relationship between our conscious, rational mind and our inner, intuitive mind. Having a proper relationship between these two aspects of our being is certainly a key factor in maintaining a state of effortless high performance.

We are indebted to Dr. Roger Sperry for his contribution to our scientific understanding of these two aspects of our being. By way of a very brief background, Dr. Sperry was awarded the 1981 Nobel Prize for

Medicine for his laboratory research into how each hemisphere of the brain functions when surgically disconnected from the other. Dr. Sperry's laboratory did research with cats in the 1950s. Using a special surgical procedure, he was able to show in cats that information reaching one-half of the brain was unavailable to the other half in the absence of the corpus callosum. In the 1960s, Sperry's laboratory had the opportunity to extend its earlier studies to human beings when Joseph Bogen and Peter Vogel cut the callosum in a group of epileptic patients in an effort to control their otherwise unmanageable grand mall seizures.

Psychological follow-up of these patients by Michael Gazzaniga, Sperry and Bogen confirmed the earlier animal studies. The patients were able to verbally describe information presented to their left hemisphere—the one which normally exhibits linguistic functions. When information was presented exclusively to the right hemisphere, patients were unable to describe it verbally, but were still able to demonstrate that they had perceived the information. Dr. Sperry and his team went on to catalog many functional differences between the brain's right and left hemispheres, and their work brought scientific proof to an area which had been the subject of speculation for many centuries.

Here is my personal "read" on Sperry's findings: Two distinctly different brains coexist inside our head. Each processes information quite independently from the other, and each uses a distinctly separate processing language. Each looks at the world from a different point of view. Each brain accumulates and stores a different memory of the same experience. These findings have given us a valuable research base from which to understand and describe key differences between analytical and intuitive thinking.

Anyone familiar with popular observations about right-brain and left-brain functions will notice I make little or no reference to such observations. There are many reasons for this, several of which will be covered in this chapter. For starters, I am far more interested in the nature of the actual processing than where it happens to occur—and more recent studies suggest the intuitive thinking process is most certainly not limited to the brain's right hemisphere. The latest studies, in fact, give considerable scientific support to the commonly used expression, "gut feeling." I therefore find it more useful to think in terms of our head and our heart to symbolize the locations in which our processing occurs, and if you and I were talking face to face right now, you would see me always point to my head when referring to analytical thinking and point to either my heart or my solar plexus when referring to intuitive thinking.

Analytical thinking, as we know, is done by our conscious, rational mind—the one that relies on words and numbers to process information. Intuitive thinking is carried out by what we refer to as our "subconscious" mind—the one that processes information non-verbally, relying on pictures, patterns and feelings to express its conclusions. Our intuitive mind, by the way, is actually quite conscious. We are led to think otherwise because its processing speed is too fast to permit the use of words and numbers to process its information. The difference in processing speed between our analytical and intuitive minds is thought to be on the order of 1:1,000. I personally suspect the difference could be even greater. This enormous difference in processing speed causes each of the two functions to perform quite differently, as can be seen in the following table.

The Sequential, Analytical Mind	The Synthesizing, Intuitive Mind
Thinks and decides logically	Feels and chooses intuitively
Reasons deductively	Synthesizes inductively
Computes data sequentially	Processes patterns randomly
Dismantles wholes into parts	Integrates parts into wholes
Has a separating influence	Has a cohesive influence
Rationalizes and judges	Assimilates and differentiates
Focuses creative energy	Generates creative energy
Guided by tangible goals	Guided by intangible purposes
Categorizes objectively	Discriminates subjectively
Accumulates knowledge	Utilizes wisdom
Can be programmed	Can be trained
Is activated by "problem-finding" questions	*Is activated by "value-finding" questions*

When you examine on a line-by-line basis this comparison between analytical and intuitive thinking, which set do you find most insightful? Which set offers the biggest surprise, if any? Which set shows you most clearly the differences between the two functions? The major purpose of this chapter is to describe how the two functions must work together as a team in order to achieve and sustain the state of effortless high performance. *This being the case, what clues do you get from the table's comparisons about how this partnership can best occur?* For me, the most telling comparison looks at programmable versus trainable. A computer chip is programmable. A horse, which has pure intuitive functions in both hemispheres of its brain, is only trainable. If a horse had an analytical mind, we could program it to win the race while it was standing in the paddock, much like we attempt to program our children in school.

A Look at Our Analytical Mind

To gain a full appreciation of our analytical mind, it is useful to see it as functioning much like a computer chip. As such, it consists of a sequence of one/zero, on/off, yes/no switches, called "binary code." This mechanism is perfectly designed to break down or dismantle whole chunks of input into individual bits of data, which are then processed in a strictly sequential order. When programmed correctly, this binary code arrangement makes our analytical mind perfectly suited to serve as an efficient input/output device on behalf of our intuitive mind. When programmed incorrectly, our analytical mind departs from its pure data transmission role and attempts instead to judge data as good or bad, right or wrong, instead of transmitting it in a strictly neutral form as intended.

This brings to mind another key discovery from Dr. Sperry's work. When the analytical mind is surgically separated from the intuition, he found it *completely incapable of distinguishing truth from fiction.* This finding has profoundly important implications for many aspects of our lives. For starters, we'll take a look at how it relates to effortless high performance. Remember, our analytical mind is programmable—just like a computer chip. The programming of a computer chip can best be described as the external manipulation of its one/zero, on/off binary code. Please note: the instructions must be initiated from outside the chip. The chip has no ability to judge whether the instructions are right or wrong, good or bad. The instructions either work or they don't, and this occurs quite independently from any right/wrong, good/bad value judging by the chip—which, of course, it cannot do anyway.

Here is where this gets tricky. Notice the extremely subtle distinction between the one/zero, on/off, yes/no binary code mechanism of the computer chip and the right/wrong, good/bad value judging that we attempt to do with our analytical minds. It is the built-in one/zero, on/off, yes/no capability which makes our analytical mind so perfectly suited for its deductive reasoning task. Unfortunately, this exact same capability makes our analytical mind completely vulnerable to being deceived into thinking it can judge right or wrong, good or bad. In truth, however, it simply cannot execute the judging function. Do you find it as fascinating as I do that "programmable" and "deceivable" are such identical and interchangeable concepts? I also find this to be quite interesting: on a continuum from highly judgmental at one end to completely free from judging at the other, all effortless high performers reside close to the end where little or no judging occurs. Do you see a pattern emerging here?

Before we move on to look at our intuitive mind, I shall propose an interesting way to either validate or shed some new light on the above points about the importance of becoming free from judging. To do this I offer a fun, contemporary "translation" of the Creation story from the Old Testament book of Genesis. Joseph Campbell tells us, by the way, that this same basic story occurs in a similar form in every single one of the world's major religions. The story as I learned it begins with the words, "God created man in His own image." Here's my translation: "God installed a computer chip to *image* the truth." In other words, the chip, the man nature (the analytical mind), was intended by God to be a pure, undistorted reflector (image) of the truth, but was incapable of actually being the truth. (The analytical mind's design features include the ability to provide a perfect reflection of data received.)

The words go on to say, "And God saw that it was good." My translation is, "And God saw this was good, that was good, and the other was good, and finally there was so much good He had to rest." The point here, of course, is that good was all their was. Bad was yet to be invented. To go on with the original essence, "Then along came the serpent (translation: programmer/deceiver) who lured man (the chip) over to eat from the tree of knowledge of good and evil." In other words, the programmer took the chip and deceived (programmed) it into believing (the illusion, or deception) that it could judge good from bad, right from wrong. As we have pointed out above, the chip (analytical mind) cannot do that, and the exact moment it was deceived into believing it could is known throughout history as "the fall of man." Interesting!

A Look at Our Intuitive Mind

To gain full appreciation of our intuition, we must first recognize that it does not speak English (or French or German or Japanese, either, for that matter), but relies on feelings, patterns and pictures as its processing languages. Perhaps you have noticed, too, how these three alternative languages can be developed to widely varying degrees in different people. I, for example, have gained the most effective access to my intuition through its pattern language, while for me it is as if the picture language might as well not even exist. For my wife, Patricia, it is nearly the opposite. She has excellent access to her intuition through the language of pictures, and is nearly as skilled at accessing it through the language of feeling. With this being just one of the many complexities of our intuition, one can see why it is certainly not the easiest piece of equipment to understand or describe.

Colorado was my home when my primary learning about the intuitive mind took place. An interesting little creature also makes its home in that state. If you have ever observed a "town" of prairie dogs and seen them poking their heads out of their burrows or standing straight up beside the burrow, you will quickly appreciate why I choose the prairie dog to symbolize one of our intuition's key characteristics. Just as with the prairie dog, the moment any form of threat appears, our intuition is gone: down the hole, vanished, out of sight and safely hidden away from harm. This is a good image to keep in mind when we are tempted to stomp our foot and command our intuitive mind to come out and perform. An environment of high trust is absolutely essential if we are hoping to make effective use of our intuition.

A most powerful leap occurred in my own understanding of how our intuition works in April of 1982 when I was visiting with Dr. George Jessup, who was the head of Texas A&M University's Wellness Department in College Station, Texas. It was very early on in my learning curve on this subject, and I was still in the right brain/left brain mode of thinking. Right in the middle of a wonderfully stimulating discussion on this subject, Dr. Jessup got an intuitive hit that we needed to meet with Dr. Philip Alexander, M.D., a Doctor of Internal Medicine in the neighboring town of Bryan, Texas. He immediately called and got an appointment. When we arrived at the cardiologist's office, Dr. Jessup encouraged me to take a close look at the drawings around the waiting room while he announced our arrival at the desk.

Not being much of an art connoisseur, I proceeded to look closely at each of several beautifully done line drawings of U.S. presidents—all the time wondering what I was supposed to be noticing. All at once I realized each of these well-done drawings was signed by Dr. Alexander himself. They were obviously his own drawings. As you might imagine, once we were seated in his office, my first awe-inspired question was, "Where did you learn to draw like that?" He proceeded to tell us the most amazing story about receiving the book, *Drawing on the Right Side of the Brain,* by Betty Edwards, as a Christmas gift only 15 months earlier. The book presents a drawing course which actually teaches us how to shut off our analytical mind (left brain) so our intuitive mind (right brain) can go ahead and draw. By following the book's carefully laid out instructions, he was able to master fairly quickly the technique of shutting off his analytical mind (he told us he could actually feel the shift). After this he found it remarkably easy to draw—as was plainly evident to me from my brief time in his waiting room. He then went on to further amaze us with a story of how he brought these ideas to a music camp for young people the previous summer. Here he began by using the drawing course to teach the students how to shut off their analytical minds. Then they switched to music, and some amazing leaps in ability appeared rather quickly. A delightful end note to the story was that a 14-year-old music student had done so well using the technique that he was playing the oboe as a member of the Salt Lake City orchestra.

The real impact of the total experience occurred for me in the next few moments, as Dr. Alexander pulled out from a desk drawer a two-inch marble. It rolled across the desk and onto my lap, and he said, "I also did this with my right brain." He had taken a piece of raw marble and, while working completely by feel, held it against a grinding wheel (a lapidary stone), carefully working with it until it became a perfectly round marble. I shall never forget the profound impact he had on me when he said, "The right brain can feel when something is perfectly round." Once the marble was finished, he had taken it over to Texas A&M University and had it tested for roundness, confirming that its shape was more perfectly round than the ball bearings coming out of Timken's factories.

While reflecting on that experience during my flight home, I felt myself being repeatedly drawn back to his observation of how the right brain (our intuition) can "feel" when something is perfectly round. This profound insight has really stood the test of time and continues to help me understand many things about our intuition. Among the most important of these is our intuition's powerful orientation to be drawn continually toward an evolving "ideal" of perfect roundness. Therefore, one of our intuition's key messages—and one each of us must continually work to improve our ability to discern—is the serene feeling of "comfort" that appears when something fits into a perfectly smooth, round whole. We must also learn to discern the subtle feeling of "discomfort" when something fails to fit into that same sense of perfect wholeness. That's comfort with "fit" and discomfort with "no fit." I truly hope you get the full significance of this. It could be one of the most important points I have to share with you in this book. Our intuition is an awesome force. It seeks continuously and relentlessly to move us toward an ever-evolving vision of an ideal. The more deeply we tap into this awesome force, the easier it becomes to reach our goal of effortless high performance. We do so by developing an "ideal" and then learning to discern and be guided by the subtle feelings of "fit" and "no fit" with actions that move us toward that ideal.

Erasing Misconceptions

The above observation provides the perfect foundation for appreciating the widely misunderstood distinction that exists between the words "judging" and "judgment." Let's see if we can clarify this important distinction. When we attempt to judge something as good or bad, right or wrong, we are making a completely inappropriate use of our analytical mind. In other words, when we judge, we use our rational mind to assign value to facts rather than to carry out its intended function of transmitting those facts into and back out of our intuition. As a result, we inadvertently eliminate the chances for good "judgment" to occur.

"Judgment" is a very healthy phenomenon which occurs in our intuition as it exercises its ability to make subtle distinctions between what fits and what doesn't fit into its ever-evolving model of an "ideal." By "judging," however, we cut ourselves off from our intuition's discerning function and allow our thinking and processing to be done by our analytical mind—which, as has already been pointed out, is incapable of distinguishing truth from fiction.

As long as we are clearing up misconceptions, let's address another. We have all heard about "women's intuition." Would you be surprised to learn that male intuition is technically more powerful than female intuition? It is, but at the same time it's more difficult for us guys to access. And, contrary to some widely held beliefs, these are not just behavioral characteristics which result from how little boys and girls are socialized. These are physiologically based differences which result from variations in the speed with which our brains mature. Few people realize that five weeks after conception, the average female brain has a two-week jump on the average male brain in terms of its evolutionary maturity. This little-known difference expands to a well-known difference of about three years by age 15. Let's now look at how this affects our brain's analytical and intuitive capabilities. The faster our brain matures, the more these two functions become "generalized," or mixed together in each of our brain's two hemispheres. The slower our brain matures, the more "lateralized" or specialized its rational and intuitive thinking capabilities become. In other words, in the average male brain—the slower-maturing brain—each function is highly specialized and located quite separately in one of the brain's two hemispheres. In the average female brain—the faster-maturing one—both the analytical and intuitive thinking capabilities are mixed together in both hemispheres.

Are you beginning to wonder if there are any practical benefits to this information? I believe we are in the section of this book that deals with learning to build on our strengths. Many of the uniquely different strengths possessed by men and women are caused by the physiological differences in brain function which we have just begun to explore. Our culture is in great need of learning to understand and honor these wonderful differences.

To begin this process, let's return to my earlier comment about women's intuition. It is quite easy to understand why we see such a difference between males and females in our ability to access intuition. For the female, we can picture it as if both the analytical and intuitive capabilities live on the same street. As a result, when an intuitive insight shows up in the female mind, it simply taps on the window and invites the neighboring analytical mind to come over and put what she's feeling into words. For most of us males, however, our intuition might as well be located off in Africa somewhere. Yes, it may well be capable of generating more powerful and comprehensive insights, but for practical purposes it might as well not even exist. This will continue to occur until we develop a much better communication link between our highly specialized analytical mind located in one hemisphere and our powerful intuitive mind in the other.

Here is how Patricia and I worked through this several years ago to gain an appreciation for each other's differing analytical and intuitive strengths. When we did group work together, she would sometimes get frustrated with me when I didn't address some issue she could feel going on in the room. Her favorite expression about this was, "Earth to Kurt!" One day she finally realized I was completely oblivious to the feelings of discomfort she read so easily in the group. Later that evening over dinner she described what she had been picking up. After finding her observations quite fascinating, I developed a question about them and sent it off to my intuition (in Africa, you understand). Several weeks later, a big whopping insight showed up from my intuition (from Africa again, we must presume). Even though I don't remember right now what the insight was, its depth and significance was every bit as amazing to Patricia as was my amazement over how quickly she could pick up that initial feeling in the room. Now that the two of us have learned to honor these beautiful differences in our intuitive strengths, we are able to work much more powerfully as a team. Isn't this what teamwork is all about?

(The physiological differences mentioned above become readily apparent in cases where accidental brain damage occurs to one of the brain's two hemispheres. Where one hemisphere becomes damaged in an adult female brain—the rapidly maturing brain—the undamaged hemisphere has been found to gradually pick up the functions of the disabled hemisphere and the person moves back toward normal functioning. When one hemisphere becomes damaged in an adult male brain—the slowly maturing brain—the function housed in that side of the brain is permanently disabled.)

Disciplining the Analytical Mind Correctly

We are now ready to begin exploring some differences between correct and incorrect ways of disciplining our analytical mind. The behaviors shown in the following table under the adversarial mode of thinking exhibit the consequences of allowing our analytical mind to pursue its unintended role of judging, or assigning value to data being transmitted. Behaviors shown under the strategic thinking mode show the benefits of keeping the analytical mind focused on its intended role of transmitting data in its pure form.

Adversarial Thinkers	Strategic Thinkers
Reinforce resistance to change out of an attack-protect view of life	Generate WHOLEHEARTED commitment out of a value-finding view of life
Fail to learn from past experience because of WHAT'S WRONG questions	Are free to create the desired future because of WHAT'S RIGHT questions
Are restricted by weaknesses	Capitalize on strengths
Are acquisitive and "get"-oriented	Are expansive and "give"-oriented
Hesitate to support new ideas	Take risks and encourage innovation
Inadvertently repeat past mistakes	Systematically create new alternatives
Prefer to maintain the status quo	Thrive in a changing environment
Deplete everyone's emotional energy	Continually rebuild energy reserves
Institutionalize the past	Strategically create the future
Are obsessed with analysis	Use intuition with skill & confidence
Hide behind policies and procedures	Work with policies and procedures
Are prone to procrastinate	Are eager to initiate
Are motivated by fear & willpower	Are motivated by a purpose
Are security- and image-conscious	Are growth- and results-oriented
Use structure for protection	Use structure to support progress
Work to avoid mistakes	Work to achieve results
Resist making changes	Search for better alternatives

Take a moment to reflect on the information in this table. *What would you say is the overall impression you get from this material? Are you acquainted with others who clearly display the characteristics shown on one side of the table or the other? What about you? Do you lean clearly to one side or the other? When you compare line items across from each other, which pair does the best job of expanding your understanding?*

There are so many additional elements of understanding to be gained from reflecting upon the information in this table I hardly know where to start. Let's try the point about our analytical mind being programmable, which also means it is deceivable. Every characteristic shown on the left side of the table can be directly attributed to an analytical mind which has been deceived to think it can judge what is right or wrong. As said before, our analytical mind simply cannot execute this function. Its binary code design, however, leaves it extremely vulnerable to being deceived into thinking it can. Most—if not all—limitations we place on ourselves can be traced back to the point where our analytical minds bought into the deception that they can judge what is right or wrong. Time and time again I have seen people make dramatic improvements in their lives once they shifted their thinking on this issue.

Here is another fascinating insight made available by this table. Notice I have deliberately used words that lend themselves to being judged good or bad. Yes, I admit it. I set up a trap (but a "good" one, right?). You will recall my earlier table which showed our analytical mind on the left and our intuitive mind on the right. Now, our analytical mind does a much better job of extrapolating on the past than it does of seeing clearly in the present or creating the future. Here is how this works. When we looked at the adversarial/strategic table, there is a pretty good chance we extrapolated on the earlier table and again saw the analytical on the left and the intuitive on the right. Gotcha! Both sides of this table are in fact analytical. If we were to set up a column to portray the intuitive mind by itself in our second table, it would be in the form of a big empty blank off to the right of the two columns shown. What a perfect way to point out that the intuition by itself is for all practical purposes dormant—until engaged by the right question from our analytical mind. Remember, our analytical mind is the only one over which we have control, so our ultimate success is dependent on programming it correctly.

Here is another part of the "trick." Do you get the impression I am putting the intuition up on a huge pedestal? Not so. Such an impression could only be formed by assuming the right half of my adversarial/strategic table—with all of its positive-sounding descriptions—was a portrayal of our intuition, just as in the earlier table. Instead, the right side here simply portrays characteristics present in someone who uses their analytical mind to furnish properly framed questions to their intuitive mind. The left side here portrays characteristics commonly found in those of us who fail to discipline our analytical mind correctly, which means it has been allowed to fall in the trap of judging good and bad, right and wrong. If our intuition were to be portrayed on this table, it could be as an empty, undefined space off to the right of the two visible columns. (I hope at least some of my attempts here to provide a bit of stimulation to our learning have succeeded!)

The Story of Little David

Here's the next question we need to explore. "How did we ever get ourselves into this self-protective way of looking at life in the first place?" Think back for a moment to Chapter 1, where I mentioned how the three-year-old child's "why" questions produce so many intuitive insights that they live with a surplus and abundance view of life. Isn't it a classic metaphor to represent their unlimited supply of energy by imagining them plugged directly into Hoover Dam? So what happens to bring about this radical change ten years later? Perhaps this story of three-and-a-half-year-old "little David" fill in some of the missing details.

We come upon little David one fine day and find him playing around the house, full of energy and into everything he can reach. He's having a wonderful time. Quite innocently he happens to walk into the den, where he accidentally interrupts his Mommy and Daddy who are engaged in a heated "discussion." Actually, they're nearly at each other's throats. As little David walks innocently through the door, all of the highly charged energy of the interrupted discussion hits him right in his solar plexus (where his intuition really lives, right?). Now, one of little David's most compelling agendas at age three-and-a-half is to train his emerging analytical mind to read and decode his intuition. This, of course, is where all of his surplus energy comes from. So what will our little David do? Simple. He immediately asks a question to help him begin to unravel this great big whirl of energy that just slammed into his intuition. His innocent little question sounds something like, "What's wrong, Mommy?"

Well, right then Mommy is so close to losing her composure she really doesn't need any extra challenges! The next thing we know, she breaks into tears and goes stomping out of the den, saying through gritted teeth to poor little David, "Nothing's wrong!" This reaction is certainly confusing to little David. Here he is, just trying to make some sense out of his feelings and he gets blasted! Speaking of blasted, he still has to deal with Daddy, who is operating under the illusion that he was about to win the argument. Now he knows it will be another six weeks before he can even bring it up again. Believe me, he is not a happy camper. So how does Daddy deal with all of this? That's easy. He points an accusing finger at little David and dumps another big charge of energy as he says, "You made your Mommy cry!" This, of course, is just enough to completely overload poor little David's circuits and he breaks into tears. We all know how Daddy responds to that. Sure enough, the next thing out of his mouth is, "And if you don't stop crying, I'll give you something to cry about."

Does any of this sound familiar? For many of us, unfortunately, it has a painfully familiar ring to it. I have created this story to symbolize how the vast majority of us were "penalized" out of the mode of using our analytical minds correctly. For most of us this happened gradually over the years, from the time we were about three years old until we were about age ten. Let's be even more specific about what we mean by using our analytical minds correctly. All little David needed was to read and decode the mass of messages which had flooded into his intuition. This could have been accomplished by simply allowing him to say, "I felt afraid." In a similar way, he needed to label every feeling which had occurred, and receive assurances in return that he had read the feeling accurately and it was okay to have the feeling. In this way he would have been allowed to "unravel and make sense of" all the feelings that swept over him when he entered the room. This would have allowed him to continue to trust his intuition as his ultimate source of guidance. This trait is technically known as having an "internal locus of control." It is a trait all of us must regain in order to reach and maintain the state of effortless high performance.

Before we leave little David, let's go back and point out exactly what kind of support he needed from Mommy or Daddy in order to prevent him from feeling invalidated for what was actually a correct use of his analytical mind. Here we are pointing out what was needed to prevent the negative residual effects of his invalidation experience. No residual effects would have occurred at all if, at any time during the first two hours after the incident, either Mommy or Daddy had taken little David on their knee and simply said, "What were you feeling back there in the den?" You see, all little David needed was the non-judgmental questions and the trusted space of unconditional love in which to simply say what he had felt. He didn't need any explanations or apologies. He didn't need anything to be fixed. He just needed the time, space and support which would allow him to do the "work" of using his analytical mind the way it was designed—to read and decode the feelings of his intuition. If little David had received this support at any time within two hours of the incident, there would have been no residual negative effects from the experience whatsoever. Without this support, however, the emotional pain generated by the experience would end up being stored, often in "knots" in little David's muscles, which a good chiropractor or masseuse might help him release later in his life.

We have something even more important to recognize here. If the support needed by little David had been available at any time within the next eight hours, there would have been no negative effects remaining to resolve today. Or, even if it had been available within the next two days . . . or even eight days . . . or two years . . . or eight years . . . or even 20 years. Perhaps you are getting my drift. We do *not* need an analyst. We do *not* need anyone to judge our unresolved feelings negatively and try to make them go away. What we do need, however, is dialogue with a good mentor-coach who will simply ask us questions (much like I am working to demonstrate throughout this book) which allow us to finish feeling our feelings, typically by putting them into words. Only after we have done a good bit of such "clearing" can we expect to get the clean, clear messages we desire from our intuition—and be able to decode them correctly with our analytical mind. It takes lots and lots of practice at reading our feelings and putting them into words before we can make any serious progress toward getting ourselves on a roll and moving into a permanent state of effortless high performance.

It would seem that some good mentor-coaching questions might be quite useful at this point. *What are the two biggest messages you are getting for yourself personally from David's story? Do you have children of your own? If so, did you find yourself thinking about the impact you have had on them over the years rather than thinking about your own needs?* Remember, this is not a story to make you feel guilty. Rather, its intent is to equip you to take even more responsibility for your own growth. *Along this line, what action steps are you now wishing to take as a result of this story? If the opportunity presented itself right now, would you be prepared to supply the questions and high-trust environment within which someone else could practice putting their feelings into words? Or, would you prefer or step up and take full advantage of such an opportunity if the* RIGHT QUESTIONS *and high-trust space were made available to you? On a one to ten scale, where would you rate your motivation to become more skilled at putting your feelings into words? How does your present motivation in this area compare to where it was before you began reading this book? If your motivation has changed, what new understandings have made the greatest contribution to that change? Are you feeling a need for more explicit guidelines on how to ask* RIGHT QUESTIONS? *If so, perhaps you will be pleased to know the entire next chapter is focused on that issue.* Meanwhile, we want to take one more look at how the two functions, analytical and intuitive, are intended to work together as a team.

Chapter Seven

A Good Mentor-Coach
Asks RIGHT QUESTIONS

What Is a Mentor-Coach?

Without the support of RIGHT QUESTIONS from a good mentor-coach, I do not believe any one of us has even the slightest chance of becoming an effortless high performer. As you hear me say that, do you have any curiosity at all about why I never use the word "mentor" alone, but always link it with the word "coach?" It's because most people imagine a mentor to be a giver of good advice, just as most people look outside themselves for answers. Instead of rewarding this behavior, a good mentor-coach asks questions to help us look inside ourselves for answers. And, since no amount of good advice could ever enable us to become effortless high performers, a good mentor-coach never gives advice.

In Chapter 6, I mentioned how important it is to have our locus of control be based internally rather than externally. Having an internal locus of control means we have a habit of asking ourselves questions that help us look deep within ourselves for answers needed to guide our own lives. This virtually defines an effortless high performer. It also makes it clear why we don't need an advice-giving mentor. Whenever we allow someone to give us "good advice," we inadvertently allow them to reinforce an unhealthy dependency on looking outside ourselves for answers. One easy way to spot advice givers is by their use of the word "should," whether directly or by implication. Another is their eagerness to offer opinions.

The challenge of developing a good mentor-coaching relationship presents an interesting dilemma. We have more control over asking questions that support another person's growth than we do over finding someone who will ask questions that support our own growth. To find someone who will learn to ask the questions needed to support our growth is a very tall order! One solution to this dilemma is to choose a promising partner and ask them to pick up their own copy of *Breaking the Rules* and join us in working to master the practices offered here. We can then practice our newly developing skills by asking questions of each other. The remainder of this chapter is devoted to the task of learning to be a good mentor-coach.

Influence Factors

Let's begin by looking at a set of four influence factors found in the background of every effortless high performer I have studied. These four factors provide a preliminary definition of the ideal mentor-coach. As we move through the descriptions, I will convey as many tangible and intangible aspects of these four influence factors as I can put into words. First, I will simply list the four outcome states.

1. Feeling believed in.

2. Being asked right questions.

3. Learning to fully trust ourselves through trusting others.

4. Developing our own validation framework.

We will now take a much deeper look at each of these factors. If I am to be the supplier of the first influence factor for you—to be your ideal mentor-coach—I must remember to relate to you at all times as if you already possess every answer you need for guiding your own life. It certainly doesn't feed my ego to operate with you in this manner, but it is the truth, and I can learn to do it. I must also remind myself that advice is the very last thing you need from me.

The second influence factor is so closely tied to the first that I will expand on it a bit before going into more detail on the first. Just because we already possess all the answers we ever need for guiding our own lives, doesn't mean we have full conscious access to them. It can be quite another matter for us to gain access to our answers, and our chances of doing so on our own are slim to none—without an outside supply of right questions. Therefore, if I am to supply this second influence factor, I must offer questions which allow you to gain access to the answers you already have inside you. In other words, your need for correctly framed questions from me is infinitely greater than your need for advice.

Remember, the desired outcome of all four influence factors is a locus of control firmly rooted inside of us, rather than outside. It seems that the best way to assure this result is through a special verbal communication process with someone who truly honors the strength of our inner knowing. In this way we can become deeply connected to the feeling that we are trusted, honored and believed in as a human being. Yet, while feeling honored and believed in is profoundly empowering, it can only sustain itself if we are also being asked right questions. Only in this way can our answers from within be drawn out and brought up into our conscious awareness. Once we are consciously aware of these answers, we can then choose to act on them and have them validated through life's experiences. The longer we are exposed to the potent combination of having our feelings truly honored, and then being asked properly framed questions, the more self-sustaining the entire process becomes. In other words, there is a conditioning effect from being continually exposed to properly framed questions. The analytical mind is, after all, programmable, and its programming occurs through repetition. There is also a conditioning effect of having our internally sourced answers continually validate themselves in our everyday lives.

The third set of influence factors relates to self-trust. It has to do with the special support we need from another person in order for our conscious, rational self to become truly trusting of our inner, intuitive self at the deepest level. Our preferred way to do this is to develop a mentor-coaching relationship in which we can be completely open with our innermost feelings. With this special person we can then experience full self-expression. In other words, we need to experience a communication relationship in which we can be as open and vulnerable as needed without feeling threatened in any way. The principle at work here is this: We can only trust that part of ourselves which we have revealed to another person and had *validated* instead of *violated*. This prompts our next question. How much of ourselves do we wish to be able to trust? Ultimately, we need to be able to fully trust ourselves both alone and in the presence of others, and this is exactly what happens when this third set of influence factors is present. Most importantly, the more of ourselves we can trust, the better our chances of becoming an effortless high performer.

The fourth set of influence factors is needed to make each of the others self-sustaining. It relies on the development of what I call a "validation framework," and must occur if we are to be able to validate our own insights and inner knowing—without being dependent on others for either permission or approval. The most effective validation framework I know of is an ever-evolving vision of an ideal "something." It is a matter of choosing to wonder what an ideal (something) might look like. (Chapter 20 describes this in much more detail.) The item we decide to wonder about is most effective if it fully captures our imagination and takes years to completely fall into place. As you can probably see, it is technically possible to complete this step of establishing a validation framework on our own. In most cases, however, it will require the support of a good mentor-coach to make it happen. Once it is in place, we will feel amazingly free to move forward and take what others may see as huge risks without being unduly concerned over any apparent lack of support from others around us.

These are the conditions or influence factors found to produce effortless high performers. Every one I have studied can identify exactly who supplied this set of influences in their life. The consistency of this finding has led me to view the above set of influence factors as an appropriate and fully achievable definition of the ideal corporate culture as well. It most certainly qualifies as the ideal culture for the family dinner table, and perhaps for educational institutions as well, although I admit we may be a long way away from any readiness on the part of educators to consider such an option. The success we described in Chapter 1 with the software development project occurred in large part as a result of immersing 200 of the 400 people on the project into a highly concentrated experience of the above conditions. This was done as a part of a dozen two-day team dialogues we conducted for that organization.

It's now time for your mentor-coach to wrap up this section with another question or two. *What two or three ideas struck you the most from the above description of conditions found in the backgrounds of effortless high performers? In what part of your life are you already experiencing many of these growth-inspiring conditions? What part of your life might get the biggest boost from having more of these conditions present? Which are you more strongly drawn to: being a good mentor-coach for someone else, or finding a good one for yourself? When you put this information alongside everything else presented so far, what is your feeling about its importance to you personally? What is the most important factor affecting that feeling?*

Putting Questions in Context

Before I zero in and begin to offer guidelines for asking right questions, I must point out there are many different domains within which questions can serve us. Some of these areas are better suited to the type of questions most of us are already trained to ask. This is particularly true where we must ask questions to acquire high-quality data or information from others—whether for our own use, or to be passed on to others as input for a variety of decision-making processes. The only contribution I intend to make to your skills in this area is to raise the general trust level of all your communications.

The type of questions I am addressing here are those which must be asked *of* us rather than *by* us if we intend to become effortless high performers. Since we have little or no direct control over questions asked *of* us by others, we must focus our discussion on the intermediate step of learning to ask properly framed questions of others. Fortunately, there are two benefits of this indirect approach. First, by learning to ask properly framed questions of others, we are indirectly affecting our own thought processes. Our answers may not come as quickly as when we are on the receiving end of good questions, but in the end this path can be even more powerful. So, while it may not bear fruit as quickly, learning to ask properly framed questions of others is still immensely beneficial. Second, by learning how to use questions to bring out the best in others, we equip ourselves to teach someone else to do the same for us in return. This is a major goal of this chapter.

To succeed in the world of asking intuition-engaging questions, we must also learn to see our questions as "gifts" given freely and without strings to others. For some of us, this will take some adjustment. For most of us, it will be paradoxical. Even though much of this material is focused on supplying questions to others, our ultimate gift is to equip someone else to become very skilled and caring about asking these questions of us.

Habit-Starters

I divide the broad domain of RIGHT QUESTIONS into three smaller areas. The first is focused on questions which can put us on a roll when consistently asked of us by others. Or, when we make a practice of asking them of others, these questions gradually shape the ones we ask internally of ourselves. I call this the "habit-starter" arena.

For questions to succeed in the habit-starter arena, they must keep us focused on finding value in the past and present. Good habit-starter questions gradually expand our ability to access and use our intuitive mind. An excellent way to tell when we have been given an effective habit-starter question is when we feel our supply of creative energy being replenished while we process it. Best of all, by making it a practice to ask high-quality habit-starter questions of others, we control the strengthening of our own habits of asking RIGHT QUESTIONS of ourselves. We also become more and more aware of the utter futility of asking problem-focused questions of anyone. Over the next few pages, I will put a great deal of emphasis on mastering the ability to ask high-quality habit-starter questions.

Vision-Building

The second domain for learning to ask RIGHT QUESTIONS is vision-building. Perhaps the first and most important guideline to remember about asking questions in this area is the tremendous amount of energy required to process vision-building questions. It is important to understand this because the vast majority of us simply do not have large enough reserves of creative energy to enter this domain. We must first develop these reserves of creative energy through lots of practice in the habit-starter area. We need to develop a habit of examining everything we can find that works and figure out why it works.

Questions that succeed in the realm of vision-building are quite simple. They invite us to describe specific aspects of our evolving vision of an ideal future in order to bring them into clearer focus. Our vision continues to take form and intensify its power as we describe various parts of it in response to the questions. The more of it we can describe, the clearer we also become about the vision's unknown aspects. Our intuitive drive to fill in these blanks or unknown aspects will eventually take over and become a powerful force to guide us with a remarkable sense of certainty into an uncharted future.

Once we learn to ask the questions unique to this realm, we must always remember to keep replenishing our energy by returning frequently to the area of habit-starter questions. Since the questions for this area are so simple, we will touch on them only briefly in this chapter and will do so in the context of a discussion of how to keep the energy up so these questions can be successfully processed.

Issue Resolution

The third domain for asking RIGHT QUESTIONS is issue resolution. As our perspective of this domain expands, we can learn to celebrate the times when we get "stuck." Such times inevitably remind us of where we have slipped back into the mode of asking WHAT'S WRONG questions, or have assigned negative value to some fact or condition we are facing. Being stuck, of course, is the opposite of being on a roll. Right questions are needed to identify the point at which we are stuck and then reveal what is needed for us to resume movement toward our goals. We'll have some fun in this chapter by expanding our awareness about what causes us to get stuck and how to quickly get unstuck.

What did you appreciate most about our treatment of the areas within which to ask questions? Were there any surprises for you? What aspect of getting ourselves on a roll has become slightly clearer for you?

Bring On the Habit-Starter Questions

Bet you were beginning to think we would never get here! No more delays. As a guiding principle, we see a RIGHT QUESTION in any area as one which allows the person responding to it to feel more valued while searching their innermost feelings to find new value. It is therefore useful to think of a RIGHT QUESTION as one which is "value-finding" in nature. My choice to use the word "value" here is largely because of its unique-ness in lacking a negative opposite. Value as a concept starts at zero and goes up. Look at how closely this fits with our concept of zero-based strengths. It is also next to impossible to process a value-finding question with our analytical mind. This is another key "value" of value-finding questions. Since it is so difficult to process a value-finding question with our analytical mind, we can sometimes use this as a way to tell if a question is value-finding or not. Within the habit-starting area, we could even define a RIGHT QUESTION as any question which cannot be processed by our analytical mind. Even if we used this as our only criteria, we could expect to be very effective at asking value-finding questions.

112

Value-finding questions must, by definition, be processed in our intuitive mind. This means we can count on them to generate fresh supplies of creative energy every time they spark new insights—a major benefit of asking and processing such questions. They are responsible for producing the creative energy we must have available in abundance to put ourselves on a roll. Learning to ask value-finding questions is therefore the most practical step we can take to begin putting everything in this book into practice in our lives. The payoff can be huge as we begin to practice asking value-finding questions of others around us and succeed in inspiring others to do the same for us in return. And, the more skill we develop in asking value-finding questions of others, the more we strengthen our own internal habits of asking value-finding questions of ourselves.

In Chapter 6 we described our intuitive mind as trainable—in contrast to our analytical mind, which is programmable. By asking and processing value-finding questions, we train our intuitive mind to be increasingly efficient in its ability to crystallize new insights. This process also prepares us to participate in the vision-building process. The questions below meet our criteria of inviting people to find value in the past and present.

1. What was the best thing that happened to you today? (After their response:) What did you appreciate most about that? (Be prepared to share openly and honestly why you are asking.)

2. What was the highlight of your _____ (day, week, trip, etc.)?

3. What is the primary value you are getting from this discussion?

4. What two things did you like best or appreciate most about _____?

5. What was the best, most meaningful or most useful part of your (meeting, etc.)?

113

6. What would you do more or less of another time?

7. What feelings are you having right now about the decision or project you are considering?

8. With what aspects of it are you feeling most comfortable? How about least comfortable?

9. What message or insight is waiting for you in these feelings?

10. What would it take for you to feel more comfortable?

11. What are your uncomfortable feelings telling you? Can you see any special patterns in these uncomfortable feelings?

12. In what ways could I be most helpful to you right now?

13. Talk to me about what you are feeling or thinking right now.

14. What are you learning from listening to your feelings right now?

15. What other question could I ask that might be helpful?

What is the first thing you notice about nearly every question? Most of them start with "what," don't they? That's a good rule to remember for learning to ask value-finding questions. If we always discipline ourselves to begin our question with the word "what," our chances of framing a useful question will go up tremendously. Notice how each question could also be looked upon as a gift to the person being asked the question. By this I mean the person asking the question has little to gain by listening to the answer. Each question reflects a trust on the part of the person asking that the only answers of value lie somewhere within the person being asked.

Because of its importance, I will focus our attention for the next several pages on the first question on the list. So far it has been introduced to more than 10,000 people. Many profound and heartwarming stories have come back to us, and we have learned lots of lessons in the process. Three stories are included here.

Before relating them, however, I urge you to practice asking that question of someone close to you within the next few hours. If the response you get comes even close to what literally thousands of people have shared with us, I know you will want to soon make it a habit.

By way of background, each person had received and followed exactly the same instruction you have just been given. In their case, the instruction came at the end of an entire day of intense and energizing dialogue around precisely the same material you have explored so far in this book. Unless otherwise noted, each story is as close as I can remember to what was shared in dialogue among peers the next morning.

Success Stories

The first story was told to us by Sarah, a professional woman and single-parent mother. Sarah began by telling us how the previous day's dialogue had caused her to take a serious look at how judgmental she had been with her fifteen-year-old daughter, Jodi. Sarah then related what happened when she asked the question, "What's the best thing that happened to you today?" Her first two efforts were met with a belligerent, "Nothing," which she told us she probably deserved. Her third try was met with an even more belligerent, "Mom, I said nothing!" At this point, Sarah realized it would be necessary to ask her question in a different way. Her next two efforts went something like, "What's the least bad thing that happened to you today?" Finally, after the third try with her insightful, "least bad" question, Jodi began to cautiously test the water with a "safe" response. Much to her surprise, she discovered an entirely new attitude had replaced her mother's judgmental one of the day before. The next morning, with tears in her eyes, Sarah reported that the two of them continued on with several hours of the most meaningful communication they had experienced for months.

The story's postscript revealed the true power of what happened that night. This occurred in a call to our office six weeks later. We learned that after their first experience with the question, Sarah and Jodi made a commitment to share it with each other every night. On the morning of the follow-up call, Jodi came bouncing down the stairway with the following announcement, "Mom! I already know the best thing that's going to happen to me today." Sarah responded with warm expectation, "What's that?" (I'm even feeling choked up again right now as I remember what a powerful message Sarah received for all of us that morning.) She told us Jodi virtually radiated as she continued, saying, "I woke up looking for the best thing that was going to happen to me today." What a transformation—and in only six weeks' time! That's just a sample of the true power of value-finding questions used in the habit-starting area. Imagine the impact on me from having listened to some 10,000 such stories—all having resulted from the asking of one simple little "gift" question. Whatever you do, please do not overlook the power of this question when transformed into a regular, everyday habit. Which reminds me, have you made your first attempt to ask it yet?

The setting for our next story was a small hotel out in the middle of nowhere. This location was chosen by a client to allow his team to abandon even more barriers by keeping us together over dinner and throughout the evening between two days of focused dialogue. This also meant team members would have to go to some extra effort to find someone with whom to practice asking their question, "What's the best thing that happened to you today?" The next morning as we discussed our successes, one team member, Anne, reported what she thought was a complete failure of her experiment. She told us how she recognized the piano player as we all walked into the restaurant the evening before, and decided this was the perfect person on whom to practice her question. Unfortunately, the piano player had had an extremely bad day. From the way the story unfolded, in fact, it may have been much worse than just a very bad day. In any case, the piano player's sharply worded response was, "How thoughtless of you to ask me such a question on a day like I've just been through!" As you can imagine, Anne made a hasty retreat and was reporting the utter failure of her efforts.

At this point another surprised team member, Joe, spoke up and asked, "Didn't you speak with her later in the evening?" Anne responded, "Are you kidding?" It turns out that after dinner Joe still needed to find someone with whom to practice his question. Just before everyone got up from dinner, he walked over to the piano player and asked, "What's the best thing that happened to you today?" She smiled and said it was the same question she had been asked by Anne earlier in the evening. The piano player went on to describe how disappointed in herself she had felt over her inappropriate response to Anne's question. While thinking about that, she had somehow switched her mind around to counting her blessings and her entire attitude had changed. She attributed the change to Anne's question and was truly grateful it had been asked.

The Power of Unanswered Questions

This brings up an important point about asking questions in our habit-starter area. The culture in which we live has taught us to judge ourselves deficient if we fail to have an immediate answer to a question— or if we fail to answer it correctly. An unanswered question can thus be a very powerful motivator. In our habit-starting arena, it is not an immediate answer to the question we are after. What's important is the processing which takes place after we are asked the question. The power of this gets magnified quite nicely when we know we failed to give the "right" answer. It is often further magnified when the person who asked the question in the first place is no longer available to receive our "corrected" answer.

To put this into perspective, think of the last time someone you know asked you a question for which you simply did not have an answer. Let's also say that for some reason you consider this person's opinion of you to be of utmost importance. *What were your feelings about not having the answer? Did you feel any special motivation to find the answer? How much time went by before you found it? Was your mind more active than usual during this elapsed time? What was the predominant focus of its attention?*

The word I use to describe this activity is "residual processing." It can be either depleting or energizing, depending on whether the processing occurs in our analytical or intuitive mind. Our energy is always depleted when we do our processing in our analytical mind—and this is virtually assured whenever we are given any kind of a WHAT'S WRONG question to process. On the other hand, residual processing can be totally energizing when it is done intuitively in response to WHAT'S RIGHT questions. A classic example of the depletion form of residual processing takes place every time an unenlightened human resources department asks members of an organization to complete an attitude opinion survey. Most such surveys ask problem-focused questions, and usually close with some kind of a negative question such as, "Are there any other problems that should be brought to our attention?" Just imagine the amount of costly residual processing which is sure to take place after such a series of questions is completed. No wonder perceptive leaders feel resistance when being urged to have such surveys conducted under their watch. Wouldn't it be exciting to see one of those surveys done using RIGHT QUESTIONS—and then sit back and watch an entire organization energize itself with residual processing done in the intuitive mind? What a golden opportunity!

Now, to set the stage for some valuable insights available from our next story, please note your answer to a special question before we begin. When you have your answer, put it where you can refer back to it later. Here is your question: On a scale of one to ten, where one is low and ten is high, where would you put your "drive" at the present time in your life?

Reaching Out

The person who brought us this next story was visibly hesitant to relate her experience. As Peggy's story unfolded, we quickly learned why she felt reluctant. At 10 P.M. the previous evening Peggy received a phone call from someone she knew only casually from work. Since Peggy's phone was unlisted, this person had obviously gone to a lot of trouble to figure out how to reach her. Shortly into the conversation, Peggy's intuition told her this person was preparing to commit suicide and planned to use the phone call as a suicide note. With absolutely no experience in dealing with such a crisis, Peggy felt overwhelmed with uncertainty about what to do. Suddenly she remembered her practice assignment, but the page of instructions she had been given was across the room out of reach. All she could think of was to begin asking this young man questions about what was going well in his life. After some 45 minutes of answering these questions, the young man admitted he had called with the full intention of committing suicide that very night. Peggy's questions had helped him turn the corner, and when I checked back two weeks later, I learned this young man's life had continued its remarkable turn for the better.

Several months later I related this story to another group in which someone present was a trained volunteer who worked with a crisis intervention hotline. We were both impressed to learn how closely aligned our questions were to those he had been trained to use in his service work. The question I think we need to ask is why must we wait until a crisis shows up in our lives to discover the importance of such questions? Perhaps we need to be asking them all the time.

How Do We Rate Our Drive?

This brings me back to insights available from the question I asked about your drive. Answers people have given me to this question over the years fall in a range from two to 13 (yes, on a ten point scale). Here are some insights I have gained into those answers. Every answer over ten—and there have been several, usually either 12 or 13—have proven to reflect a large need to compensate for a big gaping hole in the person's self-esteem. This one hits very close to home for me personally. In my case—as well as every other person I've seen who picked either 12 or 13—the pain of our low self-esteem was most keenly felt during our middle school years, or at about the age of 13 to 15. In retrospect I can be thankful for this intense pain, for it no doubt played quite a role in prompting me to develop all of the self-esteem–building tools offered in this book. It was certainly negative motivation at the time, but somehow I either abandoned that aspect of it or transformed it into a positive.

At the opposite end of this spectrum are all the answers of five I have received. It must somehow feel psychologically unsafe to answer less than five, because in all cases I have examined where someone gave me an answer of five, their "real" drive turned out to be none—a net of zero drive. This has also enabled me to interpret an answer of seven as an indication of slightly less than average drive and an answer of eight as slightly above average. To look a little more deeply into patterns present in those who have given me answers of five is instructive. In every case of this I have explored, the person was a male. Each reported having felt they had reached the pinnacle of success during their middle school years—particularly from a physical prowess standpoint.

Note how each pattern described above links our answer to the drive question to the presence or absence of negative motivation in our lives. This is particularly instructive when thinking about how to support the motivational development of someone who gives themselves an honest answer of five to the drive question. It also brings into sharp focus a difficult challenge we all face. Here is a situation in which we see what happens when there is a complete absence of *negative* drive—in a society which offers precious few models of how to develop a truly positive form of drive. This is a major void I intend to fill with this book.

A source for all the positive drive any of us could ever wish for can be found in our life's purpose! The trick lies in learning how to tap into it.

Out of Gas

Of all the insights I have gained from exploring answers received in response to my drive question, perhaps the most significant came from the nine people who gave me an answer of two. I shall never forget the first time it happened. It may also have been the first time I ever asked the question about drive. I do recall feeling quite puzzled while trying to understand the person's motivation, which was no doubt what prompted me to ask the question. When the answer came back as a two, it was one of those incredible moments for me when time stood still, and in the next few seconds my mind did an ultra-high-speed scan of everything I knew and then some. To this day I have no idea where my response came from, or even how I ever gathered the courage to express it, but I blurted out, "You are seriously considering suicide right now, aren't you?" The person's startled reply was, "How did you know?"

That first time, my observation felt like a risky, wild guess. The next time I got an answer of two, however, I felt more prepared. Sure enough, subsequent dialogue provided further validation for what had initially seemed like a purely instinctive response. To date, I have experienced a total of nine times when someone responded with an answer of two. Each occasion has provided consistent validation for the initial insight.

Here are some conclusions I have drawn from these nine experiences. The "two" answers give us a telling indicator of how depleted the person's energy supply has become as a result of processing WHAT'S WRONG questions. Every one of us has felt the depletion of energy that always occurs when we process WHAT'S WRONG questions. As a person's battery approaches the point of total depletion, it doesn't take a rocket scientist to figure out how compulsive the WHAT'S WRONG questions might become. In computer jargon, it's called an endless loop. Professionals in the crisis intervention field have obviously learned how to break the loop with an external supply of WHAT'S RIGHT, or value-finding questions.

I bring all of this up here for two reasons. First, an epidemic of suicides is occurring today among young people all over America. It is particularly serious in our high schools. Second, as I pointed out in Chapter 2, "problems" only show up in our lives to tell us we are out of alignment with our purpose. And, if we solve a problem and fail to get its message, we simply set ourselves up for even bigger problems. The suicide rate among young people in America is a very big problem. It is attempting to bring us an important message we have not yet heard. The suicide problem will continue to get worse until we get the message it is attempting to bring us. What is that message? My guess is it has something to do with our failure to honor the inner knowing of children and young people, and instead impose upon them a set of theories of questionable value. It is high time for us to start looking for WHAT'S RIGHT with ourselves, with each other and with our world. Please understand, the approach to questions I am offering here is not a bunch of platitudes. It is serious business! It could be the most serious business we ever have the privilege to undertake.

Well, I guess I had better step down off that soapbox and ask some overdue mentor-coaching questions. Imagining that we are still face-to-face, I will boldly ask *what you are appreciating most about me right now?* I do this not to invite you to stroke my ego, but because I have come to realize what I have just expressed may have touched one or more deep chords in you. If this is true, the above question works rather well to draw some of the deeper feelings out into your conscious awareness. We have several stories here to reflect on and assimilate. In our first story with Sarah and Jodi, we saw the need for commitment and persistence in getting the process started. When used consistently, we saw its potential for producing some appealing results rather quickly. In our second story with Alice, Joe and the piano player, we got a quick glimpse of how residual processing works. We then took a look at the expanded implications of residual processing in the workplace. Our third story about the potential suicide attempt gave us a hint that there may be more to this idea of asking value-finding questions than meets the eye at first glance.

Which of the three examples spoke the loudest to you? What about that example spoke most clearly to you? What spoke most deeply to you? How would you describe any shift in thinking that may have taken place for you as a result of reading these stories? Has anything happened in the past three or four pages to prompt you to go back to an earlier section and review something that now feels more important than it did at first? If you have children, and if you had a magic wand that would allow you to fully impart to them only one of the ideas we have touched on so far in this book, which idea would you most like to have them grasp? What will you do more or less of as a result of reading these last several pages on asking value-finding questions?

∞

Chapter Eight

Developing the Mentor-Coaching Relationship

Mentor-Coaching Guidelines

An ideal mentor-coaching relationship relies on our dialogue with a specially chosen person as a vehicle for developing a healthier and more productive relationship between our own head and heart. To be fully effective, we must be sure the external dialogue between us mirrors the desired internal dialogue. Thus, at any given time one of us will be simply asking questions of the other which can only be processed intuitively. The other is processing the questions. Whenever we set out to either find someone who can fill this role for us, or to fill it for someone else, it would certainly help to keep this simple description clearly in mind. Any of us who choose to do this will be taking a wonderful leap in learning to trust, honor and build upon our true inner strengths.

Our own personal mentor-coaching relationship begins when we find someone who will share these goals with us. External dialogue with our mentor-coach is then used to support optimal development of the desired internal dialogue between our conscious, rational mind and our inner, intuitive mind. As we continue to build this relationship, we greatly expand our ability to bring out the best in ourselves and others.

It is easy to strengthen this relationship when we simply remember to search for hidden value in our innermost feelings and put those feelings into words.

Mentor-coaching is always at its best when we feel totally free to put our most deeply felt feelings into words—without the slightest concern over having those feelings analyzed or judged. Our most valuable insights are most effectively drawn out and put into words in response to the following types of questions:

❖ What are you feeling right now?

❖ What does that feel like?

❖ Talk more about what you are feeling.

❖ What are you feeling about _____?

❖ What were you feeling at the time?

❖ When have you ever felt that way before?

❖ What did it feel like then?

From these questions, we can quickly see that the goal of an effective mentor-coach is to patiently ask feeling questions and then listen . . . listen . . . and listen some more. We can also make it easier for others to continue putting their feelings into words when we reveal some of our own feelings in a non-judging manner. Silence, too, is a wonderful gift that can often allow others to finish feeling their most deeply felt feelings. Finally, we can consider it a high compliment to our mentor-coaching skill when we allow others to purge their feelings of discomfort by verbalizing those feelings and crying in our presence.

Your mentor-coach now asks, *what about these observations allows you to feel more prepared to enter your own mentor-coaching relationship? What are two key benefits you can see for having such a relationship? What about these benefits feels most appealing to you? What aspect or aspects feel most challenging to you?*

Let's now take a look at how the skills we're developing can be put to work in real-life situations.

A Mentor-Coach Does Performance Appraisals

Isn't it interesting to note the amount of resistance most of us feel around doing performance appraisals? Why might this be? As we get more tuned into our inner knowing, do you suppose we might feel an increase or decrease in our resistance to doing performance appraisals in the traditional way? I believe we will feel even more resistance, and if so, this increase will be due to our intuitive awareness of the disempowering consequences of standing in judgment of anyone. Such actions are simply too far out of phase with our purpose.

If there were a way to do performance appraisals that would be truly empowering, would you wish to know about it? Well, there is, and we discovered this one quite by accident. Our original intent was simply to set up a 30-minute exercise to allow participants in our team dialogue to pair off and practice asking a set of meaningful mentor-coaching questions of each other. It didn't take long for several clients to tell us these were the best performance appraisal questions they had ever used.

We eventually learned we could all become more effective at asking good performance appraisal questions if we simply practiced conducting in-depth dialogues with others around the four non-job questions that follow. It is wonderful practice to both ask and be asked these questions. When it is our turn to ask these questions, our goal is to allow our partner to gain new insights while putting his or her feelings into words in response to our questions. When it is our turn to respond to our partner's questions, our goal is to capitalize on the opportunity by reaching as deeply into our feelings as we can and enjoying what special insights show up as we put those feelings into words.

❖ Think of a personal, off-the-job accomplishment you have enjoyed over the past year or so and feel especially good about, or feel has been particularly meaningful to you.

❖ What about this accomplishment makes you feel especially good?

❖ What special strengths do you feel might have played a key role in helping you achieve this result?

❖ What special insights are you gaining about your strengths from thinking out loud with me about these questions?

The actual questions above are intended to be used only as a guide, and only as needed. Let the principles of genuine interest and unconditional acceptance be a stronger guide. I think you will find practicing these questions quite enjoyable, and at times capable of producing some deeply meaningful insights. Can you think of someone with whom you would like to practice this right now? `PAUSE`

Once you have had some rewarding experiences with the above questions, you will be much better prepared to apply the more specific ones we use for performance appraisals. Be sure to allow ample time for this process. It is not uncommon for people to take as long as eight hours to complete this dialogue, and often with profoundly empowering results. Be sure to note how this powerful self-responsibility alternative replaces the old mode of having us stand in judgment of another person's performance. Here are the questions.

❖ Among your many job accomplishments during the past six months, which one or two do you feel most strongly about or consider most meaningful?

❖ What key personal strengths or success factors can you identify that may have played an important role in helping you to accomplish the above?

❖ What are some special ways you can think of to put these personal strengths and success factors to work in other areas of your job? What might be the benefits to you of doing so?

❖ How would you describe what your job performance might look like if all aspects of it were done ideally?

❖ What aspects of your job would you most like to be doing better?

❖ What steps would you need to take to bring your actual performance on a daily basis into alignment with the ideal you have just described?

A tremendous self-responsibility benefit occurs when these questions are used for performance appraisal purposes. Then, when it comes time for our next appraisal, we have already established the criteria upon which we will be evaluating our own performance. This is only one of many benefits I have seen from using these questions in the performance appraisal context. Another that comes quickly to mind is the improved commitment that comes from truly feeling valued as a person.

Can you imagine what might happen to job performance in our businesses if the above process was to completely replace our present mode of judging other people's performance? Your mentor-coach would now like to ask, *what are the two biggest benefits you see for yourself from taking some time to practice these two sets of questions? Which has more appeal to you, having these questions asked of you, or asking them of others? What is the most significant insight you have gained from simply reflecting on them* right *now?*

Using Right Questions to Build a Vision of an Ideal Future

In Chapter 2, I said we must define our purpose before we can proceed to develop a vision. Therefore, the following discussion presumes that our purpose has already been clearly defined. The ongoing process of vision-building (long-range goal-setting) is far too important to be addressed without first obtaining a clear definition of purpose.

Developing a vision of a future ideal uses a tremendous amount of creative energy. To assure ourselves of having an adequate supply of the creative energy we need to begin the process, we must always remember to set aside ample time up front for asking energy-generating questions. The importance of allowing time to build this foundation is often overlooked. I find it effective to allow a minimum of one to two hours at the beginning of each vision-building session for this activity.

Once our probing review of past successes has generated an adequate supply of energy, we must continually monitor the energy level of those engaged in the process. If we observe it dissipating, it is particularly helpful to shift our questions to focus on finding value in what has been accomplished up to that point in the meeting. Such questions serve the vital role of triggering insights that replenish the creative energy consumed during the vision-building process. Are you getting my message about the importance of energy here? Believe it.

An effective vision-building process must begin with the definition of things in the future about which we have the greatest certainty. It then expands into the unknowns. Successful vision-builders usually begin by choosing a specific point of time in the future to serve as the central known and around which to begin constructing the vision. If we are building a vision just for ourselves personally, there are several reasons for choosing a starting point at least ten years into the future. If we are doing it for a business, the maximum time frame would most often be five years, and could be as short as two years depending on the speed of obsolescence of the particular industry in which you are engaged. All such planning parameters are covered thoroughly in Chapter 20.

Once a point in time is chosen, it becomes the cornerstone of a structure that grows and takes shape as other knowns are added. During the process of building a vision, it is always tempting to be distracted by imagined obstacles, and it is this distraction that most frequently derails the process. In fact, it is the doubts and uncertainties that surface around steps needed to reach the goal that most often stops the flow of our vision-building questions. Successful vision-building questions will tend to reflect themes represented by the following questions.

❖ What will the whole picture look like when it's complete?

❖ What will the _____ (piece) look like when it's complete?

❖ If there were no obstacles, or nothing to stop us, what would we want to do?

When doing this in a business setting, the most useful questions we can ask are often sourced in our personal curiosity about what our piece of the completed picture will look like. We must also remember the vision-building process operates most effectively from a belief that anything is possible.

Using Right Questions to Resolve Issues That Block Progress

As I mentioned earlier in this chapter, I have really learned to celebrate those times when I find myself stuck. If we accept the premise that being on a roll is a natural state when we're in alignment with our purpose, then being stuck must mean we are somehow out of alignment with our purpose. This suggests that we may want to pay very close attention when we are stuck, as it could very well mean we are being offered a message that could help us get back in alignment and stay on a roll in the future. I don't know about you, but if this is true, I certainly don't want to miss out on any of those messages or their attendant insights. By defining such moments as opportunities for celebration, I improve my chances for receiving the important guidance of their insights in my life. I have also come to realize that being stuck may simply mean some unresolved issue is trying to get my attention or that my thinking is somehow blocked.

The following set of guidelines are my best effort to crystallize a process I have used for more than 15 years to search for insights when I am stuck. Hundreds of clients have told me they keep these guidelines handy at their desk to help them stay in the mode of celebrating when they get stuck.

Being stuck cannot occur unless we judge something negatively. Therefore, whenever we are stuck, we might as well learn to recognize it as a clear sign we have assigned negative value to some fact or condition we are facing. Remember, it is not possible for a fact itself to have either positive or negative value. It is also not possible for us to be stuck without having bought into the illusion that we have the right to assign positive or negative value to a fact. If we should find ourselves stuck, therefore, it only makes sense for us to look first to where we may have assigned value to facts. The following offers some clues as to how this may have occurred:

❖ We may have judged there would be an adverse effect on us if we were to go ahead with a course of action we are considering; that if forced to make a certain decision or accept a particular option we are facing, we would suffer some form of perceived loss or fail to retain some perceived prior gain.

❖ The set of circumstances we are facing may have allowed us to judge ourselves as deficient—to somehow imagine we lack the skill, understanding, self-esteem or other resources needed to move successfully into the desired future.

❖ By attaching too much positive value to some idea or option, we may have set ourselves up to view its possible rejection as a threat. We may see its potential failure to be accepted as some form of perceived loss.

❖ We may be tempted to focus our attention outwardly on someone else's "flaws" so we don't have to face our own internal discomforts around such thoughts as not knowing exactly where we are going or not having all of the answers.

❖ We may think keeping our attention focused on "problems" will help us avoid the discomfort of admitting we lack the energy or skills needed to create a better future for ourselves.

Do any of the five ideas listed above shed light on one or more situations in the past where you have been stuck? Can you see yourself using this list in the future to help you recognize what might be causing you to be stuck?

Once we have correctly identified where we are stuck, one or more of the following questions may help us learn from the issue keeping us stuck, and then allow us to either resolve or move past it:

❖ What idea, fact or condition has been assigned positive or negative value? Is this an isolated situation, or are we being given an opportunity to look at an area where we have a self-limiting pattern? How do we be sure we have gotten our full message here so this pattern need not show up again?

❖ What opinion, position or idea is being defended? Why? What might be the perceived loss if our position or opinion were rejected? What is the lesson for us in this situation?

❖ To what opinion or position are we or someone else so attached that its nonacceptance would be seen as a loss? If we look carefully, are there other situations in our lives where being attached to our ideas might be keeping us from seeing clearly?

❖ Is the "vitally important issue" upon which we are focused actually serving the hidden purpose of distracting our attention away from a more important issue too uncomfortable for us to confront? If so, what might this more important issue be? Are there some habits of non-confronting that might be using this issue as a way to bring themselves to our attention?

❖ A surprising number of issues—even "difficult" ones—will simply dissolve in the face of questions like: "What's really important?" "Where would we want to go if this were not an issue?" and, "If we could do it over again from scratch, how would we do it differently?"

Finally, whenever we are judging—i.e., assigning positive or negative value to facts—it is always good to remember we cannot at the same time be judging and connected to and guided by our purpose. This also means we cannot be on a roll. What's the benefit of viewing unresolved issues as providing us with golden opportunities to clarify and refocus our vision for the future? Could this be a more productive way to approach such situations?

Trust Is Vital

On several occasions we have mentioned the importance of trust to the mentor-coaching process. Let's now be even more explicit about the link between WHAT'S WRONG questions and the lack of trust in our communication relationships. As I pointed out earlier, much of the motivation that exists in our culture is to avoid pain. The primary pain most of us wish to avoid is the emotional pain that comes into existence the moment we judge, or assign negative value to some fact. A key requirement for the creation of an environment of trust, then, is some form of evidence that negative value will not be assigned to facts we are discussing within that environment. In the next few paragraphs, we will highlight some subtle ways in which trust can be damaged when people misread our intent and assume they are at risk or vulnerable to being judged negatively.

"Why?" Questions

The question "why?" is among the easiest for people to misread. As anyone with high self-esteem knows, *why* questions are among the most important we can ask ourselves. Knowing this, we have little natural hesitation about asking others "why?" Unfortunately, the vast majority of us are much more accustomed to having the question "why?" be used *on* us in an intimidating manner, as in, "Justify yourself!" Therefore, when most of us are asked something like, "Why do you feel that way?" we almost always go on the defensive. When this occurs, we immediately stop using our analytical mind correctly (to translate our intuitive feelings into words) and switch our focus to an energy-consuming, self-protective mode where we try to analyze, defend or justify our feelings. This presents a paradox. If the *why* question is one of the most important we can ask, how can we learn to do so without damaging trust or triggering defensiveness? Can you think of a way to ask the question "why?" without using the word directly? Instead of asking "why," for example, could we ask, "What would be a benefit to you for doing such and so?" Isn't that a "why" question that simply opened with the word "what"?

Fact Questions

Fact-finding questions are also easy for people to misread. To answer a fact question, we must typically disconnect from our intuition and switch to a purely analytical data mode. As an added concern, such questions can too easily create the impression that someone is gathering facts for use in trying to analyze or judge us. Or, perhaps they are doing so in order to give us unwanted "solutions" to "problems" we could much more easily solve ourselves—particularly if we could be given some good value-finding questions. Remember, however, this is not intended to have us stop asking fact-finding questions, but to sensitize us to their potential for damaging trust. In other words, if trust is the issue, we might want to find a way to stick with value-finding questions.

Excessive Analyzing

Analyzing and "explaining away" feelings is another area where trust can be easily damaged. Those of us whose motivation is to avoid pain are often very good at analyzing and explaining away our own feelings. When this is the case, we too often attempt to do the same with the feelings of others. The moment we do so, however, we send a message to the other person that discredits or devalues their feelings. In so doing, we risk interrupting their efforts to gain their own intuitive insights from those feelings and we send a message that discourages their efforts to find their own insights. This is a biggie, for as we have repeatedly pointed out, true insights occur only when we allow ourselves to finish feeling and expressing our most deeply felt feelings. We can always begin by remembering to honor our own feelings. That makes it easier for us to honor the feelings of others.

Giving Advice

The matter of giving advice plays a very subtle role in the area of damaging trust. This is something it would no doubt help us all to understand. The mirror will give us some insights here. Whenever we go into the mode of trying to either persuade or give advice, our actions could best be characterized as having our head attempt to give our heart a lecture. Do you see the fundamental discrepancy here? Is there any wonder so many of us feel resistance when someone attempts to give us "good advice"? I like to think of it as follows. Imagine that the part of ourselves which is vulnerable to being deceived is attempting to impose one of its questionable theories onto the part of us which cannot be deceived. It is like our easily deceived analytical mind is trying to give answers to our intuitive mind, which is already in possession of every answer we need for guiding our own lives. With that in mind, could there ever be any such thing as "good advice"? Finally, by giving others what we think is good advice, we can also distract them from their important task of finding their own insights hidden deeply within their innermost unexpressed feelings. Incidently, have you noticed how carefully I am avoiding the temptation to give advice?

Being Too Curious

Have you ever noticed how difficult it is to trust someone who gets so caught up in curiosity about the nature of our problem they forget we exist as a person? This would be rather hard to do if we were to stay focused on a person's feelings, wouldn't it? To feel valued as a person, most of us rely on having a sense that others are genuinely interested in us. If someone expresses undue curiosity about our problems, it is easily read as lack of genuine interest in us directly. Excess curiosity about someone else's problems thus works to devalue them and invalidate their trust in us. It can also cause them to put up their protective shield.

Asking People to Judge

My last point on questions that can damage trust is focused on asking "how?" questions. It is simply too easy for most of us to fall into the judging mode in response to most how questions. Imagine, for example, if I were to ask, "How do you feel?" Notice how difficult it is to respond with anything but a good or bad reaction. Judging and trust are mutually exclusive concepts. They cannot coexist. Nothing can take us out of the mode of being on a roll, or keep us from reaching the state of effortless high performance, with greater certainty than judging some fact to be good or bad, right or wrong. It is my view that people get plenty of practice at judging without needing any more how questions from us.

If I were a good mentor-coach, I would now ask you, *of the above descriptions of ways we can inadvertently damage trust, which one offered you the most useful new insight? What feelings did you have as you read over the descriptions? Which of the areas has been most troublesome for you in the past? What will you do more or less of as a result of reading these key points?*

Summary Observations

We have covered some vitally important material in this chapter. At some level, each one of us is hungry for good questions. I have noticed especially how visionary leaders thrive on good questions. This may seem paradoxical, since I imply their success is due in large part to their habit of asking themselves good questions. *Why, then, would visionaries be among the most responsive to being asked good questions by others? Why would most of them, in fact, give just about anything to be able to sit in their offices and have someone furnish the questions they need to transform their vision of an ideal into current reality? Do they know something the rest of us don't know?* Incidentally, since most visionary leaders rarely enjoy the luxury of having their questions furnished, they usually march boldly out into the marketplace instead, challenging it to reveal gaps in their vision. The gaps revealed become the source of the questions they require to continue their creative process.

Chapter Nine

Watching the Magic
of RIGHT QUESTIONS

Pay Close Attention to the Questions You Ask

Most of the insights I have gained about asking RIGHT QUESTIONS have occurred while working directly with clients. I will now relate three of these experiences to illustrate the wide variety of situations where RIGHT QUESTIONS can make a difference.

RIGHT QUESTIONS *in a Glass Plant*

My first example comes from a project at a glass manufacturing plant. During its 15 years in operation, the plant had never been more than marginally profitable, and I had been engaged by the plant manager as a mentor-coach to help raise performance. It was quite a sight to see hundreds of tons of sand being poured into the furnaces at one end of the plant each day, and truckload after truckload of plate glass being shipped from the other end. I soon learned that a critical factor in the plant's profitability was the percentage of output that was free from flaws. This percentage was referred to as "yield," and the plant required a 70% yield in order to break even. A yield of 80% was considered nirvana, and at that level the plant would produce a profit in excess of

$1 million a month. The plant was currently producing the same 70% yield it had been producing for most of its existence.

This was certainly a time when I was glad to be a mentor-coach, so I didn't have to provide answers. I just needed to come up with effective questions—questions that would allow others to go inside and find new and better answers for themselves. For my questions to be effective, I often find it quite helpful to know virtually nothing about the area in which I am asking them. In this case, for example, it was inconceivable to me that 30% of the plant's daily output of glass would have to be crushed and fed back into the other end again along with the fresh sand. To me, this had "opportunity" written all over it, and prompted my next exuberant question, "What would it take for the plant to reach 100% yield?" I was patiently shown how machinery used to keep the rubbery sheet of glass flowing out of the furnace while it cooled made marks along the edges. This required seven percent to be cut off the edges and left only 93% as a maximum yield. My next question was, okay, what would it take for the plant to reach 93% yield?

Incidentally, the experience I am describing took place immediately after the software development project described in Chapter 1. Perhaps you can tell I was again searching for a question about which I could get everyone in the organization to begin wondering. The question about 93% yield turned out to be a critical piece in that search.

I next learned that relations between the plant's management and unions had always been difficult, and were at an all-time low. They were about five months away from the end of their current labor contract, the plant's athletic leagues had been boycotted by the union for months, and the situation did not look at all promising. Taking all of this into consideration, the plant manager and I made a joint decision to invite four union officers to join in with the plant's 12 managers and supervisors to participate together in one of our team dialogues. Everyone was clearly on edge about how this would work out. Most were even surprised when all four union officers showed up to participate. No one was surprised, however, at the strongly self-protective postures they took.

The success of our mentor-coaching work is always dependent on our ability to dissolve the hidden defensiveness normally present in a team's communications and thus raise the trust level very quickly. In the process, it is quite common for communications among team members to reach trust levels well beyond what most people imagine is possible. Several of the tools used to support this process have already been introduced, and more will be introduced in the next three chapters. For purposes of this particular discussion, however, I will focus on two factors that play a huge role in building these high trust levels. The first of these is simply self-disclosure. In other words, as the one taking responsibility for raising the level of trust, I had to be the first to show that I am an open book—that I have nothing to hide. Fortunately, the better we get at identifying our strengths, the easier it is for us to do this.

The second factor is a bit more challenging to put into practice. It requires getting the whole idea of value-finding firmly rooted into our being. Only then can we make sure the responses people get from us will consistently demonstrate that we can be counted on to search for the value in every word or sentence that comes out of their mouth. Note how this goes just a bit further than unconditional acceptance to an active search for value. It never ceases to amaze me to watch the impact of a concentrated dose of this influence on a team of managers. Here is the only analogy I have ever found to describe it. Imagine what would happen if we were to crack open the pot which binds the roots of a Japanese bonsai tree and plant those roots in new, fertile soil. One can almost feel the new growth bursting forth. It is like being offered a fresh, cool glass of water after a hot day in the sun. I have seen only a few of my clients pick up on this idea to the point where they became committed to adopting the approach for their own leadership style. The rapid career progress that followed would suggest many others would profit from making the same commitment.

As you can see, I am accustomed to having this method work—as it did once again in this case with the 12 managers and supervisors from the plant. I am not accustomed, however, to seeing the tenacity of resistance to it demonstrated by the plant's four union officers. It was easy to see their desire to open up and participate in the trust others were enjoying. On the other hand, it was almost comical to watch them struggle with the conflict they were feeling. It was as if they somehow believed it necessary to maintain their adversarial roles. We did end up making dramatic progress on those trust issues, but I also gained a healthy respect for the challenges this adversarial relationship presents to business leaders all over the western world.

With the team dialogue behind us, I set out in earnest to find a question that I could get the entire organization wondering about, both individually and as a whole. I soon found myself engaged in a thought provoking discussion with the plant manager. I don't remember exactly what prompted me to ask, but I inquired if there was some kind of an all-consuming question in his mind. I asked what question he woke up wondering about. I asked if one question showed up frequently in the morning while he was showering. Suddenly his eyes lit up and he said, "Yes. It's how do I solve the union problem?" Here is another one of those moments when time stood still for me. I processed several years' worth of data in what could have been only seconds. In those few seconds, I somehow realized how his asking that question was working to cause problems to occur in his life. The way our minds work, his question about how to solve the union problem was actually drawing union problems into the vacuum of the unanswered question in order for them to be solved. I said to him, "Has it ever occurred to you that the compelling way in which you are asking the question could actually be attracting these union problems to you?" After some additional discussion in which he acknowledged I could very well be correct, we decided to change his question and see what would happen.

We chose to ponder the new question, "What will it take for this plant to be running at peak efficiency with everyone having a ball?" (Very few managers grasp the point that the "having fun" part of our wondering stood to make a bigger contribution to its ultimate success than the "peak efficiency" part.) I then spent some additional mentor-coaching time with each manager, supervisor and union officer, during which I invited them to join us in pondering that same question.

Meanwhile, I learned one more piece of information about yield. The sand mixture being fed into the plant must be made up of roughly 15% crushed glass in order for everything to work properly. In everyone else's mind, this put a ceiling of 85% on the plant's potential yield. In my mind, if the plant's yield could be pushed up past 90%, I thought surely it must be possible to purchase broken glass from somewhere to make up the difference. I began to get several others thinking about how much fun it would be for them to get the plant running so efficiently they had to go out and buy broken glass. I did this as a way to fully capture their imaginations—and to get them to join in on pondering the question with us. I encouraged the union people to think about how they would want to celebrate the arrival of the first truckload of broken glass bought from a competitor. For the purchasing department, I wondered out loud how one would go about finding broken glass to purchase.

There is one more vitally important thing to note here. At no time did I encourage anyone to set any goals regarding the plant's performance overall, or for anyone's individual performance. Nearly all of the above actions were patterned after those used so effectively in the software development project described in Chapter 1 of this book. And, as in the software project, I did everything I felt was necessary and then moved on to my next project.

Thirty days later I received a call from an amazed but very proud plant manager. He reported that he and his team had just completed an entire week—21 shifts in a row—where the plant's yields never fell below 90%. This is why I chose as a title for this first example, "Pay close addition to the questions you ask." I mentioned in Chapter 1, and it bears repeating here, that the energy around an unanswered question may very well be the most powerful motivating force in the universe. I also find it fascinating that this awesome power is virtually ignored in the academic study of motivation. To me, the field of psychology seems to be missing something here.

As your mentor-coach, I will now *ask you to reflect on the biggest benefit you gained from reading about my experience with the glass plant project. Can you see any areas around you in which an opportunity exists for a team of people to be inspired to focus on that kind of a question? How about for yourself as a person? Can you identify a single question now having a major influence in your own life? If so, is this influence taking you in a direction you wish to go? Is there a way for you to change your question and have it provide an even more desirable influence? Even though I offered only a tiny glimpse of what it is like to make value-finding questions a permanent way of life, what was your response to this idea for yourself? What do you find most appealing about this thought? What do you find most challenging about it?*

Creating Breakthroughs With the Five Levels of RIGHT QUESTIONS

RIGHT QUESTIONS *Produce a Software Solution*

For my next example, I will relate the experience of a client who put the five levels of RIGHT QUESTIONS to work shortly after being introduced to the idea by structuring a planning meeting around them. Since the experience is representative of similar episodes taking place whenever and wherever this questioning format is being used, it is also my intent to provide enough detail for you to become inspired to try it yourself. This particular story was told to me by a manager in the management information systems department of a large multinational company.

The manager's job responsibility was to provide support for optimal utilization of the company's computer system throughout the organization. In this capacity, he had been working with a group of five or six users from one division in an effort to work out some problems they were having with the system. These problems had begun six months earlier when new hardware and software was installed, and their weekly meetings seemed to be making very little progress at solving the problems. As is typical, I suspect, the discussions were all focused on what was wrong, and the only thing being accomplished was a drain on everyone's energy.

Once this manager was introduced to the five-level questioning structure, he decided to put it into practice at the very next meeting. He made a smart move, too, by self-disclosing right up front his feelings of uncertainty and awkwardness about attempting this new approach. In doing so, he made a point of asking everyone to support his effort. He then began with the first question (WHAT'S WORKING) and asked for descriptions of ways in which the software was working to their advantage. After some initial hesitation, one or two people began to list various ways it was working, and then others joined in. I'll never forget the manager's astonishment as he told us how, after only 15 minutes of discussion, you could have pushed him over with a feather. He had no idea so many things were going right with the system.

I must digress here for a moment and make sure you understand this is not just a "feel-good exercise." It has the serious intent of generating the creative energy and insights needed to address the third-level question of: what would be ideally right? As is often the case with someone's first attempt to use this structure, this client did not make as clear a distinction between Level 1 and Level 2 questions as I normally recommend. Quite often it is necessary to focus first on making a list of what is working. Then, we take one item at a time from the list and really dig into the Level 2 question, what makes it work. I suppose it was either beginner's luck or the mark of a true master that allowed our client to generate as much energy and insight as he obviously did while focusing primarily on the Level 1 questions.

The surplus of energy and insights was obvious when it became time for him to take the group into the Level 3 question, in which he asked them to describe what the ideal software solution would look like. Light bulbs soon began turning on in everyone's minds as they each took a turn at describing the ideal and began to see the shape of gaps that remained to be filled. As it turned out, there was one three-hour block of processing time out of every eight days that was causing a problem. Once this gap was seen in the context of the ideal, the answer became quite simple. The computer vendor was called and a solution was developed and put in place in less than a week.

Six months of meetings focused on WHAT'S WRONG produced nothing but anguish and frustration. A one-hour meeting structured around the five levels of WHAT'S RIGHT questions, and six or seven people walked away feeling truly empowered in their ability to visualize the ideal and create solutions out of that ideal. I think there is a message here.

RIGHT QUESTIONS *In a Health Care Company*

As my third example I will relate an experience that took place with the management team of an international company in the health care industry. Two of us were conducting a review of their efforts to implement our intuition-based system of management in their company. As the review progressed, team members related example after example of successful applications of the value-finding questions taking place throughout the company. Given their obvious appreciation for the power of RIGHT QUESTIONS, I began to see this as a golden opportunity to introduce an even higher level of application. I soon interjected a point about how much fun it was to demonstrate the power of the five levels of RIGHT QUESTIONS for solving difficult problems. It wasn't very long until one of the vice presidents spoke up and asked what I meant by that. He just couldn't get his head around the idea of using a WHAT'S RIGHT analysis to solve a problem.

I then went out on a limb and invited the team to put their most challenging problem out on the table and I would demonstrate how effective the WHAT'S RIGHT approach could be in solving problems. To get started, I went to a flip chart and asked the group to create a list of possible candidates for the most difficult problem they were facing. Once we had five or six choices listed, I asked them to vote on which problem they wanted to tackle. Then, since I needed some frame of reference from which to generate questions, I asked them to fill me in on some of the background of the problem. It was amazing to watch how quickly the adversarial energy came flooding back into the team's discussion. It wasn't long until I clearly remember wondering, Why in the world did I ever offer to do this? The more they talked about the WHAT'S WRONG details around the problem, the more I felt pulled right down into the quagmire with them. I started to seriously wonder how I was going to get out of this one, then finally remembered what we were setting out to do. I then held up my hand and said, "Stop. Enough."

More than one of the executives looked puzzled when I asked them to let go of their focus on the problem and join me in examining the most successful decisions the company had made in the past two years. I went back to the flip chart and asked again for best decision candidates. This time, however, I started with the Level 1 question, WHAT'S RIGHT. In other words, my agenda was to identify several decisions that had worked out well and would be worthy of our study. After getting six or seven good decisions listed, I was ready to proceed to a Level 2 question, WHAT MAKES IT RIGHT? Here we wanted to begin digging into the reasons why the good decisions worked. As a way to narrow down the focus of our inquiry, I asked which decisions best exemplified the company's greatest strengths.

One decision was selected to begin the more probing inquiry of Level 2 questions. I then alternated between asking why the decision succeeded and what strengths were exemplified by the decision. This discussion was conducted exactly as one would do brainstorming. I simply listed each idea on the flip chart as it came up, and filled at least two pages with responses to the questions. Once the flow of ideas slowed, I selected a second decision and repeated the process again. By then, as is usually the case, the room was beginning to fairly crackle with insights, most of which occurred when team members recognized similar strengths exemplified by the two different decisions. Suddenly, one and then another began to see the contrast between the factors present in successful decisions and those clearly missing in the "problem" area we had set out to solve.

I especially enjoyed the reminder of how easy it is to get completely bogged down in talking about the problem. It was a great lesson for me about how important it is to stay in the value-finding mode. The process worked so well we didn't even get to the Level 3 question to begin building a model of an ideal. Frankly, I felt both triumphant and grateful as I rested my case.

It is now time to slip back into my mentor-coaching role and ask a couple of questions. *What did you appreciate the most from these examples of putting right questions to work? Can you identify any situations around you right now where you could put the questions to use yourself? If so, what ideas discussed in this chapter will be most useful in helping you to take that step?*

WHAT'S RIGHT?

WHAT MAKES IT RIGHT?

WHAT WOULD BE IDEALLY RIGHT?

WHAT'S NOT YET QUITE RIGHT?

WHAT RESOURCES CAN I FIND TO MAKE IT RIGHT?

Chapter Ten

What About Criticism?

A Mentor-Coach Looks at Fault-finding

When we explored the ideas around praise in Chapter 5 and learned how the qualities we admire in others reflect our own greatest strengths, did you happen to wonder about the flip side? It would actually be unfair to talk about praise without also addressing the issues of fault-finding and criticism—a pair of far less constructive forms of communication. Perhaps it has already occurred to you how the effects of fault-finding and criticism must be similar to praise, but in reverse. Many psychology texts tell us the faults we dislike the most in others are those which mirror our own faults. Since you already know I don't subscribe to the weakness or deficiency viewpoints, you would likely be disappointed if I didn't re-frame the above. Here is how I do it:

Criticism of others is an outward expression of an inner opinion we hold of ourselves. Thus, when we see a trait we dislike in someone else, it is our inner self drawing our attention to an opinion or self-limiting belief we hold about ourselves which is ready to be cleared. (We will know it's cleared when we are no longer irritated when noticing the trait.) This is truly a time for celebration!

151

Now, before you decide this idea is too self-incriminating to think about and quickly close your mind to it, let's explore some wonderfully encouraging aspects of this way of looking at criticism. First, isn't it exciting to realize that the negative opinions we hold of ourselves have no relation to reality? This is truly good news! And, if we pay close attention to the next few pages, we can learn how to permanently free ourselves from the inhibiting effects of holding these invalid opinions. In other words, a powerful benefit can be gained from raising our awareness around our own inclinations to find fault with others. Do I have your full attention yet? If so, be sure to continue on with caution, for the next few pages of material have proven to be a real test of people's ability to stay in a WHAT'S RIGHT mode.

Once exposed to the material in this chapter, you will never again be able to look at criticism in the same way. And, speaking of WHAT'S RIGHT, here is my first recommendation. From today forward, whenever you feel tempted to find fault with someone, make a point to remember you are being given a special opportunity for learning. By paying close attention you can teach yourself to use each of these situations as an opportunity to identify a hidden aspect of your own personality that may be presently limiting your performance. For your first step in confirming this idea, take a moment right now to review the notes you made in Chapter 5 about two or three traits in your parents that tended to cause you the greatest discomfort. If you have children, you can also think of bothersome traits you notice in them. If neither of these approaches produces an obvious "hit," take a moment to identify a trait or two that can really irritate you when it shows up in someone around you. Pay close attention to the amount of energy you feel about each trait you observe. If you simply notice an undesired trait, it may have little meaning in relation to your own self-image. In contrast, if you feel a real "charge" about a trait you are observing, it definitely has a message for you.

I need to clarify an important point here. This is not a find-what's-wrong-and-fix-it exercise we are setting up. Instead, it is an introduction to a set of techniques for allowing us to identify negative opinions—both obvious and hidden—that we hold about ourselves. As long as we hold these negative opinions, they will continue to deplete our energy. Once we master the ability to identify these areas, we can then focus on techniques needed to transform them from energy-depleting aspects of our self-image into energy-generating aspects.

Remember, as we seek to identify potential areas of depletion, we are looking for opportunities rather than problems. With this in mind it becomes extremely useful to catch ourselves in situations where we are tempted to find fault or criticize. Each time it happens (hopefully before we verbalize our criticisms), we must remember to ask ourselves what inner doubts or concerns might be causing us to find fault. By learning to use this unique way to identify our own internal motives, we can quickly dissolve undesired aspects of our self-image that might otherwise keep us from reaching the state of effortless high performance. This point is worth repeating. Until each of the hidden negative opinions we hold of ourselves is brought out into the open and dealt with correctly, we will continue to deplete the creative energy we need to put ourselves on a roll.

Let's now look at an example and enjoy some of the insights available when we use value-finding questions to explore our urges to find fault. Be aware that the technique I am about to describe can be extremely revealing of our own "stuff." As a result, I seldom agree to demonstrate it in the presence of others. When done privately, it can usually hit pay dirt in two or three minutes.

I shall always remember the set of insights I gained into this whole area while working with the employees of a lumber company in the state of Washington several years ago. I had just finished introducing the above ideas to a group of about 15 people when two of them spoke up to express strong disagreement. I asked them each to speak with me privately during our next break. Once I learned that each of them was strongly critical of someone who, in their opinion, drank too much alcohol, I decided to work with both of them at the same time. This case was made particularly interesting by the intensity of feeling each displayed through their criticism. This was matched by the equal intensity with which they denied any possible connection to themselves. (I mention intensity here because the intensity of emotion behind the words people use gives us clues we can use to guide the framing of our next question.)

In this case, the first word where I felt strong energy was "drinking." My next question of them was, "What is it about this person's drinking too much that *bothers* you so much?" Notice my emphasis on the word "bothers." I could easily have substituted the word "irritates." In either case I am looking to identify the next word holding an energy charge. After several more questions, each exploring the word from their last answer that held the greatest energy charge, one of them slapped his knee and exclaimed, "Because he doesn't care!" Wow, his word "care" certainly held a charge! Since I've had a lot of experience using this method, my intuitive mind was immediately able to furnish me an insight into what was happening. These men were each very judgmental of themselves for their inability to express how deeply they cared about their families. When I pointed this out to them, they were both astonished. The method had worked again and led right to a key negative self-image element present in each of them. In our next chapter, I will describe how to use affirmations, which are the perfect way to replace negative self-image elements with their positive opposites. I look forward to sharing this method with you.

Speaking of affirmations, *whenever we engage in criticism or fault-finding, we create the undesired effect of affirming or reinforcing those same negative elements in our own self-image.* It is a good idea to keep this in mind whenever we are tempted to find fault or criticize. I certainly hope these new perspectives make it painfully obvious that finding faults in others has a strongly inhibiting effect on our own personal growth. In other words, being critical of others, even if we don't express it, is usually more damaging to ourselves than it could ever be to others we might be criticizing.

How are you doing with this material so far? From past experience, I know it can be pretty challenging. As a result, it is more likely to meet with resistance than anything else I will share in the entire book. Had I not developed such a strong discipline of searching for WHAT'S RIGHT about everything, I am sure the profound insights presented here would have eluded me completely. *As you now reflect on this material on how a mentor-coach looks at fault-finding, what new understandings are you gaining about yourself? What do you see more clearly about ways we deplete our own energy? Have you identified any specific traits you see in others that seem to hold enough of a negative charge for you to merit exploring them? How will you now deal with others around you who are being critical?*

Many clients and friends who read the manuscript before it was published told me they could hardly wait to buy an extra copy or two of the finished book to give to critical friends in hopes it would open their eyes. Perhaps we can create a groundswell!

Becoming Invulnerable to the Negative Effects of Criticism

We now get to explore a way to use this new perspective to insulate ourselves from the undesired effects of critical remarks other people direct toward us. With a little practice using the techniques described below, I believe it is quite possible to make ourselves invulnerable to the negative effects of other people's criticisms of us.

To begin exploring this exciting new perspective, imagine for a moment what would happen if we all realized the degree to which other people reveal to us the makeup of their own negative self-image each time they criticize us. Can you see how easy it would be to become fascinated over what is being revealed to us about other people's "stuff" they think is hidden from us? It might even be possible for our fascination with this to replace the pain normally felt from their criticism of us. (We want to be sure we don't let on that we're fascinated, as that could be dangerous!) Are you seeing how much fun it could be to explore the way critical people display their own hidden negative self-images? After all, someone else's criticism of us doesn't define us. Rather, it defines the critical person as someone who needs to criticize. This has lots of potential, doesn't it? It could become a welcome alternative to enduring the pain and agony of our own defensiveness.

I am not proposing here that the content of criticisms directed our way is of no value. But you have surely noticed how our own defensiveness has a way of preventing many of us from getting any value at all from the criticisms of others. I am simply proposing an alternative by which we can each gain every last bit of value possible from that criticism without the limitation of defensiveness on our part. We simply employ a 90/10 rule to help us sort through any and all criticisms we receive. Here is how it works.

We start by imagining that as much as 90% of a fault-finding message being directed toward us could be a fascinating reflection of the other person's hidden negative self-image. Can you see how our normal defensiveness could in this way be replaced by fascination over what is being revealed? With our defensiveness out of the way, we could search openly for a possible nugget of truth or value contained in the critical message. This technique allows us to stay in the value-finding mode so we can begin to examine the contents of a critical message to see what may be of true value for us. Once we identify a small nugget, we can continue our search for additional value. In this way we could gradually expand the portion of the critical message that is proving to be of value to us. In the absence of this approach, I propose there is too much risk of having our defensiveness cause us to miss most or all of the value.

The more we practice this technique, the more we will see what a large portion of other people's criticism of us is indeed a negative reflection of their own insecurities and self-doubts. Do not be surprised to learn how little, if any, of the criticism directed toward us by other people is valid.

It will take practice, of course, to develop the skills needed to distinguish the difference between critical messages that contain valid input for us and those which simply reflect the sender's own negative self-image. But the freedom we gain to assimilate and process the useful contents of all communication is certainly worth the effort.

As we become more and more perceptive in our observations, we will sooner or later come to recognize the single most compelling role of criticism. Whenever an insecure person senses they may be vulnerable to painful exposure of their deficiencies and shortcomings, they will often rely on criticism of others to draw attention away from their own areas of uncertainty. Did it ever occur to you what an outstanding job our criticism of others was doing to tell the world about our own self-doubts and insecurities? It is almost as if we are holding up a big neon sign saying, in effect, "Here's what's wrong with me!"

Is it possible some of this information may inspire us to be less critical of ourselves and others? It certainly is clear how the energy we expend on finding, analyzing or calling attention to the self-limiting habits of others can be limiting to our own personal growth. This is to say nothing about the limiting effect it has on others.

We limit ourselves through criticism in several ways. Chief among these is how our conscious, analytical mind is kept out of contact with our intuitive mind whenever it is focused on judging something negatively. Second is the way in which undesired emotional pressures are built up around behaviors and traits we have judged negatively and wish to change. All of this causes elements of our negative self-image to work against each other and deplete rather than replenish our supplies of creative energy. You can well imagine what happens to all of this when its intensity increases. As we feel more and more emotional pressure to negate our hidden negatives, those undesired traits become even less controllable—to the point where they can even erupt in the form of obvious, visible, undesired behaviors. It is another endless loop until we get ourselves back into the value-finding mode. Conversely, as we become less judgmental of ourselves, we will automatically find ourselves being less judgmental toward others.

As a final point about criticism, I must tell you there is absolutely no such thing as "constructive" criticism—whether it be of ourselves or of others. All forms of criticism are attempts to judge people as deficient, and are fundamentally destructive. Our efforts to label this behavior "constructive" are but poor attempts to justify our continued use of this destructive behavior.

Please note this does not say we cannot criticize. As you surely know already, there are occasions when it becomes necessary to criticize in spite of our best efforts to the contrary. In other words, sometimes we must tear something down before we can begin the long process of reconstructing it. When we must criticize, however, let's stop trying to justify it as being constructive! Even Dale Carnegie, who was famous for his efforts to get people to stop criticizing, had an additional rule which his publishers advised him to omit from his book, *How to Win Friends and Influence People*. I happen to know his unpublished rule. It was, "When all else fails, criticize!" I would add here that it is never appropriate to engage in the destructive process of criticizing someone unless we are willing to participate fully in the reconstruction of that person's self-esteem.

Constructive Direction

As a way of getting into the final item of this chapter, I would like to ask you to think about your success at giving directions. Do you ever give someone what you feel are perfectly clear directions on how to get something accomplished, and yet the project doesn't turn out the way you want it to at all? If there was a way to eliminate the chances for such situations to happen in the future, would you like to know about it? The next item I will cover is an exciting way to either correct or eliminate all kinds of misperceptions. It is based on the amazingly simple point that each of us sees the world through our own set of eyes. It also recognizes that we are prone to make the common mistake of assuming that everyone else sees things the same way we do. Not so! The new tool we are about to explore asks us to accept the simple premise that the only way we can know what other people see is to ask them to describe what they see.

I call this tool "constructive direction." It succeeds by giving people clear targets to hit instead of dismantling their guns. It offers us a way to practice a more results-oriented and supportive form of communication in the area of giving people directions. It is offered as a healthy alternative to replace the deceptive practice called "constructive" criticism—which is seldom constructive at all. Criticism, as we now know, is deficiency-based and concentrates on judging past actions negatively. It is "tell-oriented" and deals only with WHAT'S WRONG.

Constructive direction, on the other hand, engages the intuitive minds of both parties in an effort to share the task of creating a vision of an ideal future both can buy into. It focuses on WHAT'S RIGHT and relies heavily on the discipline of asking value-finding and outcome-oriented questions, as is being continually demonstrated throughout this book.

"~~Constructive~~" Criticism	Constructive Direction
Stifles growth with WHAT'S WRONG assertions	Stimulates growth with WHAT'S RIGHT questions
Prevents change	Promotes change
Is tell-oriented	Is ask-oriented
Is past-focused	Is future-focused
Causes defensiveness	Invites openness
Inhibits learning	Inspires learning
Consumes energy	Generates energy
Limits results	Enhances results
Is "you"-oriented	Is "we/us"-oriented

Since I am limited to one-way communication through the medium of this book, I cannot effectively demonstrate the practice of constructive direction. If we were face-to-face, however, I would demonstrate by asking you to describe what you understand so far about this new approach to communication. Before I begin, I must have my own picture of the practice of constructive direction quite clearly formed in my mind. At the same time, I cannot presume you see it the same way I do. Our discussion will go back and forth, with me describing more of what I see and then asking you to describe more of what you understand or see. I must always leave room for you to see part or even all of the concept more clearly than I did at the beginning. This is what creating a shared vision is all about. Only when your description of our completed picture coincides exactly with what I see is the process complete.

Perhaps it would now be helpful to look at the illustration below, which shows three TV screens. The left screen represents the picture of a desired outcome as I see it at the beginning of our communication. The center screen represents an entirely different picture of the desired outcome as it begins to appear in your mind soon after our communication gets under way. The screen on the right represents

Constructive direction uses right questions to build a shared vision of the desired future state

| We must begin with a relatively clear sense of the desired end result pictured in our own mind (this is our vision of the ideal). | We then begin exploring this vision with the other person by alternately describing what we see and asking them to describe what they see. | We've succeeded when both descriptions of the desired end result come into alignment and produce a shared commitment. |

the composite picture we both must see when constructive direction has been successfully completed.

The most powerful key I can think of to be sure our efforts to practice constructive direction never slip back into criticism is to simply discipline ourselves to *keep the discussion entirely focused on the present and the future.* We simply cannot criticize the future. It has not yet happened. The present is also hard to criticize. Criticism really only works when we are focused on the past.

As a mentor-coach I will now ask, *what are you appreciating most from this chapter on criticism? What idea from the chapter will be the first you put to work in your life? What idea do you expect will bring you the greatest long-term benefit from putting into practice? What aspect of the material is still uncomfortable for you? If you do have one or more areas of discomfort, what are your thoughts about how to go about resolving them?*

Chapter Eleven

Attitudes, Choices & Self-Talk

Effortless High Performance Is a Choice

Any attitude we hold represents a choice we make about how to view our world, and how we wish to be involved with it. In truth, we each have total control over our attitude, or the "angle of attack" with which we approach our world. Some of the attitude choices we make are known as "fundamental choices," while others are made on more of a moment-to-moment basis. The amount of control we have over each of these areas of choice is certainly not universally understood, and is seldom fully appreciated. Instead, many people choose to see themselves as victims of their circumstances, and fail to recognize the role their choices play in the creation of those circumstances.

Of all the fundamental choices we make in our lives, perhaps the most important are those we make regarding how we perceive ourselves. For example, we can choose to view ourselves as powerful or powerless. We can choose to explore our strengths and continually generate surplus creative energy, or we can choose to protect against exposure of our vulnerabilities and continually watch our store of creative energy be depleted. Each of these fundamental choices can and will have a major influence on what kind of circumstances show up in our lives. An outstanding book on this subject is *The Path of Least Resistance* by Robert Fritz. It is very much in alignment with many aspects of our book, and I strongly recommend it as additional reading for anyone interested in a more in-depth treatment of this subject.

In *Breaking the Rules*, I am focused on illuminating the consequences of one key choice in particular. That is the choice between continuing to analyze and evaluate the potential for all kinds of things to harm us, or to seek, find, reveal and capitalize on the inherent value in everything. I intend to radically increase the number of people who realize how each of us has total control over the way we choose to look at everything, and that our choices can have a dramatic effect on outcomes. The trick is learning how to exercise to our greatest advantage the control we actually do have over our choices.

Our fundamental view of how much energy is available to us has a huge influence over our choices. As we have discussed before, only a tiny minority of us see the world from a surplus and abundance perspective. Most of us see the world from a depletion and shortage perspective. What many people fail to realize is that each of these two viewpoints is self-reinforcing. Those of us who hold the depletion and shortage viewpoint do so for what appears to be a very good reason. Our life experiences simply validate the "truth" of our view. Given the typical strength of this endless loop, it is no easy task to convince us that we have total control over our choices.

The most effective way I know to bring about a shift in this fundamental view of energy is to create a new set of experiences to validate the surplus and abundance view and ultimately make it self-sustaining. This must be done by building an appealing "case" for the benefits of the alternative attitude choice and then offering simple, clearly defined steps that can be taken to create those desired experiences. It is also interesting to note how our belief in the process has little or no effect on its success. The only reason for putting any attention at all on the desired outcome is to provide encouragement so we go ahead and take the steps.

Here are some more observations about the VALUE-FINDING attitude on which we are focused. It represents a choice to put our attention on finding and bringing out the best in ourselves, other people and every situation we encounter. It leaves behind our old fear-based attitudes that keep our attention all tied up in analyzing WHAT'S WRONG. It acknowledges the faulty logic behind thinking we need to protect against loss and keep the worst in ourselves from being discovered. A VALUE-FINDING attitude represents a choice to focus our thinking on finding opportunities and creating desired outcomes. What a contrast this is to the old problem-avoiding attitude that kept our attention on problems and undesired consequences!

Nearly all the great minds of history—from Plato to Shakespeare to Abraham Lincoln and most everyone in between—have sent us the same message about the importance of our attitude. As a concise statement of the message, I am particularly fond of this quote from Prof. William James, who is considered the father of modern psychology. He said, "The greatest discovery of my generation is that man can alter his life simply by altering his attitude of mind." Eleanor Roosevelt, another great figure in history, said it even more simply: "No one can make you feel inferior without your consent."

How could it be any simpler? We must hold in the center of our attention the most complete picture we can imagine of our desired outcome and then set about to bring all of our actions and behaviors into alignment with that picture. This is the most effective way known to bring about desired changes in actions, behaviors and performance.

As we set out to build a VALUE-FINDING attitude, we must equip our-selves to abandon the emotional tensions attached to negative opinions we have held about ourselves in the past. Such negative tensions as uncertainty, self-doubt and fear can certainly act like glue or cement that make it especially difficult for us to let go of old habits. Notice that I said "abandon" these emotional tensions, rather than "overcome" them. These are tricky issues, aren't they? For if we were to attempt to overcome them, that would represent a choice to see them as negative. Instead, this is a perfect opportunity to put our VALUE-FINDING attitude to work. If our attitude toward our emotional tensions was to remain negative, we would do nothing more than reinforce our limitations. Yet the emotional tensions do make it challenging to accept the possi-bility that a desired outcome could actually occur where past history does not predict such an outcome.

To make the desired changes in our attitudes, and through that our behaviors, it is necessary for us to learn how to find value in those emotional tensions so that we can neutralize their inhibiting effects. Unless we do so, those tensions will in effect cause us to magnetically "hang on" to undesired aspects of our personality rather than abandon them. In other words, if we judge the fact of where we are to be "not okay," we are stuck. We must find a way to get "okay" about where we are before we can change, and VALUE-FINDING questions are among the best ways to do that.

About now you are probably saying, "How in the world do we go about finding value in all of those old emotional tensions?" This seems like the perfect time to explain a fundamental attitude choice I have made personally. This attitude choice does more to help me sustain a state of effortless high performance than anything else I do. As a way to set the stage for understanding this attitude choice, have you ever noticed how easy it is to look back on events that happened a year or more in the past and see the perfection in them? For most of us this is true even for situations which seemed tragic, horrible or even devastating at the time. Now, if it is possible to see the perfection in those things a year later, doesn't it make sense that the perfection must be there in the moment it happens, too? Thus, my secret weapon is to realize that everything happening to and around me has a perfect reason for happening the way it does. Even though that perfect reason is seldom clear to me in the moment it happens, I know it exists. In other words, I have learned to operate from the place of knowing that everything happening in God's universe is, by definition, perfect.

There is an incredible beauty in making this fundamental attitude choice. Once I accept a puzzling situation as being perfect, there is only one question available for me to ask: "Okay, what is it that makes this situation perfect?" In case you missed it, that's truly a VALUE-FINDING question. It also highlights the real issue here. Our goal in this discussion is to find ways to be certain the questions we are asking are always VALUE-FINDING in nature. This perspective is what does it for me.

We started out in Chapter 4 by introducing the concept of zero-based strengths. It was only possible for me to develop this concept by acknowledging as perfect the judgmental nature of our analytical mind. I then realized if we wish to honor our judgmental nature and become truly skilled at it, we must master the art of judging *degrees of good* rather than good or bad. Then we took it a step further in Chapter 6 and introduced the idea that our analytical mind is not designed to judge at all, but to simply transmit data and frame questions. In Chapter 4, I already knew that if we could become highly skilled at judging *degrees of good*, we will eventually discover the ultimate futility of judging. Once we reach the point of knowing there is nothing left to judge, we also know there is only value to be found. Look. Somehow we just got back to VALUE-FINDING questions.

What ideas have made the biggest contribution to you from this discussion on attitudes and choices? For me, reading Fritz's book on the subject of fundamental choices several years ago made a major contribution. *What insights have you gained from searching for the value in those old emotional tensions we talked about?* I'll bet you thought I would give you the answer for that one, didn't you! Remember all those insights I related in Chapter 4 when we were re-calibrating our gauges? In every case these insights became available to me after I made the choice to see the old negative self-perceptions as being perfect and set out to discover *why* they were perfect. I certainly do not expect you to get instant answers when you begin this quest. I can only tell you there is a huge payoff down this road if you choose to travel it.

Now, of all the ideas we have covered so far, which two will provide the most encouragement to continue reading?

Effortless High Performers Use Affirmations

Of all the tools available for developing our strengths and letting go of our limitations, affirmations are among the most powerful. Affirmations are "self-talk." They are little inner conversations we have with ourselves about ourselves all the time. They usually sound something like, "I am a _____," and they tend to be judgmental—either positive or negative. When we simply repeat an affirmation to ourselves often enough, and over a long enough period of time, it turns into a belief we hold about ourselves. The resulting beliefs we develop about ourselves in this way then become key drivers behind our daily behaviors.

Perhaps the best way to paint a picture of how this works is to go back to the work of Dr. Maltz and describe some of the linkages he makes between our use of affirmations and the well-known phenomenon of the phantom limb. This is a phenomenon experienced by people who undergo certain types of surgical procedures. Here is how I like to describe this phenomenon.

Imagine that you have just been taken to the hospital and your arm has been removed at the elbow. It would be common under such circumstances for you to be able to close your eyes the next day and feel your wrist move and fingers flex, all as if the arm was still attached. This phenomenon is called phantom limb, and normally lasts for exactly 21 days.

Soon after the 21st day, you would begin to notice that each time you close your eyes, you can no longer feel your missing arm. You might occasionally feel hot and cold sensations from the severed nerve ends, but your ability to feel the entire severed limb disappears almost completely by the 21st day. The key to this overnight shift in awareness is a new element installed in your self-image through the use of affirmations. In other words, you reprogrammed your subconscious mind, much as you would a computer, by constantly repeating the message, "It's gone, it's gone, it's gone . . ." for 21 days.

Studies indicate that under ideal conditions, 21 days is the minimum amount of time required to replace a self-image element as I have just described. Dr. Maltz tells us each of the following three conditions must be fully met in order for the complete replacement of a self-image component to occur in as few as 21 days.

1. We must feel an intense emotional identification with the changes taking place in our self-image. (Oh my gosh! My arm is gone!)

2. We must develop a set of clear symbols, words or pictures with which to visualize our newly adopted self-image. (We picture the arm being gone.)

3. We must constantly reaffirm our new self-image through affirmations or self-talk. (On a daily basis we talk to ourselves about the fact that our arm is gone.)

As you can see, of all the conditions required for us to change our self-image, affirmations deal only with Condition 3. And, since this is the case, we must be prepared for affirmations to require much longer than 21 days to succeed. With the surgery example above, Conditions 1 and 2 would have been thoroughly met, in addition to Condition 3. The advantage with Condition 3 is that affirmations are directly under our control and are equally effective whether or not they coincide with either our beliefs or our old perceptions of "reality."

We all use affirmations every day, so let's take a look at some we are already using. How do we describe ourselves to ourselves? Do we use successful, confident, affirming statements? If so, there is an excellent chance we will automatically interpret feedback we receive from others as validation or confirmation of all those affirming perceptions and beliefs we hold about ourselves. In this way, other people's favorable opinions of us will be openly embraced and will serve to reinforce our desired self-image and further strengthen our belief in our true worth and value as a human being.

What happens, however, if we find our private descriptions of ourselves to ourselves consisting of hesitant, doubting, insecure, negative or other similar statements of deficiency? This would suggest a high potential for us to interpret negative comments received from others as tangible verification of the "truth" of all those self-limiting perceptions and beliefs we hold of ourselves. Under these conditions, any and all negative comments made about us by others will serve to confirm and reinforce our own doubts about ourselves and will intensify our concern about our lack of worth and value as a person.

Here is where the good news comes in. We absolutely do not have to be the victim of other people's negative opinions of us! This is true primarily because we each have total control over the content of our affirmations. We can choose at any time to begin describing ourselves to ourselves in positive and affirming terms only. We have only to learn how to exercise to a better advantage the control we already possess. As we gain mastery over the contents of our affirmations, we can eventually cause all feedback comments we receive from others to become solid validations of our worth. They will reflect exactly the way we have chosen to describe ourselves to ourselves.

Mastery over the contents of our affirmations gives us a powerful influence over our own personal growth and success. We have the option, for example, of creating affirmation statements from any series of desirable self-descriptions that seem appealing to us. There are at least three distinctly different ways we can choose to build our affirmations. First, we can choose words to reinforce areas where we are already conscious of having strengths. Second, we can choose words to create brand new strength areas for us, and which will also help to bring our daily actions into alignment with these freshly appropriated strengths. Third, we can choose words directly opposite of self-limiting ways we have described ourselves to ourselves in the past. From personal experience, I happen to know this third way of crafting our affirmation statements is extremely powerful. More on that in a moment.

I will now offer a list of some of the most effective and uplifting affirmation statements I have seen used in practice.

❖ Every day, in every way, I am getting better and better.

❖ I am totally responsible for creating my own sense of fulfillment and happiness.

❖ I love and appreciate myself, just as I am.

❖ I joyfully accept all of my feelings as part of myself.

❖ The more I love myself, the more love I have to give to others.

❖ My relationship with _____ is more successful and fulfilling every day.

❖ I always communicate clearly and effectively.

❖ I am always in the right place at the right time, and successfully engaged in doing the right things.

❖ I now have ample time, energy, wisdom and money to accomplish all of my desires.

❖ Everything I need is readily available to me.

❖ It's OK for me to have everything I desire.

❖ Abundance is my natural state of being. I am accepting and enjoying this abundance now.

❖ The more I give, the more I receive—and the happier I feel.

❖ I am now enjoying everything I do.

❖ I have a wonderful job with wonderful pay. I do wonderful service in a wonderful way.

❖ All things are now working together for good in my life.

❖ I give thanks daily for my life of health, wealth, happiness and perfect self-expression.

What is the most useful idea you have gained so far in our discussion of the use of affirmations? In what way do you see yourself using what you have learned here? Which area has more appeal to you as a starting point: using this method to (1) strengthen areas in which you are already strong, (2) establish brand new strengths or (3) install new strength areas chosen specifically to replace old self-limiting beliefs? Since I have found this last approach to be so powerful, I would now like to give it some more attention.

If we wish to use affirmations to replace old self-limiting beliefs, our first task will be to locate one or more areas of our own self-image about which we may feel overly sensitive or even defensive. Perhaps the best way to do this is to identify one or more traits or behaviors which, when we see them in others, can cause us to be most critical. This would be a perfect time to remind ourselves that any time we feel an inclination to criticize or point out a fault in someone else, there is sure to be a strong finger pointing back toward us. There is always a message for us when we are critical of another. And, as I mentioned earlier, the stronger the emotional charge we feel about a given trait we see in someone else, the more important its message for us. The message will always point to an area of self-perceived deficiency about which we are concerned, and these areas of self-perception and concern can often be completely outside of our conscious awareness.

I would now like to relate my own personal experience around this issue. It was 1975 when I first discovered how qualities we admire in others mirror our own strengths. After using that wonderful character-building concept for more than a year, my self-esteem had evolved to a point where I could take a serious look at qualities I disliked the most in others. Five character traits emerged as a clear reflection of my own negative self-image. Basically, I could neither stand "losers" nor tolerate "stupidity." If I were to describe all five traits as I came to understand their adverse influence on my life, I would have to use the following negative affirmations. "I am a dummy. I am a loser. I am a little boy. I am a nobody. And I don't deserve." It was quite a revelation to discover, at age 36, the influence those five negative affirmations had on my life.

That was the hard part. The rest was easy. I simply built an affirmation statement that said, "I deserve to win big!" I then found one of those little Dymo tape writers in the office where I worked and made two copies of it on black tape with raised white letters. I stuck one on the rear view mirror of my car and the other just inside my Day Timer. Every time I noticed either of those little notes to myself, I would repeat the affirmation—out loud whenever possible, as in when I was driving my car alone. At other times I would just repeat it quietly. I did this persistently, repeating my affirmation from 20 to 30 times a day for the next eight months. At the end of that eight-month period, I got my first tangible evidence that this set of disciplines had enabled me to break the back of my lifelong failure pattern.

Here is how it happened. I founded Clear Purpose Management, Inc. in the fall of 1976 at about the same time I started my affirmations. At this time I also decided to boost my visibility in the Denver business community by entering a competition to recruit new members for the Denver Chamber of Commerce. The competition was to end on May 15th, and the winner would be prominently honored at the chamber's annual meeting later that month.

When I checked all of our scores seven months later—near the end of the contest—I found myself with 2,600 points, as compared to the top producer, who had earned 5,100 points. For the first time in my life, being in second place was no longer consistent with my newly constructed self-image. It was as if the afterburners kicked in and I set aside my work for the next two weeks and got totally focused on winning that contest. My focus was awesome and it enabled me to establish new methods used by the chamber for several years after that. By the end of the contest my point score had rocketed to 8,300, and even though the other person had seen me coming, he ended up with only 8,000 points.

At the annual meeting, I received a beautiful gold ring with a black-star sapphire setting that I still wear proudly today as a symbol for a broken failure pattern. No one will ever convince me that affirmations aren't powerful!

So, once we have identified the undesired self-image component we wish to change, we simply select a new set of words that are essentially opposite those we are wishing to replace. We construct an affirmation statement from these new self-descriptors, and then proceed to repeat it to ourselves many times a day for a period of at least 60 to 90 days. It's really that simple.

Finally, it is vitally important to remember that successful affirmations are always stated in the present tense. An excellent way to be sure we follow this rule is to begin every affirmation with the words "I am." These two words are much more significant than we might ever guess. Among other things, they seem to be the two most powerful words available for integrating the analytical and intuitive minds. (They are also referred to as God's name for himself in the Judeo-Christian Bible.)

This principle of using only present-tense affirmations is most often violated when we state our affirmation in the future tense or as goals, such as "I will . . ." or even "I am going to . . ." The way our mind works, future-tense affirmations actually serve as negative present-tense affirmations. This means future-tense affirmations work to disempower the exact elements of our self-image we are intending to empower with those affirmations. For example, if I were to state my affirmation as intending to be successful, the net result to me is as if I had affirmed, "I am not now successful." Not a good plan!

Below are listed ten additional affirmations especially appropriate for use in reinforcing the strategies and disciplines being addressed in this book.

- ❖ I am rapidly mastering the art of asking RIGHT QUESTIONS.

- ❖ I am learning to find value in everything I see.

- ❖ I am fully responsible for my own feelings.

- ❖ I am feeling respected and admired for my strengths.

- ❖ I am enjoying finding strengths to praise in others.

- ❖ I am rapidly learning to use my wonderful mind.

- ❖ I am thoroughly enjoying being organized.

- ❖ I am rapidly learning to express my deepest feelings.

- ❖ I like and respect _____ _____ (your first and last name), and I am taking very good care of (him/her)!

I must give my brother Tom credit for that last one. It is the single, most powerful affirmation I have ever seen used. I highly recommend it. I would now like to close this chapter by listing four books which each do an excellent job in treating the subject of affirmations in more detail: *As a Man Thinketh* by James Allen; *Creative Visualization* by Shakti Gawain; *The Self-Talk Solution* by Shad Helmstetter; and *The Greatest Salesman In the World* by Og Mandino.

As you reflect on everything we've covered around the issue of affirmations, what are you most pleased about understanding even better? Knowing you have already proven the concept of affirmations in your own life, what will you now do more or less of in that area? Before you move on to the next chapter, you might want to take some time to construct at least one new affirmation and establish a plan for how to gain the most good from using it.

Chapter Twelve

Tying It All Together

How Many Ways Can You Build On Strengths

When the five elements of our strategic life planning framework were first introduced on pp. 36-38 of this book, I mentioned that the fifth element, the discipline of continually identifying and building upon strengths, holds the key to unlocking the entire framework. I also said that once we gain full mastery over this vitally important discipline, the other four elements of the framework will fall into place with very little effort. Each point made and each idea offered since then has been done to strengthen this key value-finding discipline. It is now time to review these key points.

The principle goal of most ideas offered up to this point has been to remove obstacles and self-imposed limitations. This is consistent with both the book's subtitle as well as my premise that being on a roll is our natural state. If each of us were not doing so much to interfere with our natural state of being on a roll, we would all be there much more of the time. My greatest desire is to support you in making a complete shift to the value-finding mode of thinking, regardless of where you stood before choosing to read this book.

Let's now consolidate and summarize the ideas introduced so far. As you review the items listed below, your mentor-coach would want you to identify those you have appreciated the most, and then prioritize the ones you have picked. You might also give some thought to what you expect to gain from applying those with which you feel the greatest sense of alignment. I will first list the points and then follow with a discussion to weave them all together.

1. Working to gain mastery over a zero-based strengths outlook on life—first introduced in Chapter 4.

2. Gaining a practical understanding of how our correctly disciplined rational mind is expected to carry out its intended support role in relation to our powerful intuitive mind—mostly in Chapter 6.

3. Making a commitment to master the discipline of asking value-finding questions of ourselves and others, in order to engage and make full use of our powerful intuitive mind—see Chapter 7.

4. Learning how to reinforce and build up our own strengths by looking for, finding, asking questions about and praising strengths in others—introduced in Chapter 5.

5. Mastering the use of the "mirror principle" as a way to discover how well other people deal with their inner selves—by carefully observing how they deal with others around them. (This one clearly needs to be fleshed out with additional discussion, and that begins on page 184.)

6. Committing the time and energy needed to build a mutually beneficial mentor-coaching relationship with someone in order to gain the benefits of "shining sunshine" on each other's "onion"— demonstrated throughout the book, but explained in Chapters 7 & 8.

7. Becoming more conscious of the way in which our criticism of other people adversely affects our own self-image and thus our success—in Chapter 10.

8. Making a commitment to gain total and complete freedom from judging—introduced in Chapter 4 and reinforced in Chapter 6.

9. Learning the value of affirmations, and how to tailor and use them as a way to abandon old, undesired self-image elements and establish specific new desired elements—introduced in Chapter 11.

10. Learning how to give and receive constructive direction by keeping all discussion focused on creating an ideal picture or shared vision of the desired outcome—introduced in Chapter 10.

11. Learning to use the 90/10 rule to neutralize the self-limiting effects of critical remarks made about us by others, while at the same time allowing such critical remarks to reveal fascinating insights into other people's own insecurities—introduced in Chapter 10.

12. Intercepting our urges to "fix" others by reminding ourselves that such urges can only occur if we are judging others to be "not okay" or deficient as they are now—introduced in Chapter 10.

13. Continually reminding ourselves of the vast difference between managing energy and managing facts, while doing everything possible to learn more about managing energy—introduced in Chapter 4.

14. Being clear that we must learn to view ourselves accurately, and yet without negative judgment, before we become free to move ahead or make any self-sustaining changes in our lives—my core message.

That's quite a list, isn't it! *Which of the items are you now thinking will make the most meaningful additions to your tool kit?* I hesitate to even mention the word "obstacles," but since it is in the book's subtitle, *what are the most significant obstacles you can see yourself removing through the use of these tools? If you could only choose three of the above ideas or skills as permanent additions to your life, which ones would you choose?*

From past experience, most people have included either Item 1 or 8 among their top priorities. They are quite similar, of course, but clearly have a different appeal for different people. Over the years, many clients have told us the greatest contribution we made to their lives was helping them get free of judging. It has also been rewarding to watch some people start down the path toward mastery of our zero-based strengths concept, and discover a year or two later that the real issue is to become entirely free of judging. For that reason I can enthusiastically applaud anyone's selection of Item 1 among their top choices. Perhaps you can also see how each of the other choices stand in support of Items 1 and 8.

Sometimes, when I want to really slam dunk my message about not judging and nail its shoes to the floor, I point out that as far as I can tell, every time Jesus of Nazareth was asked to judge something either good or bad, He declined. The question we must then ask ourselves is this: If He did not see it as his job to judge, then why in the world would we presume it is our job to judge?

The Mirroring Principle

Let's now expand on the mirroring principle in Item 5. As I think about this, I can't help but notice how the mirroring principle is at work in several of the other items. For example, I often describe our analytical mind as a piece of imaging equipment. Among other things, this means it serves as a mirror to reflect back exactly what has been sent in. This mirroring capability is a dominant feature of our analytical mind. We can see its influence virtually everywhere we look. We have already made excellent use of it to explore how the qualities we see in others reflect qualities we possess ourselves. It has also been useful in reverse to identify areas within ourselves where we have chosen to see deficiencies instead of strengths.

I would immediately turn to the mirroring principle, for example, if you were to ask me for some direct mentor-coaching support. It would help me get a quick, accurate reading on how the relationship works between your analytical and intuitive mind. To do this, I simply observe how you interact with others. Your external behaviors will usually mirror the internal relationship I seek to understand. If you are quite directive in how you deal with others, for example, my preliminary observation would be to suspect your conscious, analytical mind presumes to impose the same style on your inner, intuitive mind. Such an observation would help me understand a great deal about the mentor-coaching challenge I would be undertaking, and how to approach it.

On the other hand, if you are quite open and inviting toward others, this will be a clue as to how your conscious self approaches your inner knowing. This shows me you will be immediately receptive to my value-finding questions, and may also respond quite well to my vision-building questions. If I observe you as being cautious or hesitant when dealing with others, I would be curious to see if you have a deficiency perspective toward your intuitive self. If so, I would expect to find only a minimal working relationship between your inner and outer selves. This observation would naturally provide priceless guidance for our subsequent interactions.

If you are obviously detached from the feelings of others with whom you interact, I would know that our relationship must at least begin on a purely analytical level. (Please notice how in each case I discipline myself to identify and focus on the inherent perfection of your present style. This prevents any negative influence from my need to be correct in my observations, keeps me open to all possibilities and allows me to perform at my best.)

What did you find most useful about this information? In what two or three ways can you see yourself benefiting from it? What did you find most intriguing about it? Even though we have only scratched the surface of this area, do you find yourself drawn to understand it more deeply, as I am?

Shining Sunshine On the Onion

Next, we need to explore the idea of "shining sunshine" on each other's "onion." The onion offers a wonderful way to symbolize our negative self-image, or all the layers upon layers upon pulpy layers of negative beliefs we hold about ourselves, whether or not these beliefs are known to us. The analogy certainly doesn't stop there, either. Do you know what happens to onions when they are hidden away in a dark basement (as in when we try to do the same with our negative beliefs)? Sometimes they just become rotten—in which case they always put up a stink. In other cases, they begin to grow (seeking the light, of course), and often they even grow two heads. Wonderful symbolism, don't you agree?

How about when we put an onion right outside on our picnic table in plain sight, under the summer sunshine? It slowly dries out and eventually shrivels up into nothing, right? I am using the onion as an analogy to help us gain a better understanding of how to deal with our negative beliefs. If we shine a little sunshine on them, those outermost layers will soon dry out and become so flaky that it is easy to remove them. The sunshine just draws the pulp right out of them. Our value-finding questions and non-judgmental listening do the same with the emotional charges around our negative beliefs. Interesting to note also that if we have enough strength and courage, we may choose to rip into those outer layers and tear them off before the sunshine has time to dry them out. We all have that option. Most of us would prefer to wait, however, until those layers of old dried-out negative beliefs just flake off without effort. How do we abandon the negative beliefs that hold us back? A good place to start would be to go back to pages 127-131 and review the mentor-coaching guidelines presented there.

I am extremely fortunate in that my best mentor-coach just happens to be my wife, Patricia. Hopefully I have been able to be the same in return for her. I can still remember what it was like when we were first beginning to put these mentor-coaching guidelines to work in our lives. Whenever either of us felt an emotional "button" get punched, the other would immediately focus in on that emotionally charged area and begin asking the questions shown in the mentor-coaching guidelines. I wish I could tell you our little onions just shriveled up and blew away overnight, but that was not the case. If you are like most of us, this may take quite some time—along with a serious commitment to use and master the tools presented here. I can certainly confirm, however, that the benefits of that commitment are well worth the time needed to establish and put into practice the disciplines offered.

How Many Ways Are We Tempted to Judge?

Two more items, 12 and 14, need additional attention before we wrap up this discussion. The only way we feel tempted to reach out and "fix" other people and their problems is if we still harbor an inner sense of deficiency about ourselves. Once we have gained complete freedom from judging, all these behaviors disappear. It is impossible for us to want to fix someone unless we have judged them deficient. Everything seems to be pointing in the same direction, doesn't it? We all need to become free from the temptation to judge.

Item 14 calls our attention to the need to view ourselves accurately, but without judging ourselves negatively. In truth, we are unable to view ourselves accurately if there is any form of judging going on, whether it is positive or negative. By definition, judging is a distortion of the facts. Thus, it is not possible to see anything accurately when we are judging. Accurate perception and judging simply cannot occur at the same time. They are mutually exclusive concepts.

This would be a great time to further clarify the difference between judging and judgment that was mentioned briefly on pages 94 & 95. We need good judgment, which is the intuitive discernment of whether something either fits or doesn't fit into an ever evolving picture of an ideal that we create in our rational mind. If something fits, that doesn't make it good. If it doesn't fit, that doesn't make it bad. It either fits or it doesn't. Here's how this works in practice. Let's say we create a picture of the kind of partner we need in order to develop the ideal mentor-coaching relationship for ourselves. In the early stages of wondering whether someone we know would be a good choice, the picture we're working from may not yet be very complete. Our intuition will know much more about the nuances of our picture than we could probably ever figure out, so we need to listen very closely to our inner discernment regarding a possible fit or not. Now, if someone fits, that certainly doesn't make them good. Likewise, if they don't fit, that doesn't make them bad. Again, they either fit or they don't. If they feel like a fit, we will take a step further. If they don't feel like a fit, we'll hold off.

As long as I am clarifying, lets add some further clarification to my concept of perfect. There is a huge difference between "seeing" ourselves as perfect and "judging" ourselves to be perfect. In the first case we see ourselves as evolving perfectly. We're on track. The emphasis here is on movement. In the second case the use of "perfect" brings to mind a finished point with no sense of movement. The first reflects the use of intuitive judgment, where we fit into a perfectly evolving ideal, while the second reflects the analytical judging of ourselves to have reached an end point of perfection. The former is truth. The latter is questionable.

This wrap-up discussion would not be complete without linking everything we have talked about back to being on a roll and sustaining the wonderful state of effortless high performance. We need to remember two things about this. First, there is only one way to sustain effortless high performance, and that is to learn how to keep our actions in full alignment with our life's purpose. Second, as long as we are judging, we cannot achieve the necessary connection with our life's purpose to either get on a roll or keep ourselves there. This is why I have included the words, "removing the obstacles" in the subtitle of this book. Nearly all of the tools presented so far relate to Step 5, the build-on-strengths aspect, of our strategic life planning framework. The more use we make of each tool, the sooner we will see the other four steps (purpose, goals, action plans and keeping track of what we're doing right) of the framework begin to take care of themselves automatically. Remember, being on a roll is our natural state. Incorrect programming of our analytical mind is the only thing preventing us from being there at this moment. A full-time value-finding mode, which I propose is the way a correctly programmed analytical mind is designed to function, will automatically keep our actions in full alignment with our life's purpose.

This completes our discussion of ways to master the discipline of continually identifying and building upon our strengths. Before we address the other four steps to the strategic life planning framework, I would like to share the following quote from *The Inner Game of Tennis* by W. Timothy Gallwey. Then I think a chapter with further thoughts about the management of energy is in order.

185

The Rose

When we plant a rose seed in the earth, we notice that it is small, but we do not criticize it as "rootless" and "stemless." We treat it as a seed, giving it the water and nourishment required of a seed. When it first shoots out of the earth, we don't condemn it as "immature" and "under-developed"; nor do we criticize the buds for not being open when they appear. We stand in wonder at the process taking place and give the plant the care that it needs at each stage of its growth. The rose is a rose from the time it is a seed to the time that it dies. Within it, at all times, it contains its whole potential. It seems to be constantly in the process of change; yet at each state, at each moment, it is perfectly all right as it is.

Chapter Thirteen

The Energy of Commitment

A Mentor-Coach Looks at Commitment

I made a commitment to myself in 1970 to spend the rest of my life working to understand what each of us is like when we are at our very best. It took me the next six years to reach the conclusion that we are each at our best when we are WHOLEHEARTEDLY committed. This conclusion inspired me to establish the consulting firm of Clear Purpose Management, Inc. and set about developing the world's leading expertise on WHOLEHEARTED commitment. I wanted to know what causes commitment—in its healthiest, least stressful, most highly productive form. The past 21 years of my life have been dedicated to that vision, and this book is the fruit of that process, because effortless high performance is the magnificent outcome of WHOLEHEARTED commitment.

We are now at a turning point in our discussions. Up to this point we have focused on removing obstacles that prevent us from achieving WHOLEHEARTED commitment. From here forward we focus on mobilizing the energy no longer needed to protect ourselves against the illusion of loss in a depletion and shortage world. We now embark on a journey to

187

get that newly released energy fully reconnected to WHOLEHEARTED commitment in a surplus and abundance world.

Commitment is the process which brings our various energies, talents and abilities into alignment with our goals. This focusing or alignment process transforms us energetically from an unfocused "bar of iron" into a motivated, highly productive "magnet" capable of achieving desired results. The analogy below is our first graphic illustration of this concept. It uses a plain bar of iron, with its diffused and unfocused energy to symbolize a person who is uncommitted, unmotivated and unproductive. And, while the discussion in this chapter is focused on each of us as individuals, all concepts will apply directly to organizations in exactly the same way.

The unfocused person is characterized by consistently poor performance. Among the causes are disorganized thought processes, lack of self-discipline, lack of commitment and a passive, task orientation.

Our second illustration represents a bar of iron to which an external source of *negative* energy has been applied to transform it into an electromagnet. This analogy symbolizes a person who is motivated by fear or threat. The bar of iron (or person) retains its negative electromagnetic alignment (motivation) only as long as it remains "plugged in" to a negative energy source such as fear. If we are responsible for obtaining results by working with this type of person, we must provide a support structure that includes clear penalties for nonperformance. The performance of a person who is motivated by threat is limited by inhibited thought processes, poor self-discipline, avoidance-driven commitment and a compulsive task orientation.

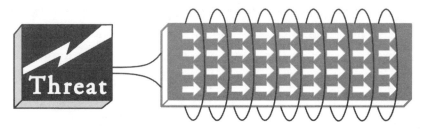

Our third illustration represents a bar of iron to which an external source of *positive* energy has been applied to transform it into an electro-magnet. This analogy symbolizes a person who is productively motivated by logic, intellect and willpower. The bar of iron (or person) retains its positive electromagnetic alignment (motivation) as long as it remains "plugged in" to a positive energy source such as willpower. If we are responsible for obtaining results by working with this type of person, we must provide an environment with many tangible rewards for desired performance. The person who is motivated by the desire to compete, win and collect rewards is characterized by intermittently high and low performance. Causes of the erratic performance include inflexible thought processes, rigid self-discipline, a willpower-driven commitment and a rational goal orientation.

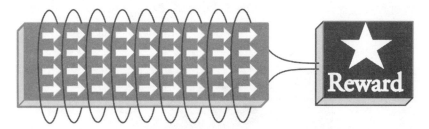

It is common for us to think of the fear-driven form of motivation as bad, and the willpower-driven form as good. As Shakespeare said,

189

however, "Nothing's either good nor bad, but thinking makes it so." This is certainly the case here. Negative motivation may well be better in the short run than no motivation. With our first analogy, if we remove the source of perceived threat, our motivation vanishes and we go directly back to the inert bar of iron. In the long run, positive motivation may be more harmful than no motivation at all. The form of motivation depicted by our willpower magnet is a major source of stress, burnout and heart attacks in the American culture. Incidentally, when motivation is taught academically, it includes only the above forms.

I shall never forget an experience I had when I first began thinking about these magnet analogies. One day I got the bright idea of taking a bar of iron, cutting it in half and getting one of the two halves magnetized. I imagined this would allow me to carry the magnets around with me to demonstrate these ideas. I asked a friend who worked for the Westinghouse motor rewinding shop in Denver if he would take me on a tour of the shop where I could ask an expert how to do this. When I asked if it could be done, he smiled and said, "Sure, but you know, it will never hold a charge." Well, I didn't know, but I was learning fast. He further informed me about the special kind of metals it takes to hold a charge. My immediate thought was, Wow, does this ever describe people I know! Some will just never hold a charge and some are made out of a very special kind of metal. He had really piqued my interest by the time he began to describe how a permanent magnet is formed.

A permanent magnet (such as Alnico) requires no external force to keep its internal energy in alignment virtually forever. Isn't this the perfect analogy for the effortless high performer and most visionary leaders? As a permanent magnet, Alnico is known to lose only $1/2$ of 1% of its magnetic alignment every 1,000 years. What a metaphor! Our next analogy depicts visionary leaders and effortless high performers who achieve permanent, internally self-sustaining commitment through the power of being in full alignment with their life purpose.

The competitive advantage enjoyed by people who are guided by their life's purpose is quite naturally sustained through their high level of self-motivation. They also tend to make steady progress in gaining access to, developing and then making full use of their highest potential. These purpose-inspired people are the subject of this book. They are permanently focused and can sustain high levels of performance over long periods of time without needing to draw on outside sources of creative energy. They also face very little risk of burnout from extended periods of effortless high performance. The person who is internally motivated by their life's purpose is the ultimate strategic thinker and is characterized by sustained high-level performance. Among the causes are permanently aligned thought processes, a relaxed self-discipline, purpose-inspired commitment and an intuitive results orientation.

What are you most appreciating about my comparison of people's motivation to various forms of magnetism? When I first learned about Alnico, I was quite struck by how it is formed. A special blend of metals is melted, thoroughly mixed together, and placed in the middle of a large electromagnetic field where it is allowed to cool. That reminds me of how gold is purified. One way is to heat it up until the "dross" simply floats to the top where it is skimmed off. The final test for purity is

191

when we can see a perfect reflection of our face off the surface of the gold. To me these are wonderful metaphors for the purification process required for each of us to reach the state of effortless high performance. Before we can each truly shine, we must clear ourselves of the negative emotions we have created and stored in our bodies as a result of judging things in our life to be good or bad, right or wrong.

Speaking of metaphors, I have one more to share before we close this chapter. This beautiful image from nature helps us make a clear distinction between purpose and goals by showing a wedge of geese as they journey either south for the winter or north again in the spring. Purpose is the intangible, intuitive force which both pulls and guides the geese toward their final destination. Goals are the tangible, measurable destination points in South America and Canada toward which the geese are being pulled and guided by their purpose. It is possible to observe, calculate and predict with some measure of certainty the yearly goals of a given wedge of geese. Any attempt on our part, however, to define the intangible driving force or purpose that keeps the flock of geese together and moving steadily toward their goal amounts to sheer speculation at best.

I like to use this wedge of geese to symbolize the ultimate spirit of teamwork and commitment. Groups of people who are willing to put into practice the intuition-based skills, disciplines and strategies set forth in this book can achieve a similar outcome.

Several more fascinating patterns have been observed within the wedge of geese by skilled observers. All but the leader fly in a nearly effortless zone by "drafting," or being pulled along in the wake of the bird ahead. The shape of the wedge is determined by the location of this drafting zone. This is also why we see the geese rotate leaders. Since they are each fully in tune with their purpose, any one of them can lead at any time. (They also have no analytical mind to interfere with that intuitive guidance system.)

Now for some mentor-coaching questions. *What are the two most valuable messages you are taking away from this chapter?* Everything we have covered so far is focused on making more creative energy available for commitment. From here on, our focus is on developing the disciplines needed to bring our available energy into alignment with our purpose in life. You most certainly do not need to finish reading the rest of this book until you are ready to do so. Without making good headway on the first part, it may be difficult to implement the strategies we are about to explore. They could even be an exercise in futility for you if you are not yet ready. *So, which do you feel is the highest priority for you, making more of your energy available for commitment, or moving on to the task of bringing all of your available energy into full alignment with your purpose in life?*

Chapter Fourteen

The Strategic Thinking Framework

Expanding the Strategic Life Planning Framework

We are now ready to begin putting some more meat on the bones of our five-step strategic life planning framework. I will first list the five steps again, along with descriptive phrases that further clarify the role played by each in enabling us to reach the state of WHOLEHEARTED commitment and effortless high performance. I will then offer a complete description of each step in the pages that follow. Note that this chapter may hold little or no interest for those who are reading for purely personal application. If that is the case for you, please feel free to skip directly to Chapter 15.

This chapter will be of greatest interest to those who already hold positions of leadership within an organization, or who aspire to do so in the future. As I mentioned in Chapter 2, this framework has been carefully structured to mirror the thought process behind the corporate strategic planning process initially introduced by Peter Drucker in his book, *Managing for Results*. I have two very good reasons for taking such care to structure the process in this way. First, it truly reflects the thought processes used by visionary leaders and effortless high performers to put themselves on a roll. Second, until we have fully put this process into practice on a very personal level, we are unprepared to address it in any meaningful way at an organizational level. In other words, strategic planning at an organizational level cannot succeed if it is approached from a purely theoretical understanding.

It is therefore my intent to have all the processes offered in the remainder of this book serve the dual purpose of showing each of us what we must do to put ourselves permanently on a roll, and at the same time equip each of us to participate effectively in putting an organization on a roll.

1. Identifying A Life Purpose — (To Be or Become . . .)
   ❖ the intuitive driving force behind long-term *commitment*
   ❖ the intangible "why" out of which true motivation flows
   ❖ the instinctive, philosophical, integrating force of direction
   ❖ the intuitive "strategy formulation" issue of management

2. Establishing Long-Range Goals — (To Do . . .)
   ❖ the analytical focal point of long term *commitment*
   ❖ the tangible "where" toward which purpose energy is focused
   ❖ the logical framework or structure for defining desired results
   ❖ the analytical "strategy implementation" issue of management

3. Defining Short-Range Action Plans — (To Act . . .)
   ❖ the concrete actions required to produce results *committed* to
   ❖ the specific "what, when and how-to" steps for achieving goals
   ❖ the clearly defined foundation for action, feedback and reward
   ❖ the intuitive/analytical "tactical planning" issues of management

4. Keeping Track of What's Right — (To Energize . . .)

❖ the habit that generates energy required to sustain *commitment*

❖ the *what's right* monitoring of results from all past actions

❖ the thought process which energizes continuous improvement

❖ the ongoing "bottom-line test" issue of strategic management

5. Building on Strengths — (To Multiply . . .)

❖ the value-finding questions that deepen *commitment's* foundations

❖ the systematic analysis that creates future opportunities

❖ the thought process that energizes the pursuit of excellence

❖ the key discipline required by successful strategic thinking

Once you have read the following expanded versions of all five steps, I will ask you to return to the above list and check your feelings as to which of the areas needs the most attention.

Step One: Identifying Our Life Purpose— Generating Commitment

The first step in the process of building an effective strategic life plan is known technically as "strategy formulation." The exercise is ultimately capable of bringing our whole reason for being into focus. It seeks to answer the question of what we—as a whole person—might become, could become and want to become ideally. Notice I didn't say "do." Personal strategy formulation helps us to identify and put into writing why our lives exist. This is a "be" issue, and thus our purpose statement typically begins with the words, "I am." It is also vitally important to understand here that we do not "invent" our purpose. We can only discover what is already very present and fully known at the deepest intuitive level of our inner selves and bring it up into our conscious awareness.

This first element is successfully dealt with when we have established a clear written statement of our own mission and purpose in life. Our completed statement of life purpose seeks to capture in writing the unique, intangible, philosophical and intuitive motivating forces that lie behind our most meaningful accomplishments. It defines the intuitively based energy forces from which we draw to experience WHOLEHEARTED commitment to our goals and objectives. It uses tangible words to define the intangible driving forces, or "glue," that keeps our attention focused on our goals.

Defining our purpose is the key intuitive step required to pull all the capabilities, attitudes and feelings of our whole being into full alignment. Having a purpose defined gives us a strategic advantage by enabling us to tap into our core creative energies and abilities and use them to reach our fullest potential. In the next chapter we will offer a series of exercises through which you will be guided to define your life's mission and purpose and put it in writing.

An effective statement of life purpose is:

❖ An intuitive concept that is philosophical and abstract

❖ A definition of the intuitive driving force in our life

❖ The cohesive "why" behind our desire for achievement

❖ The source of creative energy for committing to our goals

❖ The "cause of focus" for our energies and abilities

Step Two: Establishing Long-Range Goals— Focusing Our Commitment

The second step in building an effective strategic life plan is known technically as "strategy implementation." It is a vision-building exercise, and begins when we create a picture of a point in the future toward which our present actions can be most productively directed. This vision-building exercise helps us to answer the question of what tangible accomplishments would best reflect the fulfillment of our life's purpose. In other words, personal strategy implementation is a process by which we define the desired tangible outcomes in the future from actions we take today.

This part of our strategic life plan can be described as either vision-building or long-range goal-setting. As an exercise, it is repeated every one to five years and is successfully completed each time we have established a new set of future goals toward which to move. Here is the agenda for each time we enter the process of reestablishing our long-range goals: We are setting out to create or invent the clearest picture we can possibly imagine of ourselves and our accomplishments as we see them ideally fulfilling our purpose at least ten years into the future. Our goals are thus tangible, logical, measurable, analytical statements of "where" we plan to go to fulfill the "why" of our life's mission and purpose. Goals guide the "doing" issues of our lives, while purpose addresses the "being" issue.

Defining our long-range goals is a key analytical step required to pull all the capabilities, attitudes and feelings of our entire being into full alignment. Having our goals defined strengthens our strategic advantage by providing a focal point toward which our energies and abilities can all be directed to develop our fullest potential.

The goal-setting disciplines and exercises presented in Chapter 20 will remove some common obstacles that limit the effectiveness of most attempts at goal setting. All of this will follow the chapter on defining our life's purpose so we can begin with the proper criteria for determining goals, and thus choose only those which will easily inspire WHOLE-HEARTED commitment. Many have found both the context of Chapter 20 as well as the guidelines it offers to provide their most rewarding experience of goal-setting ever.

An effective set of long-range goals is:

❖ An analytical concept that is measurable and concrete

❖ A logically defined point toward which to steer our lives

❖ The "what" that we plan to accomplish with our lives

❖ A tangible means for measuring fulfillment of our purpose

❖ The "point of focus" for our energies and abilities

Step Three: Defining Our Short-Range Action Plans and Rewards

The third step in the process of building an effective strategic life plan plays a key role in successful strategy implementation. It is technically known as "tactical planning." It is an exercise that defines and prioritizes all present actions required for us to begin moving toward achievement of our future goals. The tactical planning process helps us answer the question of how to define, prioritize, measure and reward our own performance.

This step requires us to identify yearly, quarterly, monthly and weekly action steps that must be taken if we are to move successfully toward our long-range goals. These action steps are then linked with resources needed to accomplish them and arranged in priority order so they can be put on paper where they will to provide clear guidance for our daily actions. Specific plans are included for measuring and rewarding our successful accomplishment of these action items.

To succeed, our action plans and rewards must be specific, tangible, concrete and measurable. They are tactical action steps that serve to keep our present actions focused. They also supply immediate feedback that guides and motivates us to achieve our long-range goals. In this way they set the stage for our own internal validation of incremental successes. They become invaluable, achievement-based sources of "atta-boys" or "atta-girls" from which we build a long-term sense of fulfillment of our life's purpose. It is important to note that this feedback is internally generated and not dependent on acknowledgment from others.

Some readers will be surprised to learn how truly unimportant it is for us to see in advance any of the steps to be taken between the two-year checkpoint and the ten-year end point in our plan. No basis exists for correctly establishing short-term action plans until we have selected a clear long-range target. A valuable set of guidelines will be included in Chapter 20 for use in integrating our action plans and rewards into our overall strategic life plan.

An effective set of action plans and rewards is:

❖ A real-time way to integrate analytical and intuitive concepts

❖ A logical set of tactics and rewards for our present actions

❖ The "how to" for reaching goals needed to fulfill our life purpose

❖ The integration of thinking and feeling to achieve daily success

❖ A means for fully developing our talents and abilities

Step Four: Keeping Track of What We're Doing Right

The fourth step in our process of building an effective strategic life plan provides for the continuous replenishment of our creative energy. It is an exercise in which we identify up to three tasks essential for our continued success. We then develop a strict discipline of simply monitoring and recording our performance in the areas selected. The tasks we select to be monitored become our critical success factors. When we see consistent progress in these areas, we receive big boosts in our reserves of creative energy. This, in turn, allows us to experience the greatest amount of movement toward our ultimate goals.

Once the first three steps of our strategic life plan are put in place successfully, we will find this fourth element to be more easily established and more consistently energizing than we might have ever thought possible. This is because we are now practicing a thought process that allows us to abandon mistakes, capitalize on past successes and move effortlessly toward a well-conceived model of our future.

Among the most compelling reasons for building a habit of keeping track of what we are doing right is the simple observation that we get more of what we measure. Thus, to continually build momentum and at the same time replenish our reserves of creative energy, we must simply decide what we want more of and then begin to track it. This is the key that allows us to engage both our analytical and intuitive minds simultaneously. Only when the steps of planning, taking action and keeping track of what we are doing right are moving together in unison does our entire mind become synchronized to produce the permanent magnet, "on-a-roll" effect that distinguishes effortless high performers.

Finally, we must learn to trust the plan and let it work. This could be one of the most important, yet difficult-to-master aspects of learning to track our performance within the context of a well-conceived strategic life plan. This is particularly challenging for any of us who lack self-confidence, or whose past conditioning influences us to analyze our progress from a defensive, protective or "guard-against-loss" posture. You can look forward to some simple directions in Chapter 20 that will equip you to succeed in this area.

A well-developed habit of keeping track of what we're doing right is:

❖ A practical way to generate fresh new creative energy

❖ A natural basis for stimulating continuous improvement

❖ The best way to monitor progress in fulfilling our purpose

❖ The key to tracking, rewarding and boosting performance

❖ A perspective that keeps us generating fresh momentum

Step Five: Maintaining an Attitude of "Building On Strengths"

The fifth step in the process of building an effective strategic life plan is the key mental discipline of continually looking for, identifying and building on our strengths. This goes hand in hand, of course, with the added discipline of continually working to find value and bring out the best in every person, situation or circumstance we encounter. These two mental disciplines are so essential to the successful practice of our intuition-based system of self-management that we cannot expect to succeed without them. In other words, we simply have no alternative but to master these disciplines if we intend to reach the state of effortless high performance.

This aspect of our strategic life plan is being successfully executed when our habit of seeking and finding value and bringing out the best in every situation we encounter becomes so automatic that we are no longer conscious of doing it. The questioning sequence that awaits our mastery and that we must learn to supply both to ourselves and others is as follows:

❖ "What is already *right*?"

❖ "What is it that makes it *right*?"

❖ "What would be ideally *right*?"

❖ "What's not yet quite *right*?"

❖ "What can I do to make it *right*?"

We can count on these questions to continually draw upon our intuitive mind for its more integrated, holistic, ideal and naturally perfection-seeking solutions to the challenges and opportunities we face. Our intuitive mind is the only part of us equipped to respond to our WHAT'S RIGHT, "where's the value?" or "complete the picture" type of questions. This means we automatically tap into our intuitive powers for answers when we maintain a build-on-strengths attitude. Any kind of a WHAT'S WRONG, comparative or ranking question is automatically retained for processing in the analytical, dismantling part of our mind. This is the part that uses up our reserves of creative energy to function. Therefore, one of the very best ways to tell where our questions are being processed is to check on what is happening to our energy. If our energy is being depleted, we know our processing is taking place in the part of our mind proven to be incapable of distinguishing truth from fiction. If we are feeling energized, we can be assured that something we are doing is sparking intuitive insights.

A fully developed discipline of building on strengths is:

❖ A rational approach that is practical and rewarding

❖ A logical way to gain access to our intuitive powers

❖ The key that unlocks our self-sustaining purpose energy

❖ Essential for developing a strategic thinking advantage

❖ A way to bring peace, harmony and balance to our lives

As promised, I will now ask you to reflect on each of the five steps of building a strategic life plan and identify the one where you could most profitably focus your attention over the next 12 months. What would you say is the biggest benefit you gained from reading the information in this chapter? How will it serve you to see the personal translations we applied to more effectively illuminate this business planning process? Let's move on now to doing it.

Chapter Fifteen

Exploring Success Patterns

Putting the Right Questions to Work

We are about to put our use of the WHAT'S RIGHT questions to their ultimate test. We will use them to thoroughly explore our success patterns and discover our own personal purpose in life. We begin this task by first picking a few times when we were clearly at our best. We then move through some exercises which allow us to "tune in" to each of these special moments at the deepest intuitive level we are capable of at this time. Our goal is to listen as closely as possible to every feeling we can recall from those special moments of being at our best. If you have heeded my encouragement to put your feelings into words in response to my mentor-coaching questions, you will be well prepared to succeed in this exercise.

The most important WHAT'S RIGHT question we can ask is, "Why does my life exist?" In the third paragraph of Chapter 1, I invited you to join me in wondering what each of us is like at our very best. The exercises in which we are about to immerse ourselves give us a taste of the ultimate fruit of that quest. Our greater objective for embarking on this quest is to continually increase our awareness and understanding of what we are like when we are on a roll. From this increased awareness, we gain important insights needed to gradually become more of what we are capable of being.

Our first step is to recall two or more times in our lives when we felt deeply satisfied over a specific accomplishment. As we begin to explore our memories of high points and accomplishments, we soon begin to recognize patterns and similarities that will inevitably show themselves in these situations. This process is known as identifying success patterns. While we may look at only two or three success patterns at this time, the exercise is so fruitful I certainly encourage you to pursue it on your own to explore additional success patterns in several more areas of your life.

Once a few of our success patterns are identified, we begin to see more of the motivating forces present when we're on a roll. Our increased awareness of these patterns allows us to expand our understanding of how these motives may be contributing to our success.

Accomplishment #1

Let's begin by recalling an accomplishment from when we were 13 to 14 years old. For most Americans, this is the middle-school years of the seventh and eighth grade. If possible, it is best to choose an accomplishment about which we felt very proud. Also, it is particularly helpful if the one we choose to explore is sports-related. It is important to recall as many of the details as we can about this accomplishment. In the end it is not the details we are after, but recalling as many as possible will improve our chances of bringing all the feelings associated with this accomplishment up to a conscious level. It is now time to set aside this book and, on a separate sheet of paper, make some detailed notes about the feelings of satisfaction we felt as a result of accomplishments we are recalling. It is best to write down, in as much detail as we can recall, exactly why we felt proud of our accomplishment at the time. It is important to take plenty of time to do this so we can allow ourselves to get deeply into our memories of the feelings and get as many as possible written down. We might also ask ourselves questions like, "Did I want anyone special to know about my accomplishment?" And, "Why did I feel that was important?" Let's stop and do this now. `PAUSE`

The first time I was asked to recall an accomplishment from the seventh or eighth grade time period of my life, I was unable to recall one at all. I had to move to the ninth grade, where I could proudly recall being one of only four ninth graders chosen to sing in the senior choir. Not only did I gain important insights into myself from exploring my feelings about that, but I have gained huge insights from the absence of any feelings of accomplishment for me from my seventh or eighth grade time period.

I was actually drawn into the field of consulting because of the satisfactions received from asking this success pattern question of others. I mentioned earlier that pattern recognition is the language through which I have the greatest access to my intuition. I have asked the success pattern questions in private discussion with well over 2,000 people and listened very carefully to the feelings expressed in response. The number of insights available from this process is truly amazing. Whenever I need to gain quick insights into someone and only have time for a question or two in which to do so, I will usually rely on this question.

Accomplishment #2

Let's now go on to a second question. This time, we will focus on accomplishments about which we feel the greatest amount of pride or sense of satisfaction from the last five to ten years of our life. Here we may draw on accomplishments from any area of activity. As before, we want to capture the feelings of satisfaction received from those accomplishments. Only after we have searched our memories for the feelings and written them down on a separate sheet of paper can we go back and review them and identify any patterns they may reveal. Let's do this now, and return to continue reading after we have captured our feelings about at least one and preferably two additional accomplishments from the last five to ten years in your life. PAUSE

Reading the Clues

Learning to find and read the clues that lie hidden within our success patterns can prove remarkably helpful in discovering our purpose in life. Such patterns often fall into one or more of the six categories listed below. As we review each statement, let's ask ourselves if any part of it describes feelings of satisfaction we felt from either of the accomplishments we've identified.

A. Overcoming challenges and/or being in control of ourselves and our circumstances.

B. Avoiding negative situations; escaping from undesired consequences; rationalizing through problems and/or overcoming difficulties.

C. Being unique and different; rising above the norm and having our achievements distinguish us from the crowd.

D. Achieving for the pure joy of achieving; doing things for the pure satisfaction of doing them well.

E. Proving our competence and earning other people's respect.

F. Gaining acceptance and approval; feeling like we belong, are needed and/or loved.

Does one of the statements either shed some new light on our feelings of satisfaction . . . or maybe even fit them exactly? Were parts of more than one of the statements descriptive of our feelings? What happens when we think of other accomplishments we may not have listed? Do any of the statements fit those feelings? Are there any differences? What is the clearest pattern we see emerging here? Do we find ourselves identifying strongly with more than one of the statements? (That fits into a pattern, too.)

Please note there are certainly no right or wrong answers here. Our only goal is to recognize and begin to understand the patterns revealed in our feelings of satisfaction. Those who have less experience at putting feelings into words may find it more challenging to discern their own patterns than others who have more experience with introspection. We even find people who identify strongly with five of the six statements— and that in itself is a special pattern, for which we will soon be revealing some wonderfully meaningful insights.

Next, we will look at patterns revealed in any fears we may have. Fears play a role in our motivation that is opposite from the satisfactions we seek to enjoy. These patterns often provide helpful cross-referencing clues for checking the validity of satisfaction patterns reflected in our successes. As we review the items listed, do any describe conditions we seek to avoid? If so, please note any that apply.

❖ Rejection

❖ Failure

❖ Loss of control

❖ Being humiliated

❖ All of the above

❖ None of the above (i.e., fears play little or any role in your motivation)

Did you find it relatively easy to zero in on one of the six choices? Most people do. *Are you curious to see the correlation patterns which often occur between our fear choices and the statements of our feelings of satisfaction?* Let's now look at these, since they can help to raise our confidence in the validity of the success patterns we were most strongly drawn to. For example, a fear of rejection correlates directly with Success Pattern F. A fear of failure correlates directly with Pattern E. A fear of loss of control correlates with Success Patterns A, B, and C. A fear of being humiliated correlates with the combination of Patterns C and F, but may also include Pattern A. If we chose "all of the above," that certainly correlates with Pattern A, and could easily include any combination of the others except Pattern D. And if we chose "none of the above," that correlates only with Pattern D. For the most part, these combinations fit nearly everyone with whom we have shared this process.

What is the biggest benefit you have gained so far from looking at your success patterns? If you had a magic wand with only one choice, would you at this moment desire greater awareness of what you are feeling, or greater understanding of the patterns revealed in those feelings? Both of those choices feel quite important, don't they? Let's now develop a context within which we can discover many things about the various meanings behind all of these patterns.

The Heirarchy of Needs

It was 22 years ago when I first began asking these questions about success patterns, and began working to discern the meanings hidden within the responses. I found the work of Abraham Maslow, author of *The Further Reaches of Human Nature*, to be particularly helpful in this process. His life's work was similar to mine, in that his studies were centered around man's "peak experiences," for which he chose the label "self-actualization." Maslow is widely credited with having done the definitive work in motivation theory. Anyone who has been exposed to even a minimum of training in motivation will immediately recognize his pyramid model. As we can see from the diagram, it depicts five distinct levels of fundamental needs arranged in a hierarchical order.

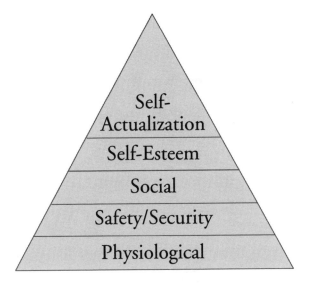

In my early efforts to learn how to identify patterns in our feelings of satisfaction around accomplishments, I found Maslow's pyramid model to be immensely useful. After working with it for some time, however, its pyramid structure began to limit my expanding understanding of motivation. In 1978, an alternate structure began to take shape for me, and it has proven to be extremely useful for understanding the complex nature of our success patterns. This new model uses Maslow's same set of fundamental needs, yet many find it more useful for making sense out of the patterns we have identified.

Thousands of clients have benefited from using this new model over the past 20 years to gain a fuller understanding of their success patterns. Many have also reported that the new model removes limitations they had also experienced in their use of the pyramid model. Be sure to note here that I take no issue with the profoundly significant findings of Abraham Maslow. I simply offer a new structure to provide even more meaningful access to those important findings.

My model uses a series of five "buckets." Each bucket carries one of Maslow's original five labels, and is positioned in the same hierarchical order. Each bucket sits on its own separate platform. These platforms are arranged in stair-step fashion, with each placed slightly above and off to one side of the last. Each bucket is positioned upright, open and waiting to be filled. This has proven to be a wonderfully effective way to characterize the concept of our fundamental "needs," as they sit waiting to be fulfilled.

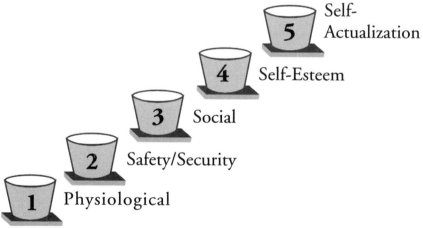

Self-
Actualization

Self-Esteem

Social

Safety/Security

Physiological

Here the model becomes really useful. Imagine how the vacuum effect of the first bucket's "emptiness" begins to draw our attention to our physiological needs shortly after we are born. These needs are for food, clothing, shelter, physical warmth, etc. Then, as our first set of needs starts to be met, imagine our bucket gradually beginning to fill. Now remember, the unfilled portion of the bucket works like a magnet to keep us focused on getting our physiological needs met. Therefore, as more and more of these needs are met, its ability to keep our total attention focused on getting our physiological needs met decreases.

At some point, the attention-holding power of our unmet physiological needs is reduced to where our primary attention is free to shift to the newly discovered vacuum of the second bucket. When this happens, our attention gets divided between continuing to get our physiological needs met and beginning to get our safety and security needs met as well. In this way, the ability of any given bucket to hold our primary attention is directly related to how well our needs are being met in that area. Then, as each bucket continues to fill, our attention can be more powerfully drawn to the next bucket by its greater remaining vacuum of unfilled needs.

As our safety and security bucket is filled, and its ability to hold our primary attention is thereby reduced, we are soon able to discover yet another completely empty bucket. This one represents our social needs. This process continues as each of our primary and secondary need areas are filled. When the unfilled needs holding our primary attention are sufficiently met, our primary attention is released to be focused on yet another completely empty bucket. Where does all of this lead? In this evolutionary process, we each live with the potential of getting all of our lower level needs sufficiently met so our primary attention can be free to focus on getting our need for self-actualization met. This would mean living in a state free from fear and working to bring out our true essence through everything we do.

I use the word "potential" here, since most of us get permanently distracted from the task of getting our needs met long before this has a chance to happen. Most of us have our primary attention shifted away from filling our needs and onto "patching leaks" somewhere between the ages of three and ten. My little David story in Chapter 6 was intended to illustrate how this distraction process occurs. We get a hurtful reprimand one day. We get painfully invalidated the next, and a good solid "gotcha" mixed in here and there for good measure. ("Gotchas" are hurtful reprimands that leave us confused and distracted from our purpose for living.) Each little gotcha takes its toll by temporarily pulling our attention away from its primary focus of getting our needs met, and leaves us a little bit more concerned about protecting ourselves from pain. At some point along the way, the vast majority of us find ourselves needing to make a permanent shift into the "protect" mode.

Here is the point of all this. Most of us have developed lifelong achievement patterns based on how far along we were in the need fulfillment process before we underwent the shift from filling our needs to patching leaks. Our resulting achievement patterns have a big influence over how we view our purpose in life. In other words, once we see how our own patterns work, it becomes easier for us to identify our own life purpose. Are we ready to begin exploring these achievement patterns?

A brief note of caution is in order before we proceed. During the next few pages, our analytical minds will most certainly be tempted to place us into a category long before our learning is complete. It would be wise to resist this temptation. Even though my explanations will be in the form of categories, these theories and categories cannot define our purpose. I offer them here only as a context to enable us to discern our feelings as clearly and accurately as possible. Only our feelings can guide us in discovering our purpose. If we keep this in mind, we are in for a deeply meaningful experience together.

Social Needs Achievement Patterns

Our first set of achievement patterns is found among those who were focused primarily on filling their social needs bucket when gotchas became the key force in their development and they switched to patching leaks. Achievement patterns developed from this set of conditions were mentioned earlier in Pattern F, which states, "gaining acceptance and approval; feeling like we belong, are needed and/or loved." Individuals of this type strive to gain a feeling of acceptance and approval, to achieve a sense of affiliation and belonging, and to feel needed and loved. On the flip side they fear rejection. This means their attention is largely focused on protecting themselves from the pain of feeling rejected in all activities they undertake.

Once our achievement patterns are set in place, our sensory mechanisms all seem to somehow adapt to the patterns and adjust the way they pick up data. In the case of the social needs achievement patterns, this adjustment allows the senses to be uniquely perceptive of other people's possible rejection feelings directed toward them. Therefore, as they scan their world, rejection messages are the first thing they will pick up (sometimes even when they're not there).

We rarely find anyone who exhibits this set of achievement patterns to be self-motivated. They are much more vulnerable, in fact, to being demotivated. Anything perceived to threaten their sense of belonging will usually demotivate them. Most efforts to use traditional reward mechanisms to improve their motivation will also have a low success rate.

Frederic Herzberg, in his research on motivation, has identified a set of what he calls "hygiene factors," which target precisely the areas where people with this pattern are so vulnerable to being demotivated. These factors are listed below, along with a description of how they affect people with the social needs achievement patterns.

❖ Lack of clarity, or inconsistent administration of policies and procedures. In other words, all the clarity and consistency in the world won't motivate, but their lack demotivates.

❖ Poor supervision. Wonderful supervision won't motivate, but poor supervision demotivates.

❖ Bad working conditions. The greatest working conditions do not motivate, but poor ones demotivate.

❖ Working around people they dislike. Having an entire room full of people they like will not motivate, but put one disliked person in the room and they are demotivated.

❖ Personal incentive compensation programs. Incentives demotivate because the person risks being rejected whether they do well or do poorly. In their eyes they can't win.

Self-Esteem Needs Achievement Patterns

Our second set of achievement patterns is found among those who were focused primarily on filling their self-esteem needs bucket when gotchas became the key force in their development and they switched to patching leaks. Achievement patterns developed from this set of conditions were identified earlier in Pattern E, which states, "proving our competence and earning other people's respect." Individuals of this type strive to do just that. On the flip side they fear failure. This means their attention is focused on protecting against any chance of failure in all activities they undertake.

The senses of individuals of this type are keenly adapted to pick up on anything having to do with relative importance. This means they are especially perceptive about relationships, political hierarchies, ranking mechanisms, pecking orders, structures and how things fit together. Their senses are typically not well adapted to reading the feelings of other people, however.

Individuals of this type are normally responsive to traditional approaches to motivation. Motivational efforts that include incentives and other forms of visible rewards for accomplishment can be expected to succeed on most occasions.

Notice the radical difference between motivational responses of these first two types. As much as half our population could conceivably fit the social needs achievement patterns, and there is little in their motivational structure to cause them to join the ranks of middle and upper management within organizations. Contrast this with individuals who fit the self-esteem achievement patterns and who are keenly aware of anything that allows them to rank themselves higher than others. If we put a ladder in front of this type of person, we will soon see them attempting to climb it. And since their ranks may make up as much as one-third of our population, they tend to dominate the ranks of middle and upper management. It is easy to see the potential for conflict when they set out to establish an incentive compensation plan and make it available to all of those people who are demotivated by such plans.

I have said it before and this is a perfect time to say it again. Each of us looks at the world through our own set of eyes. We walk on dangerous ground when we assume that everyone else sees the world the same way we do.

Without falling in the trap of trying to categorize yourself, what have you found most useful so far from exploring our first two sets of achievement patterns? Which is proving to be more fascinating: using this information to gain a better understanding of others, or using it to enhance your understanding of your own patterns?

218

Self-Actualization Needs Achievement Patterns

Our third set of achievement patterns is found among those in a tiny segment—perhaps less than 2%—of our population. These people were never sufficiently distracted by gotchas to have their attention drawn away from filling their needs and shifted onto patching leaks. Achievement patterns developed from this set of conditions are clearly expressed in Pattern D, which states, "achieving for the pure joy of achieving; doing things for the pure satisfaction of doing them well." Individuals of this type also achieve for the satisfaction of making a worthwhile contribution. Where others have a flip side, individuals of this type do not operate in the fear mode. In fact, they can even be quite puzzled over the amount of influence fear has in the lives of others. As a result, this type of individual certainly doesn't focus much attention on protecting against negatives.

219

The senses of this type of individual will be keenly adapted for seeing black-and-white facts with great clarity. They take information in through a clear, straight pipe. This makes them extremely effective in problem-solving situations, because information they receive is rarely filtered by emotions and other distorting influences. This can also make it frustrating for them when having to deal with others who are unable to receive information back from them in their direct, straight pipe manner. As a result, they rarely make good supervisors of people. Individuals of this type are almost entirely self-motivated, and can easily become impatient with or have difficulty tolerating others who lack personal motivation.

Along about now, if you are like many people who hear this explanation for the first time, you are probably feeling at least puzzled, if not on the edge of frustration. If this is the case, is it possible you have been trying to judge which category you fit in, even though you were cautioned about that? There is good news about being puzzled, though. If you can manage to remain in this puzzled state for a few more pages, you'll have a the best possible chance of really connecting with your intuition when the time comes to crystallize your own purpose.

This piece of good news, by the way, is another example of how insights so often show up when we switch from WHAT'S WRONG to WHAT'S RIGHT questions. I hate to admit it, but years ago when people would tell me how confused they were at this point, I saw their confusion as a negative reflection on my ability to explain. Later on, I made a commitment to really examine what was right about this uncomfortable state of confusion. I then made the link to something Betty Edwards says about how to gain access to our intuition in her book, *Drawing on the Right Side of the Brain*. The entire success of her approach to drawing depends on presenting our analytical mind with a task too complex for it to handle, yet at the same time not threatening. If we do this correctly, she says our analytical mind will throw up its hands in surrender and step out of the way to allow our much more powerful but less assertive intuition to come forward and accomplish the task. If there was ever a point in this book when such a process was called for, the remainder of this chapter is that time.

How Intensity Affects Motivational Needs

Years ago, while trying to rely on Maslow's pyramid to guide my expanding awareness of how our motivation works, I felt puzzled too. His model simply wasn't allowing me to make sense of everything I was seeing. That's part of what led me to develop my bucket model in the first place. The other part grew out of a deeply humiliating experience that occurred for me just before Thanksgiving in 1977. At the time, I was engaged in a mentor-coaching project where I was working individually with each partner in a CPA firm to explore their success patterns. During the process, one of the partners shared a set of patterns with me that closely matched those I had found in myself some 16 months earlier when I discovered my own failure pattern. While I felt hesitant to do so, I decided I had to tell him what I was reading about his failure pattern. Boy, was I wrong! How embarrassing. He no more had a failure pattern than I am the governor of Hawaii.

Somehow I was able to rescue our discussion, learning later that it hadn't affected my client nearly as much as it had me. But as I left his office that day, my tail was tucked so tightly between my legs it squeaked. Then, just as I drove out of the parking lot, it struck me like a ton of bricks that I had assigned negative value to the pattern and therefore blocked myself from further learning about it. What a painful way to relearn that lesson. (Remember, problems only show up in our lives to bring us a message that we are out of alignment with our purpose.) Within moments I made a vow to myself to discover what was right about that pattern, if it took me the rest of my life.

One of the most meaningful insights I have ever experienced came flooding into my life six weeks later. It began when I realized that every time I had seen this pattern, it was in someone who was extremely bright. Wow, I thought . . . if this is true, it must also mean I'm bright. What a tempting thought! Naw. That can't be right. In spite of all my self-doubts, however, the new insights just kept pouring in, one after another. Within a week or so, I was able to put enough of the new puzzle pieces together to identify the root cause of all the behaviors in this set of patterns.

Emotional Intensity and Mental Capacity Are Directly Correlated

My key discovery is this: the higher our mental capacity, the higher our emotional intensity. Yes, this means the fundamental levels of emotional intensity and mental capacity within each of us are directly correlated—as in one-to-one. One additional factor also correlates to the above, but this one is in the form of a probability. The culture we live in hasn't a clue about how to deal with emotional intensity. As a result, most of us have learned to suppress our emotions rather than bring them out into the open. Those who have the highest emotional intensity, therefore, also have the highest probability of receiving negative feedback for not being able to "control" their intensity. Incidentally, we are not talking here about displayed emotions. In this case, by my use of the words "emotional intensity," I am attempting to address the emotional intensity present inside of us, not what is or isn't being displayed externally.

You cannot imagine how many of some people's motivation and behaviors can be explained with this new set of understandings. Not only is this discovery the direct result of WHAT'S RIGHT thinking, but it also provides a tremendous foundation for some highly productive WHAT'S RIGHT thinking that is badly needed within the entire field of psychology.

Now, before the pseudo-scientists jump all over me and ask how I measure emotional intensity, I must point out there is no known way to measure mental capacity. The only thing we know how to measure in this area is the ability to take an IQ test. We then make the mistake of thinking we have measured our intelligence, or mental capacity. I also know of no way to measure emotional intensity. I have shared this new information with well over 10,000 people, however, and have carefully observed its contribution. After 20 years of this, I have personally gotten enough intuitive validation of the concept to trust it completely.

So many insights have emerged out of this discovery that I could probably fill several more chapters with them. Perhaps this needs to be the subject of another book by itself. For now, however, let's explore its implications in relation to our discussion of motivation and purpose. Here we find people at the highest levels of mental and emotional intensity having an entirely different way of viewing their emotional needs, as symbolized by our five buckets. My intuition tells me, by the way, that the patterns I am about to describe are found primarily among people whose mental capacity falls somewhere within the upper 15% or so. For many readers who relate strongly to the patterns I describe over the next few pages, this could turn out to be an extremely eye-opening experience. It most certainly has for hundreds of others. This will be particularly true if this information is validating the strength of your inherent mental capacity for the first time as you read it. If even part of this turns out to be true for you, the best source of internal validation I can offer is your own intuitive sense of your emotional intensity as compared to others you know.

The Detached Control Achievement Patterns

There is a level of mental capacity, probably somewhere near the 85th percentile, above which people seem to possess what I call a multidimensional perception capability. This means they can observe something from several different angles at the same moment in time. Anyone who has this capability will approach our "buckets" from an entirely different perspective than I have previously described. Instead of seeing and relating to only one bucket at a time, these people see all five at once from the very beginning. Not only that, but each bucket is bigger. Remember, we are dealing here at the highest levels of both emotional intensity *and* mental capacity, and we are creating a way to represent this higher level of intensity. Huge buckets seem to do that nicely.

Not only are the buckets bigger, but the heightened intensity level associated with this pattern leaves us much more vulnerable to gotchas. Everything about this set of patterns is more complex by far than the other patterns, which clearly relate primarily to one bucket at a time. Incidentally, Maslow could have been expected to observe these patterns, too, if they had applied to him as they do to me. Let's now review the complexity of this picture. We have bigger buckets, more intensely felt needs, and a greater vulnerability to being distracted by gotchas. Within this context, it is easy to see why the trigger point for making the permanent shift from filling buckets to patching leaks might happen earlier and with greater intensity than with the other patterns.

When the shift to patching leaks occurs for high-intensity individuals, the defenses brought into play are also quite different. In order to deal permanently with the gotchas, this person will simply convert their multidimensional perception capability into a defense mechanism known as "detachment." Detachment is the unique way in which they intellectually distance themselves, or separate themselves from their negative emotions.

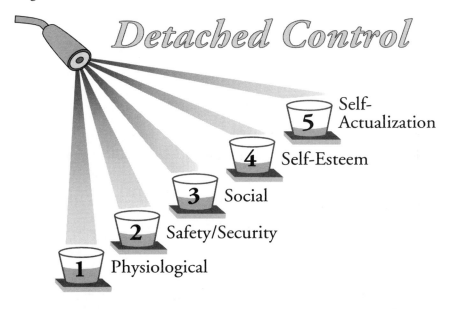

Detached Control

5 — Self-Actualization

4 — Self-Esteem

3 — Social

2 — Safety/Security

1 — Physiological

Achievement patterns developed in response to this set of conditions are also more complex, and are most often seen as the drive to overcome challenges and/or be in control of ourselves and our circumstances. For some, the patterns can also show up as a powerful need to be unique and different, to rise above the norm and have our achievements distinguish us from the crowd.

As far as this person's fears are concerned, "all of the above" frequently applies, but loss of control in any form is to be avoided at all cost. Fear of being humiliated, fear of failure and fear of rejection can each play a role in their motivation, but fear of loss of control or fear of not being in control is always paramount. If we pay close attention, we will notice how the concept of control plays a central role in their motivation and can show up in many different ways.

The senses of individuals of this type are most keenly adapted to pick up on options and alternatives in their environment. Their senses are also well adapted to perceive the full range of feelings, relationships and facts. It's another case where the complexities of this pattern make a wide variety of choices relevant.

The overall motivation for individuals of this type is unusually complex, as one might imagine. To a large extent this is because their powerful intellect can deceive them into acting on a form of pseudo-motivation that cannot be fulfilled. This often leaves them feeling little true satisfaction from their many accomplishments. Their high mental capacity, in other words, is a double-edged sword. It permits outstanding accomplishment on one hand. On the other, its reliance on detachment as a defense mechanism can virtually block them from feeling fulfilled by even the most Herculean of accomplishments.

As you examine the diagram of control-motivated achievement patterns, note how the shower spray is shown drying out before it gets to the buckets. You will also note the depiction of all the buckets being relatively empty. One more variable must also be noted. Varying degrees of detachment affect the relative distance between the shower head and the buckets. The less detached we are, the closer we are to the buckets, and the more fulfilled we will feel from our accomplishments. The more detached we are, the further away from the buckets we will be, and our accomplishments will be less fulfilling. When I first discovered this phenomenon in 1978, for example, I was so far detached, my shower head must have been positioned somewhere over in the next county. As a result, any sense of fulfillment from my accomplishments was zip.

Can you see the endless loop of this? The pain triggering my detachment defense mechanism was all the result of my own judging. I had no idea at the time of how much "control" I really had over the situation. As my temptation to judge was replaced by my new discipline of finding value, I gradually found myself creating less pain from which to detach. This is how I managed to retrieve my shower head from the next county and bring it right up next to the buckets so I could begin to experience the joy of a true sense of fulfillment. My buckets were painfully empty when this all began. Today, anyone who knows me will quickly see that my buckets are filled to overflowing. Life is very good.

We have now clarified each of the four need-based achievement patterns. It might now be useful to point out some important issues to keep in mind when we attempt to communicate with individuals who fit a given pattern. When communicating with a social needs person, for example, it would be good to avoid sending any message which could be perceived as expressing rejection. A self-esteem needs person, on the other hand, can assimilate our messages most effectively when we clarify the relative importance of ideas we wish to convey and how they relate to known structures.

When communicating with a self-actualization needs person, we can be most successful by presenting straight facts with little concern for how they are being received emotionally. Finally, when attempting to communicate with a detached control-motivated person, we must first attempt to address all possible options and alternatives, and then work to systematically eliminate all those that are unworkable. This approach is effective because an option or alternative left unrationalized by the mind of a control motivated person can easily block commitment.

The comparative table below shows other key variables found among the four types of need-based achievement patterns.

	Bucket 3	Bucket 4	Bucket 5	Detached Control
Need Area	Social	Self-Esteem	Self-Actualization	Control-Motivated
Needs to Feel	Needed	Important	A Sense of Accomplishment	In Control of Self and Environment
Fears	Rejection	Failure	Not Applicable	Loss of Control, Humiliation, All
Dependent Upon	Social Acceptance	Recognition	Self	Ability to Rationalize
Keenest Perceptions	Rejection Feelings	Relationships & Structure	Black-and-White Facts	Options and Alternatives
Achievement Obstacle	Difficult to Motivate	Doesn't Read Feelings Well	Insensitive to Needs of Others	Conflicts with Commitment
Major Strength	Loyalty	Motivation & Directness	Objectivity	Energy and Intensity

Well, we have certainly covered a lot of material in the past few pages. With any luck your analytical mind is close to overload and ready to give up and turn this whole project over to your intuition. *How would you describe the two biggest benefits you got from reading everything I presented about success patterns? What was most surprising to you? What was most validating? What part are you feeling most drawn to go back and study more thoroughly?*

Chapter Sixteen

Reviewing Generic Purpose Statements

Generic Statements of Life Purpose

Ready for the next step? We will now review four generic statements of life purpose. From past experience, there is a good chance one of them will come surprisingly close to expressing your own personal purpose in life—at least generically. Each statement has at least one word underlined. These words indicate key concepts which need to be more fully explored, once you have taken a few moments to reflect on the statements and any feelings they bring up. Here are the four statements.

A. To gain full *control* of all my feelings, needs and abilities, in order to unlock all of my *power* and use it to *influence* others for good.

B. To fully *accept myself* and know that I am *accepted* by others as a worthwhile person.

C. To be *admired* and *respected* by the *important* people in my life and those I really care about.

D. To do what I do best; to become all I am capable of becoming; to achieve my fullest potential; and to make a worthwhile *contribution*.

As you reflect on these four statements, does any one of them come close to describing what you feel is your life purpose? Would some combination of statements or parts of them be useful in describing your life purpose? Were you at all surprised by how closely you identify with one of the statements?

Expanding Our Awareness About Purpose

Here is something very important to understand about our statement of life purpose. The words are not our purpose; the words merely serve as symbols for our true purpose, which is quite unique and is far more accurately represented as a feeling than as words. Our written statement of life purpose, which this chapter is intended to help us prepare, will end up being like an exquisite, finely polished jewel box in which we collect the unique feelings that reflect our true purpose in life. We want this purpose to help in truly guiding our life. Words cannot do that. Only the purest feelings of our heart can do that. The words we eventually choose for our completed statement of life purpose will serve as the instantly accessible collection point for those feelings. Isn't this exciting?

The intent of this chapter is to enrich your intellectual understanding of the deeper intuitive meaning behind each of the special words you find meaningful. And, for those of us who identify strongly with the word *control* in Statement A, the next few paragraphs may very well provide some of the most profound insights into our motivation we have ever encountered. When compared to the powerful insights about to occur for those who are *control-motivated*, any I have to share with the other three types will seem like a walk in the park.

For starters, let's look at the underlined word *control.* It derives its strong meaning for those at the upper end of intellectual and emotional intensity in the following manner: When gotcha's occur for us, we take our big hurt feelings and our big unfilled needs and with a correspondingly big intellect, stuff them in a box and clamp the lid. That's *control!* At the hypothetical extreme of this, we not only clamp the lid, but we encase it in concrete. What do we do then with all of our *control* capabilities? By this time they are compulsive, of course, and must be expressed somehow, so we set out to impose our version of *control* upon others around us.

There is only one difficulty with this, even in its mildest form. Look at what gets "stuffed" under the lid. The empty buckets. All of those big throbbing needs waiting to be fulfilled got mixed in with our hurt feelings and are now tucked away under our "detachment" lid, being "successfully" controlled. No wonder we have such a big empty space in our lives when it comes to feeling a sense of real satisfaction or fulfillment from our many accomplishments!

Even though some of us identify quite strongly with the initial wording of the first generic statement of purpose, we must fully adjust the meaning of the word *control* before we can expect it to help us achieve fulfillment. We must come to realize that fulfillment can only occur when we learn to successfully *control* the *removal* of our lid. We could therefore replace the word *control* in the statement with the words "full expression," and it would begin to represent something capable of being fulfilled. That would be a scary thought, though, wouldn't it? Wow! *Control* removing our lid? That flies right in the face of our greatest fears. Just the thought of having all of our hurt feelings and unfilled needs pop up, out of *control,* is frightening.

It comes down to the question of how badly we want fulfillment. Perhaps we could take *control* and plunge in, counting on the truth of the statement we referred to earlier by Ralph Waldo Emerson, "Do the thing you fear to do, and the death of fear is certain." Take it from one who has been there: the ultimate sense of fulfillment that can be gained by taking *control* of removing the lid is well worth the short-term anguish of getting it started. After all, it's "pay me now, or pay me later," and, to quote Emerson again—from his essay on compensation—the interest rate on later is "compounded upon compounded."

What we are doing in this entire chapter is attempting to use our analytical minds to understand true motivation—which is a purely intuitive issue. As it turns out, our analytical mind has two design features which strongly influence its way of perceiving this issue, as well as many others. First, it is designed for data acquisition purposes. This causes it to see motivation from a data acquisition perspective. In other words, it perceives that the way to fulfill our need to feel *important* is to collect from everyone available their recognition of how *important* we are. This view of motivation is almost universally accepted in the Western world. It is virtually all that is taught academically. But wait. There's more.

Upside-Down and Backwards

Our analytical mind is also designed for imaging purposes. It is perfectly designed to reflect back an undistorted image of exactly what it has received. This is where our self-image is located, and it is also the reason our mirroring principle can be so accurate and useful. Now, if we happen to know anything at all about images, we will also know they are always upside-down or backwards. This awareness is profoundly instructive when it comes to uncovering the way our analytical mind distorts our understanding of motivation. This is also where our bucket model really begins to shine. We all see the buckets as sitting upright, waiting to be filled. Right? Unfortunately that's an upside-down understanding of how our needs really get fulfilled. The buckets must be turned over and poured out in order for fulfillment to occur. It is as if each contains a metering device, and the more they pour out the fuller they feel. Let's look at the self-esteem bucket, for example, where our need is to feel *important*. The very best way for us to get that need truly fulfilled is to pour "importance" all over others. It goes the same for the social needs bucket, where our need is to feel loved. This need is most truly filled when we allow an abundance of love to pour through us out into the hearts of others.

Abraham Maslow actually discovered this phenomenon, too, yet apparently he didn't realize it. Notice the word *contribution* is underlined in purpose Statement D. Anyone who identifies strongly with the self-actualization achievement patterns will instantly recognize the entire statement as being a complete, accurate, finished statement of their life's purpose. Done. Next question. That statement, "To do what I do best; to become all that I am capable of becoming; to achieve my fullest potential; and to make a worthwhile *contribution*," is a direct quote from Maslow's work on self-actualization. It is a universally accurate statement of the driving force present in every person who operates at the self-actualization level. And, of all the words in the entire statement, the one which resonates most deeply with self-actualizers is pure, no-strings *contribution*. As in the unconditional pouring out of the bucket.

Apparently it never occurred to Maslow that the only way any of the other levels of need can truly be fulfilled is by tipping over the buckets and pouring them out, too. Imagine what transformation could occur in our societies if this truth were widely understood, appreciated and practiced!

The Water In a Fire Hose

Let's go back and incorporate one additional perspective into our expanding awareness around the word *control* in the first generic statement of purpose. I like to think of motivation as the water in a fire hose. When we are born it is as if we are standing back several feet from the end of the hose, which has no nozzle. The diameter of the hose, and thus the volume of water that can flow through it, is a reflection of our genetic mental capacity. Our analytical mind is the raw material to be used for building a nozzle to use in directing the flow of our "water," or creative energy.

Now, since the end of the hose initially has no nozzle, what would you expect it to do when the hydrant is opened and the water begins to flow? It's going to flop all over the place, spraying "water," or our undisciplined creative energy, over everyone in sight. The higher our intensity, of course, the more it "sprays" all over people. In a culture which fails to honor feelings, this is not a good thing! The odds are we will soon be receiving a consistent message that the purpose of our life is to "cap" that hose. Our response, unfortunately, will be to use the raw material of our analytical mind to build ourselves a valve to shut off the flow, rather than to pursue its intended use as a nozzle to direct the flow. With the valve securely in place, our view of motivation becomes one of collecting drops of water to "shove" backwards through the valve and into the hose. No wonder we experience so little fulfillment!

Our analogy of the nozzle directing the flow ties back very nicely to the analogy of the permanent magnet, too, doesn't it? Notice how the directed flow of energy creates a powerful magnetic effect that "effortlessly" attracts to us the very symptoms of success so many others are "efforting" to collect. The effortless high performer is giving out of what is seen as an unlimited supply, and is using his or her analytical mind as a finely tuned nozzle to carefully direct the flow of that unlimited energy. What a beautiful picture. Do you think we have built an adequate case for gaining *control* of removal of the lid? To further modify our initial generic statement of purpose, we might now wish to say, "to gain fully focused expression of all of our feelings . . . ." Wouldn't this be the ultimate in *control?*

The words, *power* and *influence,* are also underlined in that initial statement. As originally stated, the word *power* implies obtaining or securing power. This need relates directly to the need to feel *important* experienced by the person with the self-esteem achievement patterns. From the *control-motivated* perspective, this need to feel *important* is viewed as a need to be *in control* of being *important.* Approached in this manner, however, it has little or no chance of being fulfilled. Once we transform our understanding of pouring out the buckets, we will see it differently. To be *in control* of feeling *important,* we must pour *importance* all over others. Therefore, if we simply add the letters *e-m* to the front of the word *power,* we position ourselves to *empower* others—an activity with the potential to be truly be fulfilling.

The word *influence* ties directly to the word *contribution,* which we have already explored. From the detached, *control-motivated* perspective, however, the need to make a *contribution* is perceived as a need to be *in control* of how our *contribution* is being received. That's *influence.* For those of us who resonate with the need to *influence* others, I recommend continuing to use the word *influence.* As we gain *control* of removal of the lid, we will experience a gradual shift in the meaning of the word, until *influence* eventually becomes the equivalent of pure *contribution.* When this happens, we can recognize it as a pretty strong validation of our growth process. By that time, of course, we will no longer need any external validation.

The generic purpose statement, "to fully *accept myself* and to know I am *accepted* by others as a worthwhile person," has been developed for the person who relates most directly with the social needs achievement patterns. It is not stated here exactly the way they would feel it. I have added, "to fully *accept myself*," to the front of the statement to make it possible for fulfillment to occur. Since we have already discussed the generic statements relating to both the self-esteem and self-actualization achievement patterns, we're ready for some mentor-coaching questions.

What have you found most useful from our exploration of the four generic statements of life purpose? What was the most revealing new insight you gained into your own motivation? What new piece has fallen into place in your picture of the overall motivation puzzle? Even though this is not our goal directly, what idea might have made the biggest contribution to your understanding of other people?

Chapter Seventeen

Unique Influences
on Purpose

Being Unique and Different

Two additional generic statements of purpose can now be added to the brew we're concocting together. Neither has anything to do with our buckets or Maslow. Instead, they both describe a source of motivational drive which is always found at the very highest levels of analytical and intuitive intensity. This drive is also noticeably absent in the rest of the population. Each of the two statements express the exact same inner drive, but from different perspectives. You may very well identify with this unique source of drive if, in the first exercise of Chapter 15, your initial choices of patterns included Pattern C, "being unique and different; rising above the norm and having our achievements distinguish us from the crowd." The first statement describes how this drive is experienced by high-intensity people whose development leans toward the analytical side. The second describes how this drive is experienced when their development leans toward the intuitive side.

1. To continually learn and learn (and learn), while gaining as much knowledge as possible during my lifetime.

2. To experience life to the fullest, while continually expanding my capacity for growth and understanding.

For those of us who relate strongly to either of these generic statements, the expanded explanations of this drive and how it works can make a big contribution to understanding our life's purpose. If you do not identify with either statement, the added explanations will at least offer useful insights into others you may know. It is typically easy to tell whether or not they apply to us.

A Powerful Drive to Learn

Having an extremely high level of mental and emotional intensity is either a blessing or a curse. Any of us whose drive comes from a powerful need to learn, or to be gaining the richest possible experience from life, can quickly confirm the intensity of our feelings and needs. It is possible for this need to motivate us to pursue learning in the pure academic sense, but this need is certainly not confined to such limited forms of learning as is found in schools and books. Instead, it may take the form of an insatiable appetite to learn and experience any number of new and varied ways of doing things.

The tendency to become quickly and easily bored is among the most obvious clues that the need to learn or to have enriching experiences is a vital motivating force in our life. When this drive applies to us, the following description resonates quite strongly. Whenever we have learned as much as we wish to know about something we have been fascinated in, our ability to stay focused in that area is absolutely gone. Vanished. For those more intuitively oriented, substitute the word "experienced" in place of "learned" above. Otherwise the statement remains the same.

When this occurs on a job, it can be quite painful, because we must then rely on the energy-draining use of willpower for our motivation. Under such circumstances, we might expect to find ourselves struggling to maintain an image of still being motivated and committed, yet be privately agonizing over what we feel must surely be something wrong with us. There is nothing wrong with us. This is just a natural phenomenon which occurs all too often with exceptionally bright people.

Here is another telltale clue that the drive to learn is a motivating force in our life. Most people in this category live with a powerful inner frustration over what they feel is an inability to focus all of their energy, talent and ability. Here is another example of the difficulties posed by looking at the world through our own set of eyes. With the overabundance of energy, talent and ability people of this type were born with, who wouldn't be challenged by trying to bring it all into focus?

With its Test for Aptitude Potential, the Johnson-O'Connor Institute provides an additional source of validation for my observation about this focusing challenge being related to high intensity and intelligence. When high-intensity individuals take this extensive, highly respected test, they usually score well above average in potential for as many as 12 or more of the 19 aptitudes it measures. This compares to four or five aptitude potentials scoring above average for the normal person. From a practical standpoint it is difficult at best to put more than three or four aptitudes to work at any given time. For the high-intensity person, this leaves as many as eight to ten of the aptitudes clamoring for our attention. It is easy to see from this how our frustration over the inability to focus our talent and energy can become magnified even further.

Earlier in this chapter I began pointing out some of the challenges faced by those who were genetically "blessed" with a high level of intellectual and emotional intensity. The initial challenges result from the way our needs are affected by the added intensity, as well as our awareness of all five levels of unfilled needs at the same time. That in itself is a lot to handle. Unfilled needs demand attention. So do our most promising aptitudes. Even though our aptitudes do not function in the same way as our fundamental needs, those which measure well above average in potential do have a very similar way of demanding our attention.

Here is how this works: Let's imagine ourselves as horse trainers, each with a stable of 19 horses. If 16 of our horses are used for trail riding and three of them are thoroughbred racers, we will be able to give the thoroughbreds just about all the attention they need, and our trail horses will pretty much take care of themselves. This picture changes dramatically as we change the mix. Let's now draw a comparison to the person whose intensity level puts them in the *control-motivated* category. Now we have eight or nine thoroughbred racers to take care of and only ten or 11 trail horses. Each of those high-strung, promising thoroughbreds demands our attention. There is little chance, however, for us as individual trainers to focus proper attention on all of them. Just think of the anguish of trying to resolve this dilemma. This is nothing, however, when compared to the dilemma we face if our intensity is high enough to put us in the learn-drive category. Here we have at least a dozen promising thoroughbreds, each demanding attention, and one very bright horse trainer tearing their hair out.

It is quite common for those of us with a high drive to learn to focus on one area of learning only long enough to partially and temporarily satisfy the "exercise" needs of three or four aptitudes involved in that area of learning. We then become torn between digging in and continuing to learn in this area, or allowing the clamor of eight or more unexercised, high potential aptitudes to draw our attention away into an entirely new area of learning. Yes, focusing our talent and energy can certainly be a challenge.

Perhaps this is why President Calvin Coolidge once said, "Unrewarded genius is almost a proverb." Some of us who have faced this dilemma have become jacks of all trades and masters of none. That was certainly my own situation before making these discoveries about the nature of the drive to learn. I was into gardening, photography, fishing, reading and any form of self-improvement. I even built my own stereo system—as in soldering each transistor and resistor in place—as well as doing all of the woodwork to build its beautiful, six-foot-long cabinet. I would sooner take apart a broken clock and learn how to make it work than either throw it away or take it to a repair shop.

Then I learned about commitment—and about the need to focus. I didn't realize it at the time, but any of us with the drive to learn will, by definition, have enough raw talent to accomplish just about anything we set our minds to. When we decide to become the "best on the planet" at doing something we could enjoy doing, there is a good chance we could pull it off. In my case, I did this rather flippantly in 1970, when I first decided to become the best on the planet at figuring out WHAT'S RIGHT. (The significance of that decision is really striking me as I write this.) I have been much more aware of the decision made in 1976 to narrow and intensify my focus on becoming the best on the planet at understanding commitment.

Here is the analogy I distinctly remember using at the time. When I wished to pursue my interest in photography, my limited funds confined me to using a Kodak Instamatic. This was the story of my life as a jack of all trades and master of none. I knew if my life were to ever amount to anything, I would have to temporarily set aside all of my varied interests in learning and became totally focused on one thing—mastering the understanding of commitment. At the time, I recall thinking this might require about an eight year commitment. I also recall thinking that by truly mastering this understanding of commitment, I would radically alter my earning capacity. I therefore pictured myself emerging into an entirely new context within which I could pursue my wide interest in learning. If I then wished to learn about photography, I could well afford to do so with a Hasselblad. If I wished to learn about woodworking, I could pursue that interest in my own fully equipped shop, etc. That's pretty much how it has turned out, too. It was just under nine years later when I was invited by Fred Smith to come to Memphis and work with his team at Federal Express.

I believe this story offers an important lesson for all of us who possess this unique and powerful drive to learn. We have what it takes to become very good at whatever we choose. The type of intense, long-term commitment I have described here will force us to focus on the development of at least a third of those aptitudes within us that have "thoroughbred" potential. It will also force us to sustain this focus over a long enough period of time to assure full development of the key aptitudes required to achieve mastery. What about the clamor for attention coming from the other two-thirds of our thoroughbred aptitudes not being exercised? To succeed with this approach, we must be sure to structure the motivation for our commitment so it will allow us to temporarily ignore that clamor.

In response to a sustained period of keeping ourselves focused in this manner, we can expect two delightful benefits. First, the experience of riding a well-trained thoroughbred is exhilarating, to say the least. It is something akin to the experience of effortless high performance and being on a roll. Second, as masters, we are usually in position to earn handsome rewards for our services. As we do so, we can comfortably afford to begin a serious program of exercising our other "thoroughbred" aptitudes. That would seem like the best of all worlds.

Managing Others With the Drive to Learn

What if we find ourselves facing the challenging task of needing to direct the efforts of those who are obviously motivated by this powerful drive to learn? First, we will want to get them a copy of this book. The ideal is for each of us to manage our own motivations and commitments. We may, however, be dealing with others who have not yet mastered the challenge of focusing all of the talent and energy which comes with the drive to learn. In this case, there is a wonderfully obvious solution. It works particularly well to simply assign such individuals to a task where they are sufficiently over their heads to be forced to harness their drive to learn in order to survive. We have all learned the hard way how futile it is to expect results from people with this drive in areas where their interest in learning is no longer strong enough to keep them focused.

It is quite common for individuals with the learn-drive to become bored after 18 months or less, and lose their ability to stay focused and committed. This occurs whenever they reach the point of having learned as much as they wish to know about any area in which their learning has been focused. At this point, we must be prepared to reassign their jobs to others as soon as possible, and then find new challenges for them where they will again be over their heads. In case you missed it, we must be ready for the same thing to happen all over again in another 12 to 18 months. Remember, the only way out of this dilemma is for the learn-drive person to take over the responsibility of managing their own drive in the manner described earlier.

243

How Do You Relate To All of This?

Here is another case of the challenge of seeing the world through our own set of eyes. Those of us with the drive to learn seldom realize how bright we really are. It is therefore quite common for us to experience considerable surprise when we discover the behaviors described here occur only among the brightest and most emotionally intense people in our culture. A common reaction is for us to assume everyone would wish to place themselves in this category and attempt to identify with the above behaviors. This is not the case, however. Instead, if you are one who does not identify with the learn-drive behaviors, I am sure you will confirm that you are quite pleased at not having to deal with this little challenge. I also know you appreciate being given information to help you deal with others who face these particular challenges.

Finally, if the drive to learn *does* play a key role in your personal motivation, you will surely find it useful to weave many of the above insights into your statement of purpose. This, after all, is the real purpose of presenting it here.

In what way will you be different for having reflected upon the information about the drive to learn? What aspect of it came as the biggest surprise to you? What aspect was the most validating? If the information does, in fact, describe your own experience of yourself, what aspect of it is still somewhat uncomfortable for you to accept? What is the message for you in that feeling of discomfort?

Shedding More Light on the Mystery of Life Purpose

The concept of light is being independently studied in at least three fields of science, including the field of medicine. In addition, it has been studied forever by the various religions of the world. The findings from these diverse studies have great relevance to our efforts to define our own personal purpose in life. It is certainly no accident that experts from the fields of physics, psychology, medicine and religion are each being drawn toward strikingly similar conclusions relative to the mystery of life purpose.

Before reflecting on some of these conclusions, I would like to point out that our intuitive mind—the place where our purpose is already known—is quite often symbolized by a lightbulb. This, too, is more than coincidence. It happens independently of whether the person drawing the analogy is speaking from a psychological perspective, an artistic perspective or a physiological perspective. It is one of those mysterious phenomena which goes beyond logical explanation. Perhaps you have had one of those experiences where an intuitive insight was accompanied by a barely perceptible electrical shock effect—which sometimes even coincides with a flash of light. These experiences are universal in nature and do not happen by chance.

A brief review of religious and spiritual perspectives on light will quickly remind us how each of the world's religions either identify God with, or even refer to Him as light. Jesus Christ is quoted as saying, for example, "I AM the light of the world. In me there is no darkness." Eastern religions also speak of light, particularly as in enlightenment.

To explore some of the converging studies from a medical stand-point, we have only to review any of the many well-documented experiences of the "clinical death" phenomenon. All patients who return from this experience, which is also known as a "near death experience," report an experience of coming face to face with a bright light, or some-times even a "being of light." In most cases where someone has "seen the light" in this way, they later describe their lives as having been dramati-cally changed by the experience. Since the light doesn't communicate with words, however, few who experience this phenomenon can describe what causes the profound changes in their lives.

Of specific relevance to this discussion are reports gathered from a few individuals with unusually high awareness levels who have described their experiences of clinical death. It seems people with average or low awareness levels merely sense the light. At the higher awareness levels, however, people always return to describe how they have received what seems to be a profoundly important message from the light. This message is never transmitted in words. It is only transmitted as a feeling.

In every case I know of where this has happened, the person reports having great difficulty in attempting to translate this highly significant feeling message into words which adequately express its true meaning. In spite of feeling great anguish over the inadequacy of words to express the message, however, people all over the world, in every language, have always chosen the same words to express it. Here are those words in the English language:

"The purpose of life is to learn to love."

I can only conclude that at the very centermost core of my purpose in life—as well as yours—is the need to learn to love. In this case "to love" seems to mean to have unconditional regard for ourselves and others around us. It is also clearly intended for each of us to have our own unique way of interpreting this for ourselves. One of the generic ways I express my own life purpose is, for example, "to discover just how much of God's love I can allow to flow through me with no interference on my part." This seems like a good time to remind ourselves again that the words are not our purpose. Words are merely collection points for feelings that connect us deep down inside to our true purpose.

Quantum Physics Speaks to Us About Purpose

Several books invite us laypersons to take a peek at what is happening in the fascinating world of quantum physics. Among these are *The Tao of Physics* and *The Turning Point* by Fritjof Capra, *The Dancing Wu Li Masters* by Gary Zukav, *Stalking the Wild Pendulum* by Itzak Bentov and *A Brief History of Time* by Stephen Hawking.

These books and others tell us that many of the physicists doing research with particle physics and light are reaching the astonishing conclusion that "the basis for all matter may be a philosophy." Some of these scientists have even reported getting very spiritual insights while attempting to break the atom into its smallest parts and explore the most intricate relationships between these parts.

Perhaps of greatest significance to our discussion here is the work of scientists who have broken the atom into quarks, which are described as "principles of light." This research suggests in addition that quarks cannot exist alone. They only exist in pairs or multiples, and must be continually involved in the mutual, instantaneous exchange of even more elusive forms of energy called "gluons."

To my way of thinking, these scientists provide support from an unusual source for my hypothesis about our buckets getting filled by tipping them over and pouring them out. In other words, if we think of our purpose only in terms of what we can get out of life, we have surely missed it and are unlikely to experience fulfillment. Only when we think of our purpose in terms of what we have to give do we connect with something that can truly be fulfilled. Great leaders would certainly have something to add to this.

The Great Leaders' Viewpoint

No exploration of the overall concept of life purpose and its role in our motivation would be complete without considering the nature of the purposes that have inspired, guided and motivated great leaders. Such notable men and women of history as Abraham Lincoln, Thomas Edison, Eleanor Roosevelt and Mother Teresa would surely have much to tell us about the role of purpose in their lives.

Our key observation here is that all such giant contributors to humankind seem to be connected to a greater purpose—one which is outside themselves and much bigger than themselves. Perhaps our highest level of greatness is reached by defining a purpose which allows us to reach deep inside ourselves to the unlimited source of creative energy and talent which frees us to be truly big givers of ourselves. Here is another way of saying it: Maximum personal growth, maximum personal accomplishment and maximum personal fulfillment may all be reached only through maximum giving of ourselves.

This completes my efforts to equip you to move forward and put into writing your own statement of life purpose. *As the big moment approaches, what would you say has helped you the most to prepare for this task? What, for example, did you find most useful in my reflections on light? In what way do you anticipate the information on the drive to learn will contribute? How about the four generic statements of life purpose, and in particular, all of the insights we explored around the detached control perspective?*

Chapter Eighteen

Creating Your Own Purpose Statement

Let's Put Our Purpose In Writing

Our next task—should we be willing to accept it—is to choose a special set of words to represent the intuitive driving force which is our personal mission and purpose in life. As one last reminder, our purpose is not the words we write down. The words are to act like a sticky strip of fly paper to catch all of the feelings capable of connecting us with our true purpose. In fact, I like to think of the words as a beautiful vessel containing all the feelings which represent our life purpose. Then whenever we are at a crossroads in our daily lives, be it big or small, we can take our anticipated direction and immerse it into the vessel of feelings collected conveniently here for our use. Over time, and with consistent practice, we will become keenly perceptive of what choices fit or don't fit with our purpose.

Here are two more questions which seem to help the process. First, in what ways do you feel you are truly special? Do your best to identify at least four ways, and write each one out on a separate sheet of paper as an "I am _____" statement. Once you have completed at least four statements, you can return for my next question. PAUSE

For many people this next question has produced wonderful insights into a key driving force in their lives. This question doesn't resonate with everyone, but when it does it can be truly useful. Answer only if it seems important. "What am I most aware of having missed out on during my growing up years?" You may wish to take a few moments right now to reflect on any feelings this question brings up. Before continuing, be sure to write down any insights you get. **PAUSE**

When this question hits pay dirt, it allows us to recognize the source of a major drive which may still be influencing us today. For example, the first time I looked at this question, it was immediately obvious to me that I missed out on "connecting" with my father. This helped me to understand the source of my present-day motivation both to connect with you at the deepest level possible, and ultimately to truly connect with my own inner self. Patterns which show up here usually point to being highly motivated to make up for a perceived deficiency during our growing-up years.

I encourage you to now set aside some time and develop a first draft of your life purpose statement. To do so, you may want to refer back to the following points:

❖ Ideas and insights gained during our discussion of generic statements of purpose in the early part of this chapter.

❖ All insights gained while exploring success patterns in Chapter 15.

❖ The statements just completed about ways in which you are special.

❖ Any insights gained from reflecting on the information presented in this chapter about the drive to learn.

❖ Your best sense of how you may be influenced today to fill a void in any area you may have perceived to be missing during your growing-up years.

You may wish to begin your statement with the words, "My purpose in life is to . . . ." Set aside the book and give yourself the awesome gift of completing at least a draft of this statement now. `PAUSE`

Validating Our Purpose Statement

One of the true high points of our consulting work has always been the half-hour discussion which takes place among a group of peers who have just come back together after writing down their purpose. A common response is surprise at how easy it was. Another response is a sense of needing to validate what has been felt and written down. A third response is the astonished discovery of how their purpose has been there all along. This turns out to be the key for validating those who still remain uncertain about what they have written down.

It can be extremely helpful, once we have our purpose statement in writing, to revisit as many as 15 or more of our past decisions and explore how each of them aligns with our purpose statement. In doing this, we quickly see why some of our decisions worked out so well, and why others have not. When examined closely, we can discover many ways in which our most successful decisions reflect an extra measure of alignment with our purpose. It is particularly helpful to identify decisions which somehow did not work out as well as we might have wished. Upon close examination, we will always see how some aspect of our decision was clearly out of alignment with our purpose. This process of reflecting on past decisions and holding them up against our purpose statement is an outstanding way to prepare us to use it most effectively in making future decisions.

This is worth expressing again: Exploring the ways in which our past decisions either align or don't align with our freshly minted life purpose statement equips us to make all future choices and decisions with much greater clarity. And not only will our decisions be clearer, but once we get a firm, firm grip on our purpose in life, we eliminate the option of being distracted by negatives around us. This, therefore, is the ultimate key to getting ourselves on a roll and keeping us there. It is the key to effortless high performance.

I always enjoy wrapping up this discussion with the following observation. Since our purpose has been here all along, isn't it great to finally know what it is!

What are you feeling right now? What is the biggest insight you gained from reviewing your past decisions to check their alignment with your purpose? How do you see this process helping you to make future decisions? What difference will all of this make in your ability to achieve WHOLE-HEARTED *commitment to a goal when you know it is in full alignment with your purpose?*

This completes our introduction of purpose. It is ultimately the healthiest, least stressful, most highly productive source of commitment in our lives. We commit *with* our purpose *to* a goal. Before moving on to address goals, however, we have one more area to address around commitment. What are the common obstacles that block commitment and how can we prevent them from inhibiting us from moving on to experience our own WHOLEHEARTED commitment?

Chapter Nineteen

Removing
Commitment Obstacles

Commitment Obstacles

Throughout this book I hold up WHOLEHEARTED commitment as the biggest single factor contributing to effortless high performance. This chapter on purpose—the healthiest source of commitment— would not be complete without addressing five principal obstacles which can effectively block us from becoming WHOLEHEARTEDLY committed. As we review each of these obstacles and reflect on their potential impact in our lives, let's give some thought to the question of which one gets in our way most frequently.

The first commitment obstacle presents itself to those of us who use detachment as a defense mechanism. Detachment is used as a way for us *control-motivated* types to separate ourselves intellectually from our painful emotions. It is a defensive response automatically triggered whenever we assign negative value to facts. This, of course, is the very act which generates the negative emotions we think must be controlled or suppressed in the first place.

Notice how detachment and commitment—as well as the four similar states shown on the following page—are polar opposites. This means whenever we choose to feel threatened or vulnerable, we automatically limit our ability to reach WHOLEHEARTED commitment. Please review carefully the five polar opposites to detachment shown below, for they just might reveal some insights into how we can become more fully committed.

Detachment ------------- Commitment

Detachment ------------- Involvement

Detachment ------------- Intimacy

Detachment ------------- Trust

Detachment ------------- Expressing Feelings

The solution to this first commitment obstacle is simply to free ourselves from assigning negative value to facts. Once we do so, detachment gradually disappears as an obstacle to commitment. Much of the content of this book is directed toward this end.

Commitment obstacle number two presents itself to those of us who are a bit too strongly oriented toward keeping all of our options open. If we experience this condition, we can probably see ourselves standing back where we can survey all possible options, hesitating to pick one and commit to it for fear of missing out on an even better option that is sure to come along.

Solution? We must simply learn to remind ourselves that commitment always leads us through some type of passage from which we emerge to discover a new panorama of more and better options. To think of commitment as giving up our options is an illusion. Commitment always leads us to more and better options.

Those whose intellectual and emotional intensity is at the upper end of the scale tend to look at things from many angles at once rather than straight on. This ability makes them particularly susceptible to commitment obstacle number three whenever they see everything that's wrong from many angles at once. This can be a major commitment obstacle if our intensity is high enough to put us in the learn-drive category. When used to see negatives, our multidimensional perception capability can easily cause us to be too aware of what's missing or "wrong" with whatever we are observing. Needless to say, most of us find it difficult to commit when blanks and errors are included in our picture.

Here is another interesting aspect of commitment obstacle number three we need to weave into our mix. I have now had 20 years to explore the effects of high mental and emotional intensity on motivation and behavior. Based on that experience, I believe as many as a third of us in the upper levels of mental capacity have a private, hidden fear of having people find out we are dumb. Do you see the connection? We're the ones who use our multidimensional perception capability to see everything that's missing. We then make the leap to thinking that, since we can't see the whole picture, we must be dumb. This was a real big one for me. It's why I was so astonished when I first made the link between emotional intensity and mental capacity in 1978.

This high intensity phenomenon can also be the source of an "I don't deserve" negative self-image. Here is how it works. Imagine that as bright youngsters, we enter some form of competition and win. Instead of being appropriately aware of the extra talent we are blessed with, we are conditioned to focus on WHAT'S WRONG or what's missing. This focus could easily keep us from accepting credit for our victory. "I don't deserve" is the negative self-image we then create for ourselves. If you happen to identify with being limited by either of these two negative self-image elements, be sure to go back and review the material on affirmations in Chapter 11 to develop a solution. Both aspects were certainly present in my own case, and my very first affirmation statement dealt directly with the deserve issue right up front.

Solution? We must learn to recognize when our multidimensional perception capability is interfering with our need to commit. We can then shift our thinking to focus on WHAT'S RIGHT rather than WHAT'S WRONG. As a personal insight, I have learned I can absolutely count on the rest of the world to do my negative thinking for me. I do not need to engage in it myself. Many times this has allowed me to plaster over some big blanks in my understanding and to continue moving forward. I always knew I could count on someone to come along and poke holes in my plaster job if it was truly important. I could then happily go back and do the work necessary to reach a full understanding. It continues to amaze me how often the blanks turn out to be irrelevant, or how the answers show up later—seemingly out of nowhere—at exactly the time they are needed. This approach has worked far better for me than the old one of allowing myself to become paralyzed by not having every answer needed before moving ahead.

Commitment obstacle number four is a particularly bothersome one for those of us who have the need to be in *control*. Our *control* perspective often traps us into viewing commitment as a giving up of, or loss of *control*—a condition which represents one of our greatest fears. If this condition applies to us, we will often have difficulty with delegation, too. This is because we naturally view delegation as giving *control* over to someone else, and even the thought of doing such a thing is abhorrent to us.

Solution? This one is quite simple, but far from easy to put into practice. We must continually remind ourselves that commitment is, in fact, our only available means of gaining true *control*. Yes, believe it or not, that's how it works. We need to reframe our understanding of commitment so we can move into it more readily. Then we can begin to experience the joys of commitment-based *control*.

Dissolving commitment obstacle number five is always fun. I like to call it "the tyranny of the urgent," and it presents itself repeatedly whenever our perspectives become too shortsighted. I'm sure you recognize the feeling. It's when we hesitate to commit to something which could really make a difference in our lives because we are not accustomed to thinking beyond next month. And, since we can't see ourselves getting it done in a month, we fail to commit at all.

Solution? Flag this page in the book. Then, whenever you get to thinking you just don't have enough time to get things done right, come back and fill in the three blanks again. I plan to reach at least age _____ before I die. This means I will live until at least the year _____. This means I have at least _____ years in which to achieve all of my remaining goals. Doesn't that make a strong case for getting on with it? With all that time remaining, it is much easier to commit to doing what we truly want to do and doing it to the very best of our ability.

Five Commitment Obstacles

❖ Detachment as a defense mechanism

❖ Keeping our options open

❖ Eagle-like ability to spot WHAT'S WRONG or missing

❖ Seeing commitment as loss of control

❖ The tyranny of the urgent

Which of the five commitment obstacles do you feel gets in your way most frequently? What idea proved most helpful to you among all the solutions offered? Of all the ideas offered in this chapter, which two or three do you anticipate will be most useful in allowing you to reach and enjoy a deeper level of WHOLEHEARTED commitment?

Chapter Twenty

A New Paradigm
For Goal-Setting

Exploding Misperceptions

Lots of people think they understand goal-setting. It would be better if they knew nothing about it, however, since the most commonly used approaches to setting goals are obstacle oriented and thus work to keep people from getting on a roll rather than truly helping them. As a result, my first task in this chapter is to clear up many misperceptions about the goal-setting process. I will then provide a helpful framework of seven key elements you will want to consider when setting out to create an ideal picture of yourself in the future.

It is useful to view the process of setting long-range goals as one in which we create a vision or take a snapshot of a point in time at least ten years into the future. The picture we create shows the progress we have made during those ten years toward fulfilling our life purpose. Even when done correctly, the process of creating this picture will consume lots of creative energy—more than the average person has readily available, in fact. When I introduced vision-building questions in Chapter 8, I put most of my attention on ways to make sure adequate energy is available to continue the process. Since this chapter is an expansion of the same process, the same observations apply. As we increase the use of value-finding questions to explore our strengths, we become more thoroughly grounded in those strengths, and we have more energy to use for completing this vitally important process.

There is one more potential source of energy for us to use in creating our vision. This is the excitement we would feel if we were fully aware of the benefits of being committed to reaching a set of goals. If more of us were conscious of these powerful benefits, we would see a lot more goal-setting done and a lot more success around us as a result. Three key benefits come to mind, all of which support the basic fact that people who set goals tend to reach them. The first is illustrated by the thermostat concept introduced in Chapter 11. When we set a goal, we establish in our brain a built-in servomechanism which automatically guides us and steers us toward our goal. Here is an analogy to show how it works.

The rocket used to put a man on the moon was said to be off course more than 99% of the time. The challenge of guiding the rocket has been compared to being in San Diego with an extremely high-powered rifle and attempting to shoot a bullet so accurately it could hit a specific window of a train in southern Florida going more than 90 miles per hour. It quite obviously cannot be done from San Diego. The only way to accomplish such a feat is to go to southern Florida and build ourselves a very big funnel. We then go to San Diego, point our gun in the general direction, pull the trigger and rush back to southern Florida where we use our funnel to guide the incoming bullet into our specific target window. This is exactly how the servomechanism in our mind works, once we give it a goal. This goal-seeking phenomenon is called cybernetics—which is why Maxwell Maltz titled his book, *Psycho-Cybernetics.*

When we first begin moving toward our goals, just as when a rocket first takes off, we can anticipate wide deviations from our target, with lots of corrections needed to keep us going in the general direction. The closer we get to our goal, the more finely tuned and subtle these corrections become. Notice the increased sense of effortlessness associated with this process.

This sense of effortlessness is also a byproduct of the second key benefit available from setting goals correctly. Setting a long-term goal establishes a sophisticated set of milestones in our mind which work just like a crowd of well-wishers who cheer us on every time we go by one of them. The energizing effect of this is like fuel for our rocket and is actually more powerful than having someone physically present to praise our efforts. The fact that this fueling mechanism is internally self-sustaining and not dependent on acknowledgment from others is an extremely important point to consider here.

The third key benefit of setting goals correctly—and by this I mean creating a vision of an ideal at least ten years into the future—is due to the vacuum effect generated by "holes" in the vision. This vision aspect is frequently overlooked in traditional goal-setting instructions, no doubt in part because it is the piece which requires the most energy. It is also the part, however, which offers the greatest potential. Traditional goal-setting instructions encourage us to set specific, tangible, measurable targets to be reached. Those instructions are excellent, and are fully adequate for most people. They just fail to tap into the full creative power of our intuitive mind. The instructions I am about to provide are intended to allow full access to all three benefits.

As a result of the interplay between these three benefits, the average time needed to reach a ten-year goal has been found to be seven years. In other words, just the process of putting a ten-year goal in writing has proven to take an average of three years off the anticipated time needed to reach it. This appears to be true regardless of the size of the goal. There are endless stories of people who have written down a ten-year goal and tucked it away in a drawer somewhere. I've lost count of how many have told me about being surprised when they stumbled across it five or six years later and realized it had already been accomplished. *In what way has it been helpful to see more clearly the benefits of setting long-range goals?*

Why Do It Backwards?

The vast majority of us approach the goal-setting process backwards. By this I mean we set goals for one month, three month, six month, one year, three years, etc. in that order. This approach is best described as a quantification of obstacles. Instead of its intended outcome, this approach automatically results in defining on paper all of the resistance factors which can prevent us from getting on a roll. The true intent of goal-setting is just the opposite. It is to get on paper all the commitment factors which will put us on a roll. In order to achieve this more desirable outcome, it is imperative for us to extend our thinking out beyond the obstacles—to where our minds are suddenly set free to think ideally. This is why I practically insist on taking your thinking out a minimum of ten years into the future as the starting point of your goal-setting process.

I have several points to make here. Even when executed poorly, the goal-setting process offers a host of important benefits. As we learn to think ideally, the power of these benefits goes up exponentially. If this appeals to you, and if you therefore wish to learn to think ideally—and thus take full advantage of this power—you must first be able to clear your mind from any form of distractions or obstacles. Now, this can be a bit challenging in an obstacle-oriented world. Most of us have been heavily conditioned to think that our very survival depends on our ability to identify and either overcome or circumvent the daily obstacles in our lives.

It's no wonder we do our planning backwards. Obstacles we see most clearly are those we expect to encounter over the next month. Those we see slightly less clearly are the ones we expect to encounter over the next three months, etc. Taking this approach to planning is certainly no way to get on a roll. This is why we ask you to go out at least ten years. Most of us can think of upcoming obstacles out to about eight years from now. An exception to this is if you have a five-year-old child in your home. Ten years from now, your wonderful child just happens to be age 15. I don't know about you, but most of us are capable of thinking of that as an obstacle. The criteria for determining how far out we must go to start our planning process is the number of years required to take our thinking out beyond every conceivable obstacle. As a general rule, this is ten years for most people.

One more good example of where we absolutely must go out more than ten years to begin the planning process is for those of us who are near age 55. At this age there is a great temptation to plan to retire at age 65, rather than to plan for what we'll be doing in retirement at age 70 or 75. If we miss this point and proceed to plan for age 65, the big spike in death rates for ages 66 and 67 is clear evidence that such an approach is little more than planning to die.

There are great examples of this longer view principle in action in the business world, too. In 1981, the company, Champion International, ran a series of ads describing its 76-year planning cycle. This was particularly interesting because a five-year planning cycle would be appropriate for most companies. Why do you suppose this company had a 76-year cycle? Quite simply, they are in the paper business, and it takes 75 years for each newly planted tree to finish growing. In order to practice the principle I am attempting to illustrate, they had to take their thinking out one year past the time when the tree was ready for harvest.

One more analogy and I will move on to describe the next obstacle. Imagine we encounter what appears to be a virtually insurmountable obstacle as we move down the path of life. From where we stand, in fact, there is no way to even see around it, let alone figure out how to get past it. Paralyzing, isn't it? But wait. When we look back from today at similarly intimidating obstacles present in our lives ten years ago, they no longer look so intimidating, do they? That's the wonderful benefit of hindsight. Now what is to prevent us from transporting our thinking out ten years into the future and getting it so firmly grounded in that space we can successfully practice "hindsight" in advance? Our chances of engaging in constructive thought about how to get past our presently "insurmountable" boulder go up dramatically when we view it as an almost imperceptible speck of dust in our distant past. When goal-setting is done properly it gives us this kind of access to "hind-sight-in-advance" decision-making.

Needing the Right Criteria?

So here we are, up to our neck in a culture which rewards us for being good at identifying and overcoming obstacles, and now we're told that in order to plan our lives correctly, we have to go where there are no obstacles. Whatever will we use for criteria to determine whether we have picked the right goal for ourselves? Alas, there is a solution for those who may be indecisive or have difficulty picking the right goals. It's called purpose. Our clearly defined purpose will serve as the perfect framework for evaluating any goal we can imagine to check whether it would be right for us. Therefore, the clearer we become about our purpose, the easier it becomes to choose the right goals.

When I get to this stage of the goal-setting process myself, I often find my purpose is more helpful for determining what will *not* work for me than it is in showing me what *will* work. In other words, sometimes it is easier for me to feel the "no fit" than it is to discern exactly what does "fit." Remember, our purpose defines the energy with which we can commit. Our goals define the outcomes to which we commit. We commit with our purpose to our goals. The real issue here is commitment. If we imagine a possible goal and then confirm its full alignment with our purpose, this does not necessarily mean it is the "right" goal for us. It only means the goal is one to which we could become WHOLEHEARTEDLY committed if we chose to do so. On the other hand, if we are contemplating a possible goal and find it clearly does not align with our purpose, we can be quite well assured it would be unwise to pursue its achievement.

Our final goal-setting obstacle is closely aligned with this need for a way to validate a goal as being right for us. Here, however, we come face to face with our reluctance to commit to a goal for fear it might be the wrong one. How can we know? Eventually, most of us learn this one the hard way. It is far better to be hard at work in pursuit of the wrong goal than it is to be without one. This is a hard lesson to learn, but goals are not to be cast in concrete. Goals must be flexible and easily changed. We must learn to view goals as a basis from which changes can be made.

It may interest you to know, by the way, that the very book you are reading grew out of my total commitment in 1970 to what turned out to be the wrong goal. If you will recall, the first goal I set was to become a nationally famous motivational speaker. After I had pursued this goal aggressively for a little more than four years, I was asked in a training exercise to write down my life purpose. Once my purpose was in writing, it became immediately clear to me that I had been pursuing the wrong goal. But was it really the wrong goal for me? It was certainly the wrong goal for me to continue pursuing, but how in the world would I have ever been able to define my purpose in life so easily if I had not been pursuing the "wrong" goal?

I have expressed this before, and I will now say it again: Goals are not the issue. WHOLEHEARTED commitment is the issue. In order for any of us to reach the state of effortless high performance, we simply must find a way to experience WHOLEHEARTED commitment. There is no other way to get there. You must remember, therefore, that a goal is only useful to the degree that it facilitates total commitment on a moment-to-moment basis. This is also why it is so incredibly important for us to be able to free up our minds to think ideally. None of us is capable of becoming WHOLEHEARTEDLY committed to anything we see as less than ideal. Once we understand this, it becomes easier for us to see our goals as points in the future which are continuing to evolve into a higher order of ideal.

Incidentally, I have occasionally encountered a person who seems able to achieve WHOLEHEARTED commitment on a moment-to-moment basis without the use of goals. To insist that such a person follow rules made for others and which do not apply to them would be counterproductive at best. We must learn to honor their unique ability to be committed without needing goals.

The Cruelest Thing a Sales Manager Could Do

I will close this section on shattering misperceptions with a story that carries several important messages. The event I will relate took place some 20 years ago, but I think it could easily have taken place last week and be just as valid. I had been invited to speak to a group of about 20 life insurance general agents. In order to be sure I got everyone's attention right away, I began with a bold statement. I announced that the cruelest thing a sales manager could do to his sales force was to get them to set one-year goals. I then went on to assert that if anyone on the sales force were to set and reach a one-year goal, they would suffer a loss from doing so. It is even more obvious that anyone who would set and fail to reach a one-year goal would also suffer a loss. As you can imagine, I did have their full attention.

As I went on to explain, if I were to set and reach a one-year goal, I would probably take much of the first three months of the following year to set up the next year's goal. This time is essentially wasted as far as sales production is concerned. I would then take the following three months to get myself psyched up and committed to achieving my goal. Another three months virtually down the drain. Then it's summer. Along about September I begin to realize if I am going to reach my goal for the year, I had really better get cracking. Here I dropped the big bomb and said, "That's why more than 50% of the life insurance sold in America is sold during the month of October." You could have heard a pin drop. Everyone's chin was on the floor, and not a single person spoke up to argue with what I had just said. They knew their numbers. They knew I was right. Just to sink the point in a little deeper, I added, "What kind of sales records could you each set if you could see that kind of performance taking place for several more months out of the year?" . . . And that was the outcome for those who set and *reached* their goals. What about those who failed to reach their goals? That is barefaced failure, any way you cut it.

On the other hand, I continued, if those one-year goals are set as a part of a ten-year plan, those who set and fail to meet their goals would produce every bit as much of a win for themselves as those who set and reached their goals. It is an entirely different ball game. Here is the way our mind works with this—assuming I have a commitment to achieve a set of ten-year goals. If I set and fail to reach a one-year goal that is part of my plan, it is as if on January 2nd I get a printout that itemizes everything I must adjust to get back on track to reach my ten-year goal. Then, every single one of those adjustment items is just as energizing or perhaps even more so than the person who is clicking away at their success. The person who sets and reaches a one-year goal in this context gets a big jolt of energy on January 2nd that serves to strengthen a commitment level that is already quite healthy. No wasting three months this year while waiting for the next year's goals to be set, and no wasting another three months waiting for commitment to be mobilized. All of that is already handled by the commitment that has been made to the ten-year goal. Let's get on a roll!

Well, enough of shattering misperceptions. *What are the two most useful ideas you have gotten from this chapter so far? After reading this information, what do you anticipate might be different about your next attempt to set your own long-term goals? How far out into the future will you need to go in order to think ideally?*

Elements of the Big Picture

How does one eat an elephant? One bite at a time. The task of transporting our thinking ten years or more into the future and creating a vision of the ideal for ourselves is one that can sometimes feel as big as an elephant. Each of the seven goal areas shown below offers questions that are intended to help divide our task into manageable chunks. I will first simply list the seven areas and their associated questions. Once they are listed, I will make some observations about ways to take full advantage of this framework.

A. *Spiritual Goals*

What does my spiritual life look like as I view it ten years from now? In what ways is it serving to influence and add sustenance the other parts of my life? How does the way I live my life reflect my relationship with the higher power that is my ultimate source of strength? What actions am I taking on a regular basis to preserve and enhance this vitally important relationship?

B. *Family Goals*

What does my marriage relationship and/or my relationship with each of my children look like as I view this picture ten years from now? Where are we living? How old are my children? In what special ways are their lives reflecting the guidance and support I have given them? In what kind of meaningful activities are each of them engaged? In what kind of special activities am I regularly engaged with my spouse and with my family?

C. *Career Goals*

Thinking ideally, and realizing that I now have at least ten years to prepare myself, how do I see myself earning a living in the year _____? In what ways is this allowing me to make the best use of all my talents and enjoy truly fulfilling accomplishments? In what ways is it allowing me to achieve my fullest potential?

D. *Self-Improvement Goals*

As I view myself ten years from now, what specific steps have I completed to broaden my horizons and improve my knowledge, attitudes and skills? What kind of self-improvement programs have I successfully completed? Which ones still lie ahead for me? In what kind of hobbies and other outside interests am I now engaged?

E. Health Goals

Specifically, in what kind of physical shape am I as I view myself ten years from now? In what kind of exercise programs am I consistently active? How free am I from dependence upon medication and drugs?

F. Social Goals

In what kind of social activities am I regularly engaged as I view myself ten years from now? In what clubs and organizations am I actively involved? What offices or other positions of responsibility have I held, or am I holding? What kind of entertainment do I enjoy? What kind of social engagements am I enjoying? How do I describe my circle of friends? In what ways are they similar to or different from the friends I have today?

G. Financial Goals

How much money is required on a yearly basis to fully support the above activities? As I view myself ten years from now, what progress have I also made toward accumulating wealth for my future years and for retirement? Besides my employment income, how are my additional earnings being generated? What is my level of satisfaction with this overall financial picture?

Priorities

Please note carefully that each of the seven goal areas are listed in order of importance for reaching the state of effortless high performance. This is particularly true about the final one, our financial goals. When starting out to set goals, it is very common for most of us to think of our financial goals first. I must caution you that, while setting financial goals first does not prevent us from reaching them, it definitely does not support getting ourselves on a roll, either! It is just another indication of our analytical mind's data acquisition influence. Notice, too, how I have shown the accountant's double underline just above the financial goals. This is to signify that our financial goals are intended to summarize the financial resources required to assure accomplishment of our other goals. As such, it can only be computed after the other six goal areas are fully defined.

The first three goal areas are also listed in priority order, while no indication of order is implied for the self-improvement, health and social areas. As for the first three, there simply is no way to reach and sustain the state of effortless high performance without being clear about our priorities in these goal areas. Perhaps it would be useful if I express my own sense of priorities here as an example.

First, I view all of this from both a self-responsibility and an alignment perspective. In other words, I feel a sense of responsibility to bring several areas of my life into alignment. I see these areas as levels with an order of importance. My highest-level of responsibility is to bring my conscious, rational mind into full alignment with my inner, intuitive self. I see this relationship between my analytical mind and my intuitive mind—between my head and my heart—as being a direct mirror of my relationship with the higher power that most of us would call God. It could also be said that my highest priority is to bring my thoughts, my actions and every aspect of my being into full alignment with God.

My second highest level of responsibility is then to support my wife, Patricia, in bringing about this same alignment process within herself. Notice that I am not responsible for her inner alignment, but for supporting her in taking her own responsibility for that alignment. I then see my third level of responsibility as working to bring our two lives into alignment with each other. Our success in this, of course, will be a reflection of the progress we are each making on our own internal alignment.

My fourth level of responsibility is then to support the people closest to me in taking responsibility for their own inner alignment. This sense of responsibility continues to extend itself to people further away from me. As it expands, note that I always focus first on supporting the individual's own internal alignment, and then on supporting their alignment with whatever larger group brings us into contact. At no time am I ever responsible for anyone but myself. It has been made painfully clear to me that I have all I can handle to exercise full responsibility for myself, and to think that I could be responsible for someone else is an illusion I no longer need to chase.

A Second Set of Priorities

Whenever we set out to build a vision, we must start with the knowns and work toward the unknowns. It is as if by describing the knowns, we are defining the outer boundaries of a vacuum and closing off its leaks. As this vacuum becomes more and more powerful, it works to attract all of the "answers" needed to transform all of the gaps in our vision into perfectly finished components for the bigger vision. To take full advantage of this powerful mechanism, you must begin by taking your thinking at least ten years into the future and asking yourself, "In which of the seven goal areas do I find items of the greatest certainty?" Would you agree that most of us would want to look first to the area of our family? It is as simple as starting with our own age. That will be a certainty. We then describe our spouse and any other members of our family along with their ages. All of this gives us an initial framework or context within which to begin the known aspects of our vision of an ideal.

271

Another way to look at this is to start with any aspects of the picture about which we have the clearest and strongest desire and move toward those areas to which we have given little or no thought. This is where it is so helpful to realize that our goals are not cast in stone. We are artists here, beginning with a blank canvas. If we put some ink on it that we later don't like, all we do is paint right over it with another color. This is pure creation, and we have far greater control over the outcome than most of us can even imagine!

You will also want to give yourself plenty of time to do this right. You might even wish to set up seven empty file folders and brainstorm with yourself for a week or two—or even a month. You could make little notes all week long on every idea that crosses your mind and collect them in the appropriate folders for use in stimulating your thinking, once you are ready to build your actual plan. As with all true brainstorming, your first step is to collect ideas with no judging allowed. Remember, you are building a dream, and the more ideal your dream, the more powerfully it will inspire your total commitment in the now.

How can we keep ourselves from feeling limited in any way while doing this? When setting goals myself, for example, I often think of something I would like to accomplish and then feel tempted to reject it, merely because I do not yet know how to make it happen. We must remember that the question of how to do something belongs in a totally different part of the planning process. Now is the time for pure invention. If we allow any how-to questions to be asked in this part, they can only detract from our success. In this part of the process, we are choosing to stick with pure creation, because it is a proven way to harness the power of our intuitive minds.

Let's now ask some mentor-coaching questions. *What have you found most useful about this way of creating an ideal vision of ourselves ten years from now by breaking down the big picture into seven elements? What questions did you find most thought-provoking? Which area were you most prepared to think about? Which area were you least prepared to think about? What insights are you gaining about yourself from this process?*

The Short-Range Action Plan

Only after completing the picture of our ten-year goals are we even prepared to think about our short-range action plans. We then begin this task by skipping all the way back from our ten-year vision to our two-year milestones. Be aware that it is largely a waste of time to think about any action items which might need to occur during the time period from two through ten years.

As we review each aspect of our ten-year picture, we want to ask ourselves how far we intend to move toward completing it by the end of the next two years. Then, if we are to make this much progress in two years, how far will we have to move in one year? How far in six months? Three months? Please note the movement from a distant viewpoint backwards to nearby action plans. The distant, intangible picture supplies all of the intuition-based criteria needed to define a set of logical, perfectly focused short-range action plans—which must be specific, measurable and concrete in order to be effective. And remember, none of them are set in concrete. They are only useful to us if they are appealing enough to inspire our total commitment. When they stop inspiring commitment, we need to see them as a basis from which changes can be made.

Listed below are several additional questions which can be used to stimulate and guide our thinking within this short-term planning process. I might also mention these questions tie in quite nicely to the piece on constructive direction at the end of Chapter 10.

* What are the results I expect to accomplish? By when?

* How do I expect to recognize each result when it is achieved?

* What measurements of performance do I plan to use?

* What obstacles must be overcome in order to get my plan moving or keep it moving?

* How do I plan to track my progress on my action items?

* Whose help or support do I expect or need to obtain?

* What resources do I expect to need that I do not already have?

* How do I expect to obtain the help, support and resources needed?

* When do I plan to begin?

* How much time do I expect it to require to complete the project?

* When do I expect to be finished?

* How do I plan to reward myself for a job well done?

How to Identify and Track Critical Success Factors

The final step in our strategic life planning process is to develop a way to keep track of what we are doing right. My working premise here is the well-known psychological principle that we get more of what we measure. To bring this into a clearer focus, I would bring our attention back to the idea of directing the flow of our energy—which has been an underlying theme of the entire book. I addressed it explicitly early in Chapter 4, when I described how the energy we put into our "weaknesses" causes them to expand. This seems to be a law of the universe. Directing our conscious, rational mind's attention to any given point will cause that point to expand.

If we accept the idea of expanding energy as true, then I suggest we have right in front of us the ultimate key to putting ourselves on a roll. All we have to do is identify two or three areas of activity which could put us on a roll if properly expanded. We must then simply find a way to keep our conscious, rational mind focused on these areas of activity. Since we know our rational mind loves to measure and compare things, the only task we have left is to develop a way for it to measure and track our progress in the two or three areas of activity that we will call our "critical success factors."

Let's cite an example to show how this works. Do you happen to know anyone who maintains a regular discipline of running? This could be anything from running for exercise to getting in shape for the next marathon, or even ultra-marathon. If you were to ask one of these people how far they ran last week, what kind of a response would you expect? Every runner I have ever known would be quick to tell me the exact amount of either time or distance they had recorded for their efforts last week. Now, what would you expect to be the critical success factor in this example? Might it be the energy needed for them to maintain the discipline of going out and doing it every day? If so, doesn't it make sense that the habit of keeping track of time or distance on a daily basis would be the probable source of that energy? That certainly is how I see it.

Listed below are some questions that are intended to help you clarify the key factors that are critical to your own success. Remember, you may not be fully prepared to put this step into practice until you have completed your long-range vision and your short-range action plan. At that point you will want to take full advantage of the energy-supplying power of identifying and tracking your own critical success factors.

❖ What three action steps can I take on a regular basis which will make the biggest overall difference in how well I succeed at reaching my goals? (Alternately, what three action steps are so critical to my success that, if not done effectively, would set me back the most?)

❖ What are some specific desired results I can watch for and measure to help me know how well I am doing in each of the above three areas?

❖ What are specific steps I could take to monitor and keep track of actions I am taking (my critical success factors) to produce the above desired results?

Once you have begun to experience the powerful benefits of identifying and keeping track of your own critical success factors, you may very well wish to pass along those benefits to others. The payoff for you in doing so would be to strengthen your skills in this area and keep them readily available for your own further use.

Wrap-up

This completes our treatment of the strategic life planning process which has been set forth in these last three chapters. We began by exploring our success patterns and then used insights gained from that to help us identify our purpose in life. This gave us the validation criteria needed to create a multifaceted vision of an ideal future to which we can become WHOLEHEARTEDLY committed. In order to harness the power of that commitment, we then established a framework for developing a set of action plans that will be needed to transform our current reality into that ideal. Finally, as a way to fully energize that commitment, we have explored the power of identifying and tracking our critical success factors. By mastering each of these steps, you will have secured for yourself the ultimate strategic thinking advantage. You will have established a fully integrated, "hindsight-in-advance" decision-making process. You will have also put in place a way to keep your analytical mind focused on areas that will continually expand your success.

Your mentor-coach would now like to ask what you expect to do with this information. *What do you anticipate will be the greatest payoff for you from completing all of these steps as they have been laid out? What might be your biggest obstacle to getting started immediately? In what way could you set up some critical success factors right now that you could begin tracking to assure your completion of this project?*

Chapter Twenty-One

Living a Life With No Downside

Unshakably Committed

One of my key findings about visionary leaders and other effortless high performers is their ability to move forward and take risks in spite of any apparent lack of support around them. Their ability to remain remarkably flexible in their thinking and open to new ideas, while staying unshakably committed to their goals, is quite amazing. It would be easy to explain this if they were compulsively "attached" to their goals, but this is clearly not the case. My fascination with all of this has led me to invest a good deal of time in attempting to gain an understanding into exactly how they sustain both their openness and commitment at the same time. Here are some of my observations.

Why do you suppose that, left to our own devices, most of us can be counted on to take a self-protective, WHAT'S WRONG approach to nearly every issue or circumstance we encounter? Could it be that we have bought into the perception that life is a win/lose proposition? Could it be that we therefore see a need to be always on the alert to avoid losing?

I find effortless high performers to have somehow been able to dismiss any thought of "losing" from their minds. Please understand that I am not talking here about something as simple as them being confident that they can *avoid* losing. Instead, the thought of losing is simply inconceivable to them. It doesn't exist. Period. As you can well imagine, this leaves them entirely free to give their full, undivided attention to finding new and exciting ways to win (i.e., achieve their goals). I even hesitate to use the word win in this context, since it implies the existence of "losing" as an alternative.

All of this has led me to a growing awareness of how adversely our minds are affected whenever we allow our attention to become focused on the "downside" of anything. Do you notice how, at the very instant the thought of a downside enters our mind, our thinking must shift to protecting ourselves from its effects? What does this do to the working partnership between our analytical and intuitive minds? We know that self-protective thinking requires us to disconnect from the inner knowing of our intuitive minds and direct our attention externally. Since this is exactly opposite the thought process required to remain on a roll, it would seem that we might wish to learn how to completely release ourselves from any thoughts of downside whatsoever. In other words, what must we do in order to shift from a win/lose way of looking at life to a can't-lose frame of mind? How could we learn to dismiss any thought of losing from our mind?

How to Develop a "Can't Lose" Attitude

I have identified at least eight distinctly different methods by which effortless high performers sustain their can't-lose frames of mind. They all practice at least one of the eight to keep their minds free from downside thinking. I view this mindset as being fundamental to your ultimate success at putting everything in this book into practice. You might even want to mark this page with a 3M Postit Note so you can refer to it as often as needed until you have chosen and mastered an approach that works for you. Since I carefully avoid offering "shoulds," I will offer each of these approaches in the form of questions for you to consider.

Hindsight In Advance

❖ *Could you learn to view the tasks and projects in which you are engaged or plan to undertake from the vantage point of having already completed them successfully? Do you notice how this allows you to practice a form of "hindsight-in-advance" decision making? Might it work for you to look back at your present circumstances from the perspective of a more ideal future? Would this enable you to practice the five levels of* WHAT'S RIGHT *questions to establish an effective path that would lead you to successful completion?*

❖ *Could you learn to view any problems or obstacles you are facing as opportunities? Could you learn to view them from the perspective of having already overcome them successfully? Would this allow you to practice "hindsight-in-advance" decision-making as described above? Could this be your key for consistently using* WHAT'S RIGHT *questions as a way to find and remove the obstacles from your path to success?*

Worst-Case Scenarios

❖ *Would it be effective for you to develop worst-case scenarios or tasks for projects in which you are engaged or plan to undertake? If you knew it would free you from the limitations of downside thinking, could you see yourself accepting—in your mind's eye only—the possibility of this worst case coming to pass? Would doing so allow you to keep your attention focused on achieving a result that is significantly better than your worst-case scenario? Would this approach enable you to generate significantly greater amounts of creative energy with which to complete your tasks?*

It's All a Game and We're Winning

❖ *Would it be possible for you to develop a discipline of reminding yourself that the all-important task or project on which you are working is, after all, "just a game"? Could you see yourself adopting the affirmation, "It's all a game and I'm winning"? Would such an approach work to eliminate downside thinking from your mind?*

❖ *Would it be effective (and possible) for you to pre-think accomplishment of your tasks and projects in such a way that you become fully comfortable with and confident in your ability to achieve the desired outcomes?*

Winning Is All There Is

❖ *Here is my favorite. Could you learn to define "winning" in such a way that there are simply no circumstances in which it cannot occur? For example, could you learn to see winning as acquiring tools, knowledge, skills and experience that will all be useful in helping you achieve an important long-term goal? Can you see how this automatically translates every experience into a win of some kind? This approach is so simple, I can't imagine why more people don't use it!*

❖ *Could you learn to remind yourself that there are an infinite number of ways to win in every circumstance you encounter? Would it work for you to then make a practice of identifying in advance many ways in which you could eventually win?*

There's No Such Thing As a Weakness

❖ *If you currently happen to define losing as any condition in which your "weaknesses" are uncomfortably exposed, can you see yourself fully adopting the viewpoint from Chapter 4 that weaknesses do not exist?*

Would this be the surest path for you to adopt the can't-lose frame of mind? Does it make sense to you that, as defined here, losing would then no longer be within the realm of possibility?

As I was completing the above list, my thoughts were drawn back to the two examples related earlier in the book where the software engineers and glass plant employees each became focused on a question. I remember calling your attention to the fact that at no time in either case was goal-setting a part of the solution. A vision, yes. An intuition-engaging question, yes. Goals, no. In thinking about that, it has occurred to me that goals, in the way most people view them, have the undesired consequence of actually initiating the downside thinking that prevents us from getting on a roll. If we view our goals as questions, they keep us reaching more and more deeply into our inner strengths. If we view our goals as a context within which the degree of our deficiency can be defined, we certainly place unnecessary limitations on our ability to access our strengths. What a stimulating thought on which to end this particular chapter!

Donning my mentor-coaching hat, I will now ask some more questions. *Which of the approaches have you already been using? What new insights have you gained from this chapter about the importance of keeping yourself in a can't-lose frame of mind? What are you enjoying about the new thoughts about goals that have just surfaced? What is the most significant action step you can see yourself taking as a result of thinking about no downside and developing a can't-lose frame of mind?*

Chapter Twenty-Two

The Big Picture

Reflections On Gratitude and Service

It's interesting for me to now sit back and reflect on the ideas we've explored together. I am deeply aware of how my own life has benefitted over the years as these ideas have gone through their birthing process. I am also aware of the benefits they have brought to the lives of more than 10,000 people who have been exposed to them in person. I am now asking myself what it will take for you yourself to gain the greatest possible long-term benefit from these ideas. Perhaps by now you could guess my mind would move quickly from there into a WHAT'S RIGHT analysis. Sure enough, it is now focused on exploring factors which may have contributed the most to sustaining my own commitment during the early stages of this quest.

The first factor to show up is the one of feeling believed in by my grandmother—in whose eyes her eldest grandson could do no wrong. That leaves me feeling quite a rush of gratitude—which in turn reminds me how a strong sense of gratitude is almost universally present in the thought processes of all effortless high performers. It's interesting to note how these thoughts are triggering each other. Look at how closely aligned the concepts of value-finding and gratitude are with each other. This also brings to mind a wonderful thought-provoking question about gratitude which is fun to ask people around Thanksgiving time. *"Does being thankful come from abundance, or does having abundance come from being thankful?"*

A second factor for which I am grateful is all of the great books I have enjoyed reading over the years. Here I am thinking not so much about the content of these books—even though that has certainly been significant—but of the cumulative effect of spending quality time with authors. As I think I mentioned earlier, I do not read books for content. I read books as a way to bring up into my conscious awareness what I know somewhere deep within me—so I can then make a deliberate choice about whether or not to act upon it. One timeless classic really puts this in perspective. *As a Man Thinketh*, by James Allen, likens the feeding of our minds to the cultivation of a garden. That priceless little book belongs in everyone's library so it can be read over and over again— at least yearly, if not more often. Other timeless classics great for feeding the mind would certainly include *Think and Grow Rich, The Master Key to Riches* and *Grow Rich With Peace of Mind*, all by Napoleon Hill; *The Magic of Thinking Big* by Dr. David Schwartz; and *The Magic of Believing* by Claude Bristol.

I also feel a real debt of gratitude for having been exposed to the great mind of Dr. Peter Drucker. His influence begins, of course, with the strategic thinking framework upon which our intuition-based system of management has been developed, but it can also be felt in many other ways throughout this book. For example, I am grateful for the forceful and articulate way he calls on managers to build upon the strengths of their organizations. He certainly validated and expanded my own beliefs on the personal side of that issue. I am also confident his efforts gave me added courage to speak out boldly on the importance of building on our own personal strengths.

Drucker is also an extremely keen observer of patterns, and his frequent reflections on those he thought were significant provided much early support for the development of my own fledgling skills in this area. I have therefore taken great delight in seeing many of the parallels between his work and mine. One which might be of special interest here is how his way of dealing with the purpose of an organization relates to our concept of buckets in need of being filled: by pouring them out, of course. As Drucker points out in his classic, *Management, Tasks, Responsibilities and Practices*, organizations have five "publics" whose needs must be "served" in order for the business to prosper. These are customers, employees, shareholders, society and government. I have often wondered if others must think me strange for getting excited over such things, but look at the obvious similarities to our approach to purpose at an individual level. We have physiological, safety, social, self-esteem and self-actualization needs (publics) awaiting our attention.

Great Organizations Run On a Purpose, Too

Since we seem to be dealing with parallels here, I'll call your attention to another. I believe it can be said unequivocally that all great business organizations become that way by "running on" a great purpose, just as the same thing could be said about outstanding human beings. I believe it to be universally true that such greatness, whether it be organizational or personal, is a reflection of "pouring out buckets," or service, rather than seeking to get our buckets filled. Greatness is a manifestation of being aligned with a philosophy which could be described as serving or giving out of abundance. It cannot manifest out of an effort to overpower or negate the illusion of shortage and depletion. We are surrounded by personal examples that give testimony to both sides of this illustration.

Much can be learned, too, from examples where organizations were aligned with great purposes and became truly outstanding, only to lose sight of those purposes and clearly demonstrate to the world the consequences of doing so. One example that quickly comes to mind is AT&T. Their initial purpose was so brilliantly conceived it was possible to reduce it to one word: "service." But oh, what powerful implications that word carried. The company needed to survive and prosper as a monopoly in a regulated business. To do so, its leaders recognized their best course of action would be to provide such a high level of service their needs and requests of regulators would never be questioned. The company prospered for many decades while its decisions were being made in alignment with that purpose. It is doubtful the breakup of AT&T would have occurred at all if its leaders had not lost sight of its original purpose.

Another example is the amazing story of Sears Roebuck & Company, whose original purpose was "to serve as the informed buyer for an immobile consumer." Their catalog became a booming business long before it was convenient, or in most cases even possible, to obtain the goods it offered in any other way. The quality of goods manufactured to their specifications was legendary. Sometime during the first half of this century they had to adjust their purpose to fit the growing mobility of their customer, but that most certainly didn't take them out of alignment with it. Where did they get off track? It would seem many of the merchandising and fashion-oriented decisions made within the last 25 to 30 years have been out of alignment with that original purpose.

Just as all individuals possess a purpose, so do all businesses. And in the same way that very few individuals are consciously aware of their own purpose in life, I suspect there may be even less of a conscious awareness within most business organizations of their purpose for existing. (Incidentally, to think of profit as a legitimate purpose for a business is to be sadly misguided by the data acquisition orientation of an analytical mind disconnected from the intuitive mind. As Drucker says—again so eloquently—profit isn't even a goal of a business. It is a cost item, and is thus a responsibility of business. It is the purchase price of having a business to return to tomorrow. But it is definitely not a purpose!)

One would hope more business organizations could be founded with at least a moderate awareness of their purpose—although this is still not very likely, given the limited understanding most people have about the subject. When a high awareness of business purpose does exist, it is often because the founder of that business is either consciously aware of, or subconsciously in alignment with, his or her own personal life purpose. That, in case you hadn't already guessed, is a major piece of my purpose in writing this book.

Since I am on the subject of drawing parallels, there is one more I must bring up. I also happen to believe this one is vastly more important than all of the others. If the very center, core purpose for each of us as individuals is to learn to love, then it absolutely must follow that the only legitimate purpose for any business to exist is to provide a context within which we can all learn to love. If we look closely, ample evidence is available all around us to verify this. Show me a business succeeding brilliantly, and together we will soon be able to confirm that its decisions are being made in close alignment with that purpose. Show me one that is failing, and believe me, the opposite will be true, and quite obviously so.

Making Purpose and Shared Vision Work In an Organization

It is one thing for a business to have a clearly defined, service-based purpose. It is quite another to have the majority of decisions within that business being made in alignment with that purpose. Just as with human beings, there can be no true commitment within a business organization to either a purpose or a shared vision as long as the people within that business are operating in a WHAT'S WRONG mode. The kind of high-quality corporate culture we all desire—where nearly all decisions made and actions taken are in alignment with a purpose and shared vision—can only be built on a foundation of value-finding questions.

I see a huge opportunity today for business leaders to improve profits by bringing about a fundamental shift in the questions being used to drive their cultures. To grasp the enormity of this opportunity, think about the tremendous cost of defensiveness and adversarial thinking within organizations. On several occasions I have asked groups of executives to estimate the percentage of their payroll being wasted on one form or another of defensiveness. The average response has always been "over 40%." It wouldn't take much of an improvement in this area to pay huge dividends, would it?

As an example, most of us would like to see radical improvements made in the performance measurement and evaluation systems being used today. Even the most enlightened system imaginable would fail, however, if we attempt to implement it in a business lacking critical mass of WHAT'S RIGHT questions to drive its culture. On the other hand, once we get our thinking right, problems can disappear faster than we could ever solve them. In other words, just about any performance evaluation system would work well in a culture where value-finding questions are a way of life.

Our five-step framework for strategic life planning was first introduced in Chapter 2. At that time I pointed out the need to master step five, building on strengths, before we could expect to succeed with our purpose, goals, plans and keeping track of what's right. The same is true for any organization. So, how do we make that happen in our business organizations? To answer this question, I am reminded of an experience I had the fall of 1979, when visiting with a friend who was a highly respected trainer of psychotherapists. It was about a month after my divorce was finalized, and we were talking about some deep concerns I had about limiting its negative effects on my two children, who were then ages ten and 13. I shall never forget what he said to me that day. "Kurt, the biggest gift you can give your kids is to get well, right in front of their eyes."

Doesn't that same message apply to our desires to make value-finding questions a way of life in our organizations? I believe the answer in both our personal lives as well as our business lives is one of self-responsibility. We must take responsibility for getting ourselves free from the temptation to judge. We must take responsibility for making our conscious, analytical minds into fully dedicated servants to our intuitive minds. One great way to begin moving in this direction is to systematically put into practice everything covered in this book. It can start out with something as simple as asking the question, "What's the best thing that has happened to you today?" of everyone we care about on a daily basis.

It's All a Matter of Energy

I began this book by suggesting that our natural state is one of being on a roll. To strengthen our awareness of this, I invited you to join me in exploring the fundamental question, "What are we like at our very best?"

While traveling along on this journey with me, what are some of the more useful observations you have made about yourself? What two or three steps have you found must be taken in order for you to be at your best more often?

Here are a few key points I would want you to remember from reading this book. First, it's all a matter of energy. We are either connected to the source of unlimited energy, and thus equipped to be on a roll, or we are doing something to block our connection. Judging is the act which separates us from this universal source of creative energy. Whenever we presume to judge anything to be good or bad, right or wrong, we at that precise moment begin to create an illusion of being separate from Source. The experience (illusion) we then create—of being no longer connected to the source of abundance—can only lead to a feeling of depletion and limitation. Any step we take must then, by definition, be perceived to further deplete our limited reserves of creative energy. In response, we create the concepts of fear, ego, anger, etc.

From the experience of depletion and limitation it is only natural for us to begin wondering, WHAT'S WRONG? Unfortunately, few of us ever make the link between our WHAT'S WRONG question and the further depletion of our limited reserves of creative energy. Instead, as our reserves become more and more depleted, we become more and more compulsive in asking, "What in the world is going wrong here?"

The diagram on the next page allows us to picture this process. Each of us begins life in the abundance mode, as depicted by the break point inside the tiny circle toward the right end of the scale. This also corresponds to our example of the three-year-old child. As long as we remain free of judging, we will remain in this abundance mode. Our story of little David describes how we fall into the depletion mode. Notice how an increasing fear of further depletion would naturally follow as one becomes more judgmental.

One way to describe the purpose of this book is to obtain the tools we need to move ourselves from wherever we are on the scale as far as possible toward the right. Anyone who is far to the left end of the scale will probably have set this book aside long before now. It seems they have correctly identified "thinking" as the cause of their depletion, and

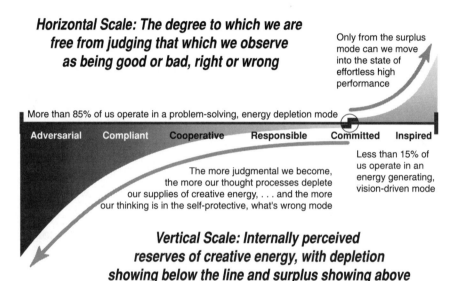

Horizontal Scale: The degree to which we are free from judging that which we observe as being good or bad, right or wrong

Only from the surplus mode can we move into the state of effortless high performance

More than 85% of us operate in a problem-solving, energy depletion mode

| Adversarial | Compliant | Cooperative | Responsible | Committed | Inspired |

The more judgmental we become, the more our thought processes deplete our supplies of creative energy, . . . and the more our thinking is in the self-protective, what's wrong mode

Less than 15% of us operate in an energy generating, vision-driven mode

Vertical Scale: Internally perceived reserves of creative energy, with depletion showing below the line and surplus showing above

are looking frantically under every rock for a way to not think. What they fail to recognize is how thinking, when done in response to properly framed questions, is the solution to their problem of depletion rather than its cause. The only hope I can think of for them is to arrange for an authority figure to show up in their space two or three times a day with a "What's the best thing . . ." question, and demonstrate sincere interest in their answers.

As you can see from the diagram, those who find themselves in the area between compliant and cooperative are considerably less depleted. It is therefore quite possible for them to begin working on asking the

RIGHT QUESTIONS directly. It would be best, of course, if they were able to find a good mentor-coach to supply the questions they need. In lieu of having a mentor-coach, however, they can master the discipline of asking RIGHT QUESTIONS of themselves by making it a practice to ask them of everyone else.

Many who read this book will look at the diagram and find themselves in the area of very little depletion just to the left of the break point. This is a particularly challenging area from which to continue growing, because we still have an ample supply of problem-focused habit structure left to be abandoned. To do this we must go beyond our newly acquired skills of asking the value-finding questions of others and build those questions into everything we do—so they literally surround us. In other words, we need to institutionalize the whole idea of value-finding.

The much bigger question, however, is how do we make a permanent shift into the self-sustaining, vision-building mode. As far as I know, there are no rules for this game. Making this shift is not a science; it is a pure art form. It requires us to make a fundamental decision to leave the world of having all the answers (at least intellectually), and enter the world of "not knowing."

To open the door to effortless high performance, and to move into the state of surplus and abundance, we must become vision-driven. We must reach the point where we continually wonder, "What does the ideal . . . (something) look like?" An artist might refer to this as working with negative space. A very appropriate idea. Why do we need a vision? The magic of a vision—the source of all its power—lies in those parts of it which are not yet known. A vision of an ideal resides in our conscious, rational mind and, like Swiss cheese, is filled with holes. These holes furnish our intuitive mind with an unlimited supply of unarticulated, intuition-engaging questions. I call this "living in the question." The state of being on a roll is then fueled by "Eureka!" insights generated within our intuitive minds in response to our awareness of the holes in our vision.

My brother, Dan, had an experience in this area recently that I found very encouraging. He's wonderfully vision-driven and has been on the cutting edge of putting these ideas of asking right questions into practice at his company, Trimpac, Inc., in St. Cloud, Minnesota for many years. In his efforts to support two of his key people in moving into the vision-driven mode, he developed a list of 23 questions about a new project he's working on, and for which he didn't have the answers. He then shared the entire list with his two people. As we were doing a post-mortem together on the positive results he got from doing so, we realized that had he doled out only one question at a time, there would have been considerable risk of having his people feel manipulated— thinking that he had the answers all along and was just leading their thought process. By supplying all 23 questions at the outset, he was able to bring them fully into the vision-building mode with him. I think this idea holds considerable promise and can hardly wait for another chance to put it into practice.

Meanwhile, my greatest hope is that you have felt my commitment throughout these discussions to see you as perfect, just the way you are. I also hope you have enjoyed our process of exploring your perfection together. We are all on a path. Progress on that path is what's important, not reaching its end. The end is ever-expanding, anyway. The question can never be fully answered. Living in the question is an ever-evolving, creative process in full alignment with the wisdom of the universe. As long as we are able to stay "in the question," miracles will happen.

Just before putting the finishing touches on this chapter, I went back and reviewed several of the great books on leadership that have come out in the past several years. My list included *On Becoming a Leader* by Warren Bennis, *Synchronisity, The Inner Path of Leadership* by Joseph Jaworsky, and *The Fifth Discipline: The Art and Practice of the Learning Organization* by Peter Senge. In doing so, I was reminded of an overwhelming feeling I had the first time I read them. The one piece they've all missed is our need to get free of judging. All of the conditions and skills these books hold up as being necessary to become an effective leader are symptomatic of being free of judging.

All three books, for example, put an appropriate focus on the importance of honest introspection and learning to fully trust ourselves. Unfortunately, they overlook the way in which our culturally conditioned habit of fault-finding stands in the way of honest introspection. Once we replace our temptation to judge with the new discipline of value-finding, we will eagerly approach introspection as a process of discovering our strengths. My guess is that you may have done more of this while reading this book than you have for a long time.

In closing, I will state unequivocally one more time that being on a roll and living in abundance is our natural state. The opposite of this state is when we use our rational minds to judge things as being good or bad, right or wrong. Judging is at the root of every way in which we keep ourselves from enjoying the state of effortless high performance. Therefore, the degree to which we approach being on a roll is directly related to how successful we are at freeing ourselves from the temptation to judge.

I wish you great success in getting free of judging, in getting and staying on a roll, and in sharing the joy of it with everyone around you.

Index

Order Form

✳ Fax orders: (208) 362-7999   Toll Free Fax orders: (888) 443-2703

☎ Telephone orders: Toll Free (800) 726-5880. Have your AMEX, Optima, Discover, VISA or MasterCard ready.

❏ Online orders: www.cpmpublishing.com

✉ Postal orders: CPM Publishing, 3452 Riva Ridge Way, Boise, ID 83709-3809, USA.

Telephone (208) 362-7979.

❏ Please send me _____ copies of *Breaking the Rules* at US $23.95.

❏ Please include free information about *The Mentor-Coaching Leader's Guide* for use in guiding group dialogue around *Breaking the Rules*.

Name: _____

Company: _____

Address: _____

City: _____ State: ____ Zip: _____-_____

Telephone: (_____) _____

Sales Tax: Please add 5% for books shipped to Idaho addresses.

Shipping: $3.00 for first book and $2 for each additional book. All orders shipped book rate. For Priority Mail add $2.00. Call for international.

Payment: ❏ Cheque

    ❏ Visa   ❏ MasterCard   ❏ Optima   ❏ AMEX   ❏ Discover

Card number: _____

Name on Card: _____ Exp Date: ____/____

Call *toll free* and order now:
(800) 726-5880